REEFER MADNESS

AND OTHER TALES FROM THE AMERICAN UNDERGROUND

■

ERIC SCHLOSSER

ALLEN LANE
an imprint of
PENGUIN BOOKS

ALLEN LANE
THE PENGUIN PRESS

Published by the Penguin Group
Penguin Books Ltd, 80 Strand, London WC2R 0RL, England
Penguin Putnam Inc., 375 Hudson Street, New York, New York 10014, USA
Penguin Books Australia Ltd, 250 Camberwell Road, Camberwell, Victoria 3124, Australia
Penguin Books Canada Ltd, 10 Alcorn Avenue, Toronto, Ontario, Canada M4V 3B2
Penguin Books India (P) Ltd, 11, Community Centre, Panchsheel Park, New Delhi – 110 017, India
Penguin Books (NZ) Ltd, Cnr Rosedale and Airborne Roads, Albany, Auckland, New Zealand
Penguin Books (South Africa) (Pty) Ltd, 24 Sturdee Avenue, Rosebank 2196, South Africa

Penguin Books Ltd, Registered Offices: 80 Strand, London WC2R 0RL, England

www.penguin.com

First published in the USA by Houghton Mifflin Company 2003
First published in Great Britain by Allen Lane The Penguin Press 2003
1

Copyright © Eric Schlosser, 2003

The moral right of the author has been asserted

Portions of this book have appeared in slightly different form in the
Atlantic Monthly, *Rolling Stone* and *U.S. News & World Report*.

"Devil's Harvest" poster, p. 12, courtesy of Something Weird Video.
Photograph of a strawberry worker, p. 76, copyright © by Andrew Lichtenstein.
Photograph of Reuben Sturman, p. 110, courtesy of Richard N. Rosfelder, Jr.

Set in Adobe Minon
Printed in England by Clays Ltd, St Ives plc

ISBN 0–713–99658–7

For Cullen Murphy and William Whitworth

Sapere aude.
Dare to know.

—HORACE

contents

THE
UNDERGROUND

ADAM SMITH BELIEVED in a God that was kind and wise and all-powerful. The great theorist of the free market believed in Providence. "The happiness of mankind," Smith wrote, "seems to have been the original purpose intended by the Author of nature." The workings of the Lord could be found not in the pages of a holy book, nor in miracles, but in the daily, mundane buying-and-selling of the marketplace. Each purchase might be driven by an individual desire, but behind them all lay "the invisible hand" of the Divine. This invisible hand set prices and wages. It determined supply and demand. It represented the sum of all human wishes. Without relying on any conscious intervention by man, the free market improved agriculture and industry, created surplus wealth, and made sure that the things being produced were the things people wanted to buy. Human beings lacked the wisdom, Smith felt, to improve society deliberately or to achieve Progress through some elaborate plan. But if every man pursued his own self-interest and obeyed only his "passions," the invisible hand would guarantee that everybody else benefited, too.

Published in 1776, *The Wealth of Nations* later had a profound effect upon the nation born that year. The idea that "life, liberty, and the pursuit of happiness" were unalienable rights, endowed by a Creator, fit perfectly with the economic theories of Adam Smith. "Life, liberty and estate" was the well-known phrase that Thomas Jefferson amended slightly for the Declaration of Independence. The United States was the first country to discard feudal and aristocratic traditions and replace them with a republican devotion to marketplace ideals. More than two centuries later, America's leading companies—General Motors, General Electric, ExxonMobil, Microsoft, Wal-Mart, Boeing, et al.—have annual revenues larger than those of many sovereign states. No currency is more powerful than the U.S. dollar, and the closing prices on Wall Street guide the financial markets of Tokyo, London, Paris, and Frankfurt. The unsurpassed wealth of the United States has enabled it to build a military without rival. And yet there is more to the U.S. economy, much more, than meets the eye. In addition to America's famous corporations and brands, the invisible hand has also produced a largely invisible economy, secretive and well hidden, with its own labor demand, price structure, and set of commodities.

"Black," "shadow," "irregular," "informal," "illegal," "subterranean," "underground"—a variety of adjectives have been used to describe this other economy. Although defined in numerous ways, at its simplest the American underground is where economic activities remain off the books, where they are unrecorded, unreported, and in violation of the law. These activities range from the commonplace (an electrician demanding payment in cash and failing to declare the payment as income) to the criminal (a gang member selling methamphetamine). They include moonlighting, check kiting, and fencing stolen goods; street vending and tax evading; employing day laborers and child laborers; running sweatshops and chop shops; smuggling cigarettes, guns, and illegal immigrants; selling fake Rolexes, pirating CDs. Economists disagree about the actual size of the underground economy and how to measure it. Some studies look at the discrepancy between the amount of personal income declared on tax returns and the amount of money that is actually spent. Other studies examine changes in currency supply, the velocity of money, levels of electricity usage. Each of these methodologies has its merits. All have produced conclusions that are debatable. There is general agreement, however, on two points: America's underground economy is vast—and most of its growth occurred in the past thirty years.

Any estimate of illegal economic activity is bound to lack precision, since it attempts to quantify things that people have carefully tried to hide. Nevertheless, the best estimates convey a sense of scale and proportion. In 1997 the Austrian economist Friedrich Schneider calculated the rise of America's "shadow economy" by tracing changes in the demand for currency. According to Schneider, in 1970 the size of the underground was between 2.6 and 4.6 percent of America's gross domestic product (GDP). By 1994 it had reached 9.4 percent of the GDP—about $650 billion. Using a different methodology in 1998, Charles Rossotti, the commissioner of the Internal Revenue Service, told Congress that during the previous year Americans had failed to pay about $200 billion of federal taxes that were owed, an amount larger than the government's annual spending on Medicare. Assuming an average federal tax rate of 14 percent, that means Americans somehow neglected to report almost $1.5 trillion in personal income. The IRS estimate did not include undeclared earnings from criminal activity.

Two other periods in modern American history were marked by thriving underground economies. From 1920 to 1933, the prohibition of alcohol led to widespread trafficking and the rise of organized crime. At the height of Prohibition, Americans spent about $5 billion a year on alcohol (roughly $54 billion in today's dollars). This black market constituted about 5 percent of the U.S. gross national product at the time. When Prohibition ended, some bootleggers became well-respected businessmen. During the Second World War, the imposition of rationing and price controls created even larger black markets. A system designed to distribute scarce commodities fairly had some unanticipated effects: a burgeoning trade in ration books and a hidden cash economy. Perhaps 5 percent of the nation's gasoline and 20 percent of its meat were soon bought and sold illegally. According to one estimate, by the end of the war Americans were failing to report as much as 15 percent of their personal income. The underground subsided amid the prosperity of the Eisenhower era. Wages increased, tax evasion decreased, and no illegal commodity generated the sort of profits once supplied by bootleg alcohol. And then at some point in the mid- to late 1960s the underground economy began to grow.

Conservative economists point to high income tax rates and excessive government regulation as the fundamental causes. Liberals contend that declining wages, unemployment, union busting, and the business deregulation of the Reagan years were much more responsible for shifting economic activity underground. The explanations offered by the left and the right are not mutually exclusive. A stagnant economy prompted Americans of every background to work off the books. The hippie counterculture of the 1960s and the anti-tax movement of the late 1970s shared common ground in their dislike of government, encouraging defiance of the IRS. A new drug culture provided new opportunities for organized crime. The expansion of America's underground economy over the last thirty years stemmed not only from economic hardship and a desire for illegal profits, but also from a growing sense of alienation, anger at authority, and disrespect for the law.

During roughly the same period similar phenomena occurred throughout the western industrialized world. The underground economy of the European Union may now be larger than that of the United States. Years of high unemployment, high tax rates, illegal immigration, and widespread disillusion with government have created enormous undergrounds. According to Friedrich Schneider's estimates, these shadow economies range in size from an estimated 12.5 percent of GDP in Great Britain to an estimated 27 percent of GDP in Italy. Countries that were once part of the Soviet Union have even larger black markets. In Estonia the underground is now responsible for an estimated 39 percent of GDP; in Russia, for an estimated 45 percent; in Ukraine, for an estimated 51 percent. The underground is sometimes the most vibrant sector of these transition economies, the place where free enterprise has finally bloomed. But in many ways the growth of black markets in the developed world represents a step backward. An expanding underground economy is often associated with increased corruption and a greater disparity in wealth. For years government officials and members of the Communist Party secretly profited from the Soviet Union's "second economy," offering services and commodities unavailable through the mainstream. The largest undergrounds are now found in the developing world, where governments are corrupt and laws are routinely ignored. In Bolivia the underground economy is responsible for an estimated 65 percent of GDP. In Nigeria it accounts for perhaps 76 percent.

The U.S. dollar now serves as the unofficial currency of this new global underground. During the late 1960s and early 1970s American economists began to notice that the amount of currency in circulation had grown much larger than the amount ordinary citizens were likely to use in their everyday transactions. The discovery led to the first inklings that an underground economy was emerging in the United States. While business publications heralded the advent of a cashless, credit-based economy, the use of banknotes quietly soared. The $100 bill soon became the underground favorite, not just in the United States, but overseas as well, thanks to its high face value and the relative stability of the dollar. During the late 1970s the outflow of currency from the United States averaged about $2 billion a year. By the 1990s, about $20 billion in U.S. currency was being shipped to foreign countries every year. Today approximately three-quarters of all $100 bills circulate outside the United States.

The supremacy of the dollar in the global underground has proven a boon to the American economy. The outflow of U.S. currency now serves, in essence, as a gigantic interest-free loan. Every time the U.S. Treasury issues new banknotes, it purchases an equal value of interest-bearing securities. Those securities are liquidated only when the currency is taken out of circulation and put into a bank. In 2000 the U.S. Treasury earned an estimated $32.7 billion in interest from its banknotes circulating overseas. The 1996 redesign of the $100 bill was partly motivated by fears that Middle Eastern counterfeiters had created a convincingly real $100 bill, a "supernote" that might threaten the role of U.S. currency in unofficial transactions. The latest threat to the $100 bill comes not from organized crime figures, but from the central bank of the European Union. The new 500-euro note is perfect for black market activity. It has roughly five times the value of a $100 bill, allowing drug dealers and smugglers to lighten their suitcases. Portugal has banned the 500-euro note for those reasons, and its acceptance in other foreign undergrounds is not yet certain.

The three essays in this book shed light on different aspects of the

American underground—and on the ways it has changed society, for better or worse. "Reefer Madness" looks at the legal and economic consequences of marijuana use in the United States. Pot has become a hugely popular black market commodity, more widely used throughout the world than any other illegal drug. The enforcement of state and federal laws regarding marijuana guides its production, sets the punishments for its users, and suggests the arbitrary nature of many cultural taboos. Americans not only smoke more marijuana but also imprison more people for marijuana than any other western industrialized nation.

"In the Strawberry Fields" examines the plight of migrant workers in California agriculture, who are mainly illegal immigrants. The state's recruitment of illegals from Mexico started a trend that has lately spread throughout the United States. Many employers now prefer to use black market labor. Although immigrant smuggling looms as a multi-billion-dollar business in its own right, the growing reliance on illegals has far-reaching implications beyond the underground, affecting wages, working conditions, and even the practice of democracy in the rest of society.

"An Empire of the Obscene" traces the history of the pornography industry through the career of an obscure businessman and his successors. It describes how a commodity once traded only on the black market recently entered the mainstream, turning behavior long thought deviant into popular entertainment. Profits from the sale of pornography that used to be earned by organized crime figures are now being made by some of America's largest corporations. The current demand for marijuana and pornography is deeply revealing. Here are two commodities that Americans publicly abhor, privately adore, and buy in astonishing amounts.

Linking all three essays is a belief that the underground is inextricably linked to the mainstream. The lines separating them are fluid, not permanently fixed. One cannot be fully understood without regard to the other. The vastness and complexity of the underground challenge the mathematical certainties of conventional economic thinking. Hard numbers suddenly appear illusory. Prices on Wall Street rise or fall based on minuscule changes in the rate of inflation, the unemployment rate, the latest predictions about the GNP. Billions of dollars may change hands because an economic measurement shifts by one-tenth of a percent. But what do those statistics really mean, if 20 percent, 10 percent, or even 5 percent of a nation's economy somehow cannot be accounted for? America's great economic successes of the past two decades — in software, telecommunications, aerospace, computing — are only part of the story. Marlboro, Camel, and Philip Morris are familiar names, and the tobacco industry is one of the most powerful lobbies in Washington, D.C. But Americans now spend more money on illegal drugs than on cigarettes.

The proper role of the state and the proper limits on the free market are central themes of this book. The political system of the United States and the economic system proposed by Adam Smith are ostensibly dedicated to freedom. Since 1776 Americans have been willing to fight and to die for freedom. You will search long and hard to find an American who thinks freedom is a bad thing. The question that has been much more difficult to answer is: Freedom for whom? Should the government be protecting the freedom of workers or employers? Of consumers, or manufacturers? Of the majority who live one way, or the minority who choose to live differently? In the abstract, freedom is always easy to celebrate. But adherence to that lofty ideal seems impossible to achieve. Despite the best of libertarian intentions, giving unchecked freedom to one group usually means denying it to another.

What happens in the underground economy is worth examining because of how fortunes are made there, how lives are often ruined there, how the vicissitudes of the law can deem one man a gangster or a chief executive (or both). If you truly want to know a person, you need to look beyond the public face, the jobs on the résumé, the books on the shelves, the family pictures on the desk. You may learn more from what's hidden in a drawer. There is always more to us than what we will admit. If the market does indeed embody the sum of all human wishes, then the secret ones are just as important as the ones that are openly displayed. Like the yin and yang, the mainstream and the underground are ultimately two sides of the same thing. To know a country you must see it whole.

[1]

REEFER MADNESS

I N THE STATE OF INDIANA, a person convicted of armed robbery will serve about six years in prison; someone convicted of rape will serve about eight; and a convicted murderer can expect to spend twenty-five years behind bars. These figures are actually higher than the national average: eleven years and four months in prison is the typical punishment for an American found guilty of murder. The prison terms given by Indiana judges tend to be long, but with good behavior, an inmate will serve no more than half the nominal sentence. Those facts are worth keeping in mind when considering the case of Mark Young. At the age of thirty-eight, Young was arrested at his Indianapolis home for brokering the sale of seven hundred pounds of marijuana grown on a farm in nearby Morgan County. Young was tried and convicted under federal law. He had never before been charged with drug trafficking. He had no history of violent crime. Young's role in the illegal transaction had been that of a middleman — he never distributed the drugs; he simply introduced two people hoping to sell a large amount of marijuana to three people wishing to buy it. The offense occurred a year and a half before his arrest. No confiscated marijuana, money, or physical evidence of any kind linked Young to the crime. He was convicted solely on the testimony of co-conspirators who were now cooperating with the government. On February 8, 1992, Mark Young was sentenced by Judge Sarah Evans Barker to life imprisonment without possibility of parole.

Marijuana is such a familiar part of youth culture in the United States, and the smell of pot smoke is now so commonplace at high school and college parties, that many Americans assume a marijuana offense rarely leads to a prison term. In fact, there are more people in prison today for violating marijuana laws than at any other time in American history. About 20,000 inmates in the federal prison system have been incarcerated primarily for a marijuana offense. The number currently being held in state prisons and local jails is more difficult to estimate; a reasonable guess would be an additional 25,000 to 30,000. And Mark Young's sentence, though unusual, is by no means unique. Dozens of marijuana offenders may now be serving life sentences in federal penitentiaries, without hope of parole. If one includes middle-aged inmates with sentences of twenty or thirty or forty years, the number condemned to die in prison may reach into the hundreds. Other inmates—no one knows how many—are serving life sentences in state correctional facilities across the country for growing, selling, possessing, or even buying marijuana.

The phrase "war on drugs" evokes images of Colombian cartels and inner-city crack addicts. In many ways that is a misperception. Marijuana is and has long been the most widely used illegal drug in the United States. It is used more frequently than all other illegal drugs combined. Approximately one-third of the American population over the age of twelve have smoked marijuana at least once. About twenty million Americans smoke it every year. More than two million smoke it every day. Unlike heroin or cocaine, which must be imported, anywhere from a quarter to half of the marijuana used in the United States is grown here as well. Although popular stereotypes depict marijuana growers as aging hippies in Northern California or Hawaii, the majority of the marijuana now cultivated domestically is being grown in the nation's midsection—a swath running from the Appalachians west to the Great Plains. Throughout this Marijuana Belt drug fortunes are being made by farmers who often seem to have stepped from a page of the old *Saturday Evening Post*. The value of America's annual marijuana crop is staggering: plausible estimates start at $4 billion and range up to $25 billion. In 2001 the value of the nation's largest legal cash crop, corn, was roughly $19 billion.

Marijuana has well-organized supporters who campaign for its legalization and promote its use through books, magazines, Web sites, and popular music. They believe marijuana is important not only as a benign recreational drug but also as an herbal medicine and as a commodity with industrial applications. Marijuana's opponents are equally passionate and far better organized. They consider marijuana a dangerous drug—one that harms the user's mental, physical, and spiritual well-being, that promotes irresponsible sexual behavior, that encourages disrespect for traditional values and threatens the nation's youth. At the heart of the ongoing, bitter debate is a hardy weed that can grow wild in all fifty states. The two sides agree that countless lives have been destroyed by marijuana, but disagree about what should be blamed: the plant itself, or the laws forbidding its use.

The war on drugs launched by President Ronald Reagan in 1982 began largely as a campaign against marijuana, organized by conservative parents' groups. After more than a decade in which penalties for marijuana offenses had been reduced at both the state and federal levels, the laws prohibiting marijuana were made much tougher in the 1980s. More resources were devoted to their enforcement, and punishments more severe than those administered during the "reefer madness" of the 1930s became routine. All the legal tools commonly associated with the fight against heroin and cocaine trafficking—civil forfeitures, enhanced police search powers, the broad application of conspiracy laws, a growing reliance on the testimony of informers, and mechanistic sentencing formulas, such as mandatory minimums and "three strikes, you're out"—have been employed against marijuana offenders. The story of how Mark Young got a life sentence reveals a great deal about the emergence of the American heartland as the region where most of the nation's marijuana is now grown; about the changing composition of the federal prison population; and about the effects of the war on drugs, more than twenty years after its declaration, throughout America's criminal justice system. Underlying Young's tale is a simple question: How does a society come to punish a man more harshly for selling marijuana than for killing someone with a gun?

the plant in question

"MARIJUANA" IS THE MEXICAN colloquial name for a plant known to botanists as *Cannabis sativa*. In various forms, it has long been familiar throughout the world: in Africa as "dagga," in China as "ma," in northern Europe as "hemp," in India as "bhang," "ganja," and "charas." Although cannabis most likely originated in the steppes of central Asia, it now thrives in almost any climate, spreading like milkweed or thistle, crowding out neighboring grasses and reaching heights of three to twenty feet at maturity. Marijuana has been cultivated for at least 5,000 years; it is one of the oldest agricultural commodities not grown for food. The stalks of the plant contain fibers that have been woven for millennia to make rope, canvas, and paper. Cannabis is dioecious, spawning male and female plants in equal proportion. The flowering buds of the female—and to a lesser extent those of the male—secrete a sticky yellow resin rich with cannabinoids, the more than sixty compounds unique to marijuana. Several of them are psychoactive, most prominently delta-9-tetrahydrocannabinol (THC). Marijuana's effects on the mind and body were first recorded by the Chinese emperor Shen-Nung in the twenty-eighth century B.C. The ancient Chinese used cannabis, mixed with wine, as an anesthetic during surgery and prescribed it to cure a variety of ailments. The ancient Egyptians also praised the medicinal properties of cannabis, and Roman women inhaled its smoke to relieve labor pains.

Dr. Lester Grinspoon, an emeritus professor of psychiatry at Harvard Medical School, thinks marijuana will someday be hailed as a "miracle drug," one that is safe, inexpensive, and versatile. In his book, *Marihuana, the Forbidden Medicine,* Grinspoon provides evidence that smoking cannabis can relieve the nausea associated with chemotherapy, prevent blindness induced by glaucoma, serve as an appetite stimulant for AIDS patients, act as an anti-epileptic, ward off asthma attacks and migraine headaches, alleviate chronic pain, and reduce the muscle spasticity that accompanies multiple sclerosis, cerebral palsy, and paraplegia. Other doctors think that Grinspoon is wildly optimistic, and that no "crude drug" like marijuana—composed of more than 400 chemicals—should be allowed in the modern pharmacopoeia. They argue that effective synthetic drugs, of precise dosage and purity, have been developed for every one of marijuana's potential uses. Dronabinol, a synthetic form of delta-9-THC, has been available for years, though some clinical oncologists find it inferior to marijuana as an anti-emetic. Recent inquiries by the National Academy of Science and Great Britain's House of Lords suggest that cannabis may indeed have legitimate medicinal uses. There have been remarkably few large-scale studies that might verify or disprove Grinspoon's theories about marijuana's efficacy. He says that the federal government has always been far more interested in establishing the harmful effects of cannabis than in discovering any of its benefits, while major drug companies have little incentive to fund the necessary research. As Grinspoon explains, "You cannot patent this plant."

The long-term health effects of chronic cannabis use, and marijuana's role as a "gateway" to the use of other illegal drugs, are issues surrounded by controversy. Marijuana does not create a physical dependence in its users, although it does create a psychological dependence in some. It appears to be less addictive, however, than heroin, cocaine, nicotine, alcohol, or caffeine. People who smoke marijuana are more likely to experiment later with other psychoactive drugs, but a direct cause-and-effect relationship has never been established. Marijuana's potential role as a "stepping-stone" to other drugs is most likely determined by cultural, not pharmacological, factors. Delta-9-THC is highly lipid soluble and has a half-life of five days, which means it diffuses widely throughout the human body and remains there for quite some time. An occasional marijuana user can fail a urine test three days after smoking a single joint, while a heavy user may test positive after abstaining from marijuana for more than a month. Delta-9-THC's persistence within various cells and vital organs (also a characteristic of Valium, Thorazine, and quinine) raises the possibility that it could exert subtly harmful effects; none has been proven. Studies of lifelong, heavy marijuana users in Jamaica, Greece, and Costa Rica have revealed little psychological or physiological damage. More research, however, needs to be done in the areas of cognition, reproduction, and immunology.

Some studies have suggested that short-term memory deficiencies among heavy smokers may endure long after the cessation of marijuana use. Other studies have demonstrated, in vitro and in laboratory animals, that marijuana may have a mild immunosuppressive effect, but no study has conclusively linked delta-9-THC to immune system changes in human beings. Well-publicized horror stories from the 1970s — that marijuana kills brain cells, damages chromosomes, and prompts men to grow large breasts — proved to be unfounded.

Smoking marijuana may damage the pulmonary system, in some of the ways that inhaling tobacco smoke does. In an ongoing study of people who have smoked three or four joints a day for more than ten years, Dr. Donald P. Tashkin, of the University of California at Los Angeles Medical Center, has found substantial evidence that habitual marijuana smoking may cause chronic bronchitis, changes in cells of the central airway which are potentially precancerous, and an impairment in scavenger cell function which could increase the risk of respiratory infection. A joint seems to deliver four to five times as much carcinogenic tar as a tobacco cigarette of the same size. Tashkin expects that some heavy marijuana users will eventually suffer cancers of the mouth, throat, and lungs. Oddly enough, the more potent strains of marijuana may prove less dangerous, since less of them need to be smoked.

There is much less controversy about the short-term effects and toxicity of marijuana. According to Dr. Leo Hollister, a former president of the American College of Neuropsychopharmacology, occasional use of marijuana by a healthy adult poses no greater risks than moderate alcohol consumption. For a variety of reasons, however, schizophrenics, pregnant women, and people with heart conditions shouldn't smoke pot. Although the misuse of over-the-counter medications such as aspirin, acetaminophen, and antihistamines kills thousands of people every year, not a single death has ever been credibly attributed directly to smoking or consuming marijuana in the 5,000 years of the plant's recorded use. Marijuana is one of the few therapeutically active substances for which there is no well-defined fatal dose. It has been estimated that a person would have to smoke a hundred pounds of marijuana a minute for fifteen minutes in order to induce a lethal response.

criminalized, decriminalized, recriminalized

THE FIRST AMERICAN LAW concerning marijuana, passed by the Virginia assembly in 1619, required every household to grow it. Hemp was deemed not only a valuable commodity, but also a strategic necessity. Its fibers were used to make sails and riggings, and its byproducts were turned into oakum for the caulking of wooden ships. Maryland, Virginia, Pennsylvania, and other colonies eventually allowed hemp to be used as legal tender to boost its production and relieve colonial shortages of currency. Although a number of the Founding Fathers, including George Washington and Thomas Jefferson, later grew hemp on their estates, there is no evidence that they were aware of its psychoactive properties. The domestic production of hemp flourished, especially in Kentucky, until after the Civil War, when it was replaced by imports from Russia and by other domestic materials. In the latter half of the nineteenth century marijuana became a popular ingredient in patent medicines and was sold openly at pharmacies in one-ounce herbal packages and alcohol-based tinctures, as a cure for migraines, rheumatism, and insomnia. Dr. Brown's Sedative Tablets contained marijuana, as did Eli Lilly's One Day Cough Cure.

The political upheaval in Mexico that culminated in the Revolution of 1910 prompted a wave of Mexican immigration to the American Southwest. The prejudices and fears that greeted these peasant immigrants also extended to their traditional means of intoxication: smoking marijuana. Police officers in Texas claimed that marijuana incited violent crimes, aroused a "lust for blood," and gave its users "superhuman strength." Rumors spread that Mexicans were distributing this "killer weed" to unsuspecting American schoolchildren. Sailors and West Indian immigrants introduced marijuana to port cities along the Gulf of Mexico. In New Orleans newspaper articles associated the drug with African Americans, jazz musicians, prostitutes, and underworld whites. "The dominant race and most enlightened countries are alcoholic," one prominent critic of marijuana argued, expressing a widely held belief, "whilst the races and nations addicted to hemp . . . have deteriorated both mentally and physically." Marijuana was depicted as an alien intrusion into American life, capable of transforming healthy teenagers into sex-crazed maniacs. In 1914, El Paso, Texas,

enacted probably the first local ordinance banning the sale or possession of marijuana; by 1931, twenty-nine states had outlawed marijuana,
usually with little fanfare or debate.

Amid the rise of anti-immigrant sentiment fueled by the Great Depression, public officials from the Southwest and from Louisiana pe-
titioned the U.S. Treasury Department to ban marijuana. Their efforts were aided by the Hearst newspaper chain's lurid reporting about
the drug. "Murder Weed Found Up and Down Coast," one headline
warned; "Deadly Marijuana Dope Plant Ready for Harvest That Means
Enslavement of California Children." Harry J. Anslinger, the commissioner of the Federal Bureau of Narcotics (FBN), at first doubted
the severity of the problem and the need for federal legislation. But he
soon responded to political pressure and assumed leadership of the
drive for a nationwide marijuana prohibition. In public appearances
and radio broadcasts Anslinger asserted that the use of this "evil weed"
led to cold-blooded murders, sex crimes, and insanity. He wrote sensa-
tional magazine articles with titles like "Marijuana: Assassin of Youth."
In 1937 Congress passed the Marijuana Tax Act, effectively criminaliz-
ing the possession of marijuana throughout the United States. A week
after it went into effect, a fifty-eight-year-old marijuana dealer named
Samuel R. Caldwell became the first person convicted under the new
statute. Although marijuana offenders had been treated leniently under
state and local laws for years, Judge J. Foster Symes, of Denver, lectured
Caldwell on the viciousness of marijuana and sentenced him to four
hard years at Leavenworth Penitentiary.

Harry J. Anslinger is a central figure in the history of American drug
policy. He headed the FBN from its inception through six presidential
administrations spanning more than three decades. Anslinger had
much in common with his rival, J. Edgar Hoover. Both were staunchly
anti-Communist proponents of law and order who imbued nascent
federal bureaus with their own idiosyncrasies. Anslinger did not believe in a public health approach to drug addiction. He dismissed
treatment clinics as "morphine feeding stations" and "barrooms for
addicts." In his view, strict enforcement of the law was the only proper
response to illegal drug use. He urged judges to "jail offenders, then
throw away the key." Anslinger's outlook was consistent with that of

most Americans, though his opinions proved more resistant to new scientific evidence. When the New York Academy of Medicine issued a report in 1944 concluding that marijuana use did not cause violent behavior, provoke insanity, lead to addiction, or promote opiate use, Anslinger angrily dismissed its authors as "dangerous" and "strange."

America's drug problem was often depicted by the FBN as the work of foreign powers. During the Second World War Anslinger accused the Japanese of using narcotics to sap America's will to fight; a few years later he asserted that Communists were attempting the same ploy. The Boggs Act, passed by Congress at the height of the McCarthy era, specified the same penalties for marijuana and heroin offenses — two to five years in prison for first-time possession. As justification for the long sentences contained in that act and in the Narcotics Control Act, which followed in 1956, Anslinger stressed marijuana's crucial role as a "stepping-stone" to narcotic addiction. Like Hoover, he maintained dossiers on well-known entertainers whose behavior seemed un-American. Anslinger hated jazz and kept a special FBN file, "Marijuana and Musicians." It was filled with undercover reports on band members who played with Cab Calloway, Louis Armstrong, Les Brown, Count Basie, Jimmy Dorsey, and Duke Ellington, among others. For months Anslinger planned a nationwide roundup of popular musicians — a scheme foiled by the inability of FBN agents to infiltrate the jazz milieu. He did, however, manage to secure the arrest of a well-known marijuana user in Hollywood, the actor Robert Mitchum.

Although Anslinger's opposition to drug use was both passionate and sincere, he allowed some notable exceptions. In the 1940s he collaborated with the Office of Strategic Services (OSS), the wartime precursor of the Central Intelligence Agency (CIA), on various mind control experiments using narcotics. With help from the FBN, peyote and sodium amytal were combined to produce a "truth drug" for OSS interrogations of enemy prisoners. When that combination didn't work, Anslinger suggested using cigarettes laced with marijuana derivatives. That didn't work either, and the OSS search for a truth drug proved unsuccessful. Nevertheless, Anslinger later worked closely with the CIA on MK-ULTRA, a notorious mind control program in which hundreds of people were given lysergic acid diethylamide (LSD) without their knowledge or consent. George White, one of Anslinger's top agents, ran bordellos for the CIA during the late 1950s, observing the behavior of customers after their drinks were spiked with LSD. He not only dosed unsuspecting men and women with a variety of powerful psychoactives, but also took the drugs himself in order to gauge their effects. "I toiled wholeheartedly in the vineyards because it was fun, fun, fun," White later recalled about his work for MK-ULTRA. "Where else could a red-blooded American boy lie, kill, cheat, steal, rape, and pillage with the sanction and blessing of the All-Highest?" Activities that could bring ordinary Americans long prison sentences were deemed permissible and even patriotic for members of the FBN. In his memoir, *The Murderers,* Anslinger confessed to having arranged a regular supply of morphine for "one of the most influential members of Congress," who had become an addict. Anslinger's biographer, John C. McWilliams, believes that well-connected addict was Senator Joseph R. McCarthy.

By 1962, when Harry J. Anslinger retired, many states had passed "little Boggs acts" with penalties for marijuana possession or sale tougher than those demanded by federal law. In Louisiana, sentences for simple possession ranged from five to ninety-nine years; in Missouri, a second offense could result in a life sentence; and in Georgia, a second conviction for selling marijuana to minors could bring the death penalty.

As the political climate changed during the 1960s, so did attitudes toward drug abuse. A series of commissions appointed by Presidents John F. Kennedy and Lyndon Johnson repudiated some of the basic assumptions that had guided marijuana policy for over fifty years, denying a direct link between the drug and violent crime or heroin use. As marijuana use became widespread among white middle-class college students, there was a reappraisal of marijuana laws that for decades had imprisoned poor Mexicans and African Americans without much public dissent. Drug abuse policy shifted from a purely criminal justice approach to one also motivated by interests of public health, with more emphasis on treatment than on punishment. In 1970 the Comprehensive Drug Abuse Prevention and Control Act finally differentiated marijuana from other narcotics and reduced federal penalties for the possession of small amounts.

That same year, President Richard Nixon appointed a bipartisan commission to study the health effects, legal status, and social impact of marijuana. In 1972 the National Commission on Marijuana and Drug Abuse reached an unexpected conclusion: marijuana should be decriminalized under state and federal law. The commission unanimously agreed that possessing small amounts of marijuana in the home should no longer be a crime. Growing or selling marijuana for profit, using it in public, or driving under the influence would remain strictly forbidden. "Recognizing the extensive degree of misinformation about marijuana as a drug, we have tried to *demythologize* it," the commission explained. "Viewing the use of marijuana in its social context, we have tried to *desymbolize* it." Society should strongly discourage marijuana use while devoting more resources to preventing and treating heavy use. "Considering the range of social concerns in contemporary America," the commission argued, "marijuana does not, in our considered judgment, rank very high." President Nixon felt betrayed by the commission and rejected its findings; he privately blamed the agitation for marijuana law reform on "the Jews." Nevertheless, eleven states, containing one-third of the country's population, decriminalized marijuana in the 1970s, and most other states weakened their laws against it. The American Bar Association, the American Medical Association, and the National Council of Churches all supported the decriminalization of marijuana—as did President Jimmy Carter. It seemed long prison sentences for marijuana offenders had been consigned to the nation's past.

But they had not. One of the seminal events in the creation of the modern American antidrug movement was a backyard barbecue held in Atlanta, Georgia, during August, 1976. In the aftermath of their daughter's birthday party, Ron and Marsha Manatt crawled through the wet grass in their pajamas, at one in the morning, with flashlights, finding dozens of marijuana roaches, rolling-paper packets, and empty bottles of Mad Dog 20/20 discarded by their twelve- and thirteen-year-old guests. Alarmed by these discoveries, the Manatts gathered local parents in their living room and formed what was soon known as the Nosy Parents Association, a group dedicated to preventing teenage drug use. Marsha Manatt wrote to Dr. Robert DuPont, the head of the National Institute on Drug Abuse (NIDA); he helped arrange her introduction to Thomas Gleaton, a professor of health education at Georgia State University. There soon arose the Parents' Resource Institute for Drug Education and the National Federation of Parents for Drug-Free Youth, two organizations backed by top officials at NIDA and the federal Drug Enforcement Administration (DEA) which would exert a tremendous influence on the nation's drug policies. Thousands of other parents' groups soon formed nationwide, and Ross Perot helped launch the Texans' War on Drugs.

Marijuana use seemed epidemic; a survey in 1976 found that one out of twelve high school seniors smoked pot on a daily basis. The 1960s youth counterculture had celebrated marijuana's reputation as a drug for outcasts and freaks. "The slogans of the revolution are going to be pot, freedom, license," one Yippie leader confidently predicted. "The BOLSHEVIKS of the REVOLUTION will be long-haired pot smokers." Conservative parents' groups took such words to heart and similarly invested marijuana with great meaning. Robert DuPont, who at NIDA had once supported decriminalization, later decried the "tumultuous change in values" among the young—their pursuit of pleasure, their lack of responsibility to society—and argued that "the leading edge of this cultural change was marijuana use."

During the 1980 presidential campaign, Ronald Reagan endorsed the view that marijuana "is probably the most dangerous drug in America today." With strong support from the conservative parents' groups, his election brought the war on drugs to the White House. In 1982 President Reagan signed an executive order creating a new post in his administration—head of the White House Drug Abuse Policy Office, soon known as the "drug czar"—and appointed a chemist, Carlton Turner, to the job. Turner had for many years directed the Marijuana Research Project at the University of Mississippi, running the government's only marijuana farm. According to a profile in *Government Executive* magazine, Turner thought that marijuana use was inextricably linked to "the present young-adult generation's involvement in anti-military, anti–nuclear power, anti–big business, anti-authority demonstrations." He also thought that smoking pot could turn young men into homosexuals. In 1977 the DEA had acknowledged that decriminalization was worth considering; three years later it called marijuana the most urgent drug problem facing the United States.

Richard Bonnie, a professor at the University of Virginia Law School who was the associate director of President Nixon's marijuana commission, believes that advocates of marijuana law reform were pushed out of the mainstream by the growing influence of the parents' groups. Political moderates soon abandoned the issue. Amid their silence, philosophies of "zero tolerance" and "user accountability" revived the notion that what drug offenders deserved most was punishment. Once again, drug abuse was depicted as a moral, not a medical, problem. The Comprehensive Crime Control Act of 1984, the Anti–Drug Abuse Act of 1986, and the Anti–Drug Abuse Amendment Act of 1988 raised federal penalties for marijuana possession, cultivation, and trafficking. Sentences were to be determined by the amount of pot involved; "conspiracies" and "attempts" were to be punished as severely as completed acts; and a hundred marijuana plants now carried the same sentence as a hundred grams of heroin.

the caprice of geography

MARIJUANA IS CURRENTLY CLASSIFIED as a Schedule I controlled substance, implying that it has a high potential for abuse, no officially accepted medicinal uses, and no safe level of use under medical supervision. Heroin, LSD, and peyote are other Schedule I drugs; cocaine and phencyclidine (PCP) are listed in Schedule II, allowing doctors to prescribe them. Under federal law, it is illegal to possess any amount of pot anywhere in the United States. Penalties for a first marijuana offense range from probation to the death penalty. Moreover, it is illegal to use the U.S. Postal Service or other interstate shippers for the advertisement, import, or export of such marijuana paraphernalia as roach clips, water pipes, and, in some instances, cigarette papers—a crime that can lead to imprisonment and fines of up to $100,000.

Under civil forfeiture statutes, real estate, vehicles, cash, securities, jewelry, and any other property connected to a marijuana offense are subject to immediate seizure. The federal government need not prove the property was bought with the proceeds of illegal drug sales, only that it was involved in the commission of a crime—that marijuana was grown on certain land or transported in a particular vehicle. A yacht can be seized if a single joint is discovered on it. A house can be seized if a single marijuana plant is found growing there. Property may be seized and forfeited even after a defendant is found innocent of the offense, since the strict burden of proof that applies to people—"beyond a reasonable doubt"—does not apply in accusations against inanimate objects. Property can be forfeited without its owner ever being charged with a crime. On top of fines, incarceration, and forfeiture, a convicted marijuana offender may face the revocation or denial of more than 460 federal benefits, including student loans, small-business loans, professional licenses, and farm subsidies. Americans convicted of a marijuana felony, even if they are disabled, may no longer receive federal welfare payments or food stamps. Convicted murderers, rapists, and child molesters, however, remain eligible for such benefits.

State marijuana laws were also toughened during the 1980s and now vary enormously. Some states classify marijuana with drugs like mescaline and cocaine, while others give it a separate legal category. In New York State possessing slightly less than an ounce of marijuana brings a $100 fine, if it's a first offense. In Louisiana possessing the same amount of pot could lead to a prison sentence of twenty years. In Montana selling a pound of marijuana, first offense, could lead to a life sentence, whereas in New Mexico selling 10,000 pounds of marijuana, first offense, could be punished with a prison term of no more than three years. In some states it is against the law to be in a room where marijuana is being smoked, even if you don't smoke any. In some states you may be subject to criminal charges if someone else smokes, distributes, or cultivates marijuana on your property. In Idaho selling water pipes could lead to a prison sentence of nine years. In Kentucky products made of hemp fibers, such as paper and clothing, are not only illegal but technically carry the same penalties associated with an equivalent weight of marijuana.

Crossing an invisible state line with marijuana in your car can result in vastly different punishments. If you are caught with three ounces of marijuana in Union City, Ohio, you will probably be fined $100. But if you're caught in the town of the same name literally across the road in Indiana, you could face six months to three years in prison, a fine of up to $10,000, a felony record, suspension of your driver's license, forfeiture of your car, and charges of marijuana possession, of possession with intent to distribute, and of "maintaining a common nuisance" (for the criminal use of an automobile). That one arrest in Indiana might cost you the $10,000 fine and at least $5,000 in legal fees, plus the value of your forfeited car. Wide discrepancies in punishment occur not just between states but also from county to county within a state. In La Salle County, Illinois, a first-time offender arrested with 300 pounds of marijuana might be sentenced to four months in boot camp. Sixty-five miles to the south, in McLean County, the same person convicted of the same crime would likely receive a prison sentence of four to eight years.

In at least twenty states, federally mandated "smoke a joint, lose your license" statutes now suspend a person's driving license after a conviction for any marijuana crime, regardless of where that person was arrested. A person who has never operated a vehicle under the influence of marijuana may still lose the right to drive. Indeed, being caught smoking a joint on the couch of your living room, with your car parked safely in the driveway, can lead to a harsher punishment than being arrested for driving drunk.

About 724,000 people were arrested in the United States for violating marijuana laws during 2001 — more than were arrested for heroin or cocaine. Almost 90 percent of the marijuana arrests were for simple possession, a crime that in most cases is a misdemeanor. Those arrested may spend a few days in jail. But possession of more than an ounce of marijuana — roughly equal to the amount of tobacco in a pack of cigarettes — is in many states a felony. Conviction may lead to a few months or a few years behind bars and the loss of a house or a job. People who use marijuana as medicine must either buy it from drug dealers or grow it themselves, often in violation of the law. James Cox, a cancer patient in St. Louis, was found guilty of growing marijuana and sentenced to fifteen years in prison. After the verdict, both he and his wife attempted suicide. Orland Foster, an AIDS patient in

North Carolina, served fifteen months for growing marijuana; one of his cellmates served less time for killing a woman.

In perhaps the most extraordinary case of this kind, Jim Montgomery, a paraplegic immobilized from the waist down who smoked marijuana to relieve muscle spasms, was arrested in Sayre, Oklahoma, when sheriffs found two ounces of pot in the pouch on the back of his wheelchair. Montgomery was tried and convicted by a jury for possession of marijuana with intent to distribute, for possession of paraphernalia, for unlawful possession of a weapon during the commission of a crime (two handguns inherited from his father, a police officer), and for maintaining a place resorted to by users of controlled substances. His sentence was life in prison, plus sixteen years. Both the judge and the prosecutor were appalled by the sentence chosen by the jury; the judge subsequently reduced it to ten years. Montgomery spent ten months in a prison medical unit, where he developed a life-threatening infection, before being released on bond. After spending more than $30,000 in legal fees and losing an appeal, he was returned to prison briefly, then freed on medical grounds. The government's effort to seize Montgomery's home, shared with his widowed mother, proved unsuccessful.

Oklahoma today has a well-deserved reputation for being the worst place in the United States to be caught with marijuana. On June 11, 1992, Larry Jackson, a small-time crook with a lengthy record of non-violent offenses, was arrested at a friend's Tulsa apartment. On the floor near Jackson's right foot a police officer noticed a minuscule amount of marijuana — 0.16 of a gram, which is 0.005644 of an ounce. Jackson was charged with felony possession of marijuana, convicted, and given a life sentence. In Oklahoma City, Leland James Dodd was given two life sentences, plus ten years, for buying fifty pounds of marijuana from undercover officers in a "reverse sting."

Oklahoma is not alone in handing out life sentences for buying marijuana from the government. In Tuscaloosa County, Alabama, William Stephen Bonner, a truck driver, was sent away for life without parole after state narcotics agents delivered forty pounds of marijuana to his bedroom. Raymond Pope, a resident of Georgia, was lured to Baldwin County, Alabama, with promises of cheap marijuana; he bought twenty-seven pounds from local sheriffs in a reverse sting, was convicted, and sentenced to life without parole. Pope's criminal record consisted of prior convictions for stealing televisions and bedspreads from Georgia motels. Douglas Lamar Gray purchased a pound of marijuana from a government informer at an Econo Lodge in Morgan County, Alabama. After paying $900 for the pot, which seemed like a real bargain, Gray was arrested, charged with "trafficking in cannabis," tried, convicted, fined $25,000, sentenced to life without parole, and sent to a maximum-security prison. Gray is a Vietnam veteran with an artificial leg. Under the stress of his imprisonment, Gray's wife attempted suicide with a pistol, survived the gunshot, then filed for divorce.

Although the penalties for buying, selling, or possessing marijuana are often harsh, the penalties for growing it can be even more severe. In Iowa, cultivating a few plants can lead to a five-year prison sentence; in Missouri, to a seven-year sentence; in Tennessee, to a fifteen-year sentence. In the state of Virginia, where hemp cultivation was once mandatory by law, the recommended punishment for growing a single marijuana plant is now a prison term of five to thirty years.

a farm in morgan county

IN NOVEMBER OF 1988 Claude Atkinson and Ernest Montgomery met at a Denny's near the airport in Indianapolis to discuss setting up a large-scale marijuana-growing operation. Atkinson, a fifty-nine-year-old Indiana native, was by all accounts charismatic and highly skilled at cultivating marijuana. Ostensibly a used-farm-implements dealer, Atkinson had organized huge marijuana farms in Illinois, Indiana, and Kentucky. His knowledge of growing techniques was much more impressive than his skill at eluding capture. In 1984 law enforcement authorities had linked him to a pot farm in Paragon, Indiana. The following year, he was caught growing marijuana with artificial light in an immense Indianapolis warehouse. And in 1987 a deer hunter stumbled upon thousands of his marijuana plants in an Indiana field. Claude Atkinson had cut a series of deals with the government, informing on others after each arrest and serving brief terms in prison, where he recruited employees for future ventures. Now fresh out of custody and broke, he was ready to get back into the growing business. Ernest Montgomery was an unemployed truck driver in his early forties who wanted to make big money. They agreed to form a partnership, with Montgomery supplying the capital and Atkinson the expertise. Soon after their meeting Claude Atkinson went to the Indiana statehouse and formed a dummy corporation, R.P.Z. Investments, using one of his many pseudonyms, Arno Zepp.

That fall Atkinson supervised the construction of a large "grow room" in the basement of a secluded cabin that Montgomery owned in Gosport. Montgomery enlisted his younger brother, Jerry, a gravedigger with a slight drinking problem, to help with the task. Together the three men drilled holes in the concrete floor for drainage, built a cooling system, assembled ballasts and reflectors, suspended grow lights with thousand-watt halide bulbs from the ceiling, and planted marijuana seeds in small pots. They installed a generator so that the operation would not be detected through an incongruously high electric bill. Montgomery invited David Lee Haynes, a young lumberyard ripsaw operator from Louisville, Kentucky, and the son of an old friend, to come live at the cabin and tend the plants. After digging graves all day, Jerry Montgomery would visit the dark basement in the evenings, tending and pruning. By spring the group had 12,500 small marijuana seedlings growing in sixteen plywood flats. What they needed next was a farm.

In May of 1989, Martha Brummett, an elderly woman hard of hearing, agreed to lease her farmhouse halfway between Eminence and Cloverdale, in Morgan County, to R.P.Z. Investments. It came with about forty acres, a barn, and an option to buy. Martha Brummett was surprised that when a "Charlie Peters" arrived to sign the lease, the woman with him remained in the car and never entered the house. Nevertheless, Brummett innocently signed over her farm for $10,000 in cash, which she then took straight to her bank.

After Ernest Montgomery and his wife, Cindy, secured the house, David Haynes moved into it to "babysit" the operation, having obtained a sham rental agreement from R.P.Z. Investments as a legal buffer from what was about to happen on the land. The group plowed and tilled the field, fertilized it, and planted corn. Once the corn had reached a good height, they planted marijuana, hiding it amid the stalks. Over the summer they walked the fields, "sexing" the marijuana—eliminating all the males. The females, left unpollinated, would produce a much higher level of delta-9-THC in their buds, and would thus become a much more valuable crop: sensimilla. In late September, before the corn leaves turned golden brown, the group harvested the marijuana and then cured it in the barn for two weeks and cut it into "books" about a foot wide and three feet long. The books were hauled into the farmhouse or driven to the cabin in Gosport for manicuring; the stems, orphan leaves, and fan leaves were separated from the precious buds. So far the operation had gone smoothly. Soon there would be about 900 pounds of high-quality marijuana to sell. Now the group needed buyers. Ernest Montgomery thought that Mark Young, a man whom he'd met a few times with Cindy, might know the right people to call.

Mark Young was thirty-six and had been smoking marijuana on a daily basis since his late teens. He'd grown up in Christian Park Heights, a middle-class neighborhood on the east side of Indianapolis. His father left the family when Mark was two. He and his sister, Andrea, were raised by their mother, Mary, who worked as a waitress or a hostess to pay the bills. Young was a willful, stubborn, charming boy always getting into trouble. He seemed to have, throughout his pranks and petty thefts, the sort of bad luck that is almost uncanny—often he would get caught while his friends got away. Young dropped out of high school after a year, became a father at the age of sixteen, married to give the child his name, divorced, worked as a carpet-layer, washed dishes, laid concrete, tended bar, sold used cars, and rebuilt Harley-Davidson motorcycles. He kept an album filled with pictures of his favorite Harleys. He knew all the local biker gangs, but remained apart; Young seemed to get into enough trouble on his own. He dated many women, lived a fast life, and slowly acquired a criminal record—nothing violent, just misdemeanors for driving without a license, for possession of marijuana, for taking a girlfriend's stereo. He also earned two felony convictions: one at the age of twenty-one, for attempting to obtain diet pills with a fraudulent prescription, and the other, at the age of twenty-five, for possession of a few amphetamines and Quaaludes. Each felony brought a suspended sentence, probation, and a $1 fine. When Ernest Montgomery called, Mark Young was rebuilding motorcycles, selling used cars wholesale, and looking for new income. He had held a financial interest in a number of massage parlors, which were now closed. His dream was to get some money, move to Florida, build custom Harleys, and work part-time as a fishing guide on Lake Okeechobee.

Claude Atkinson, Ernest Montgomery, and Mark Young met in the family room of Young's home in early October. The price of the marijuana was set at $1,200 a pound. If Young found buyers, he would receive a commission of $100 for every pound sold. Not long after, Atkinson and Montgomery returned to Young's house, where they were introduced to two men from Florida who were acting on behalf of someone seeking to buy all the marijuana the group could supply. Atkinson offered a hundred pounds a week; the marijuana was still being manicured and couldn't be delivered all at once. Within days a man from New York City arrived at Young's house with $120,000 in a cardboard box. While the New York buyer inspected the marijuana at Montgomery's Indianapolis house, Atkinson remained behind, counting the money. The deal was completed, and Young was handed $10,000 in cash. The New York buyer eventually paid for 600 more pounds, in transactions that took place at Montgomery's house. By Christmas all the high-quality marijuana was gone, the last 200 pounds either distributed to workers who'd helped with various tasks or sold to an acquaintance of Montgomery's in Illinois.

The town of Eminence, Indiana, is about twenty-five miles west of Indianapolis. Near its only intersection is a Citizens Bank, a small church, a convenience store, and a post office built of concrete bricks and painted royal blue. The town boasts 180 inhabitants and looks as though it has not seen much new construction since the interval between the world wars. There are countless small towns like Eminence across the Midwest, slightly faded but still eulogized as the heartland of this country. To reach the farm used by R.P.Z. Investments, one must leave Eminence on a narrow country road and then turn onto a dirt road and drive for a long stretch, past fields of fifty to a hundred acres where corn, hay, soybeans, and wheat are grown, past modest farms with collapsing outbuildings, an occasional trailer home, and rusted cars on cinder blocks. Farther west the land is flat, the acreage of each plot enormous, but here the countryside feels long settled, with hedges and trees marking boundary lines. After cleaning out the barn, Atkinson and Montgomery allowed the lease on Martha Brummett's property to expire. The one-story farmhouse has been painted beige by its latest occupants; the barn remains bright red. There is a porch on the front of the house, an enclosed patio on one side, and a swing set on the lawn. Looking at this humble American farm, one would hardly believe that more than a million dollars' worth of marijuana had been grown there in the space of about three months.

inside the industry

STEVE WHITE LOOKS LIKE AN ORDINARY Indiana farmer, with slightly unkempt hair, a graying beard, teeth stained by nicotine, and strong hands. The day we met, he wore an old flannel shirt, gray pants, and battered work boots. His voice had a low rural twang. He seemed to belong in an old pickup, riding through a vast dusty field. At the time, White was the Indiana coordinator for the Drug Enforcement Administration's Cannabis Eradication/Suppression Program. He'd spent the previous twenty years as a DEA agent in Indiana, working undercover. He knew the state backwards and forwards — had walked it, driven it, and flown low over it every summer, scrutinizing hills and farmland. He got along well with rural people. Nobody ever thought he was a cop. He grew up in New York City and went to elementary school there. His father worked on Wall Street. In addition to pursuing drug dealers, Special Agent White traveled to London every year to indulge a passion for collecting antique English toy soldiers. He would be an implausible character in any work of fiction. Savvy, articulate, self-deprecating, and blunt, White defied easy categorization and knew more about growing marijuana than most of the people he arrested.

Claude Atkinson was an extremely talented grower with a "good product," White told me—"a super salesman." The operation near Eminence was of average size for that time. It is difficult, even from the air, to find marijuana hidden in corn. "Remember *North by Northwest?*" White asked. "Cary Grant in the cornfield? We don't have cornfields like that anymore, with wide rows. They broadcast the stuff, and it's just thicker than hell." Sometimes patches of marijuana will be distributed here and there amid hundreds of acres. Discovering one may not lead to the others. Growers tend to be much more concerned about hiding their marijuana from thieves than from the government. A rural American underworld has emerged around marijuana, secretive and unknown to outsiders. Booby traps are being laid in cornfields. There is now a group of people in the Midwest, known as "patch pirates," who earn a living solely by stealing marijuana from growers, whom they follow. White acknowledged that the booby traps are aimed at patch pirates, not his own men. Nevertheless, fish hooks strung at eye level on fishing line are nondiscriminatory.

Outdoor marijuana farms have become smaller to avoid detection, though White's agents had recently found "60,000 beautiful plants" on a farm in Tippecanoe County. The case proved a disappointment; the DEA found the suspected grower, but prosecutors declined to press charges. "What I want is bodies," White explained. "I don't give a damn about the dope, that's just something we're going to burn up." His job involved a daily cat-and-mouse pursuit of marijuana growers, with both sides changing tactics, adopting new technologies, and often, after an arrest, amicably discussing tricks of the trade. White harbored no animosity toward his prey. "These are not heroin or cocaine dealers," he said. "They're not violent. I find a lot of them personally engaging." They were violating the law, however, and White loved tracking them down.

Take a map of the United States and draw a circle, including within its circumference Indiana, Illinois, and Michigan, with portions of Ohio to the east, Kentucky and Tennessee to the south, and Missouri, Iowa, and Nebraska to the west. According to Steve White, the region within that circle produces most of the marijuana grown in the United States. Some of the most expensive marijuana is cultivated indoors on the West Coast, but for sheer volume, no other area approaches the American heartland. White does not find this surprising. During the Second World War, the U.S. government encouraged farmers throughout the Corn Belt to plant 300,000 acres of marijuana, in the hopes of replacing fiber supplies from Asia that had been cut off by the Japanese. The program, whose slogan was "Hemp for Victory," turned out to be a financial disaster and left marijuana growing wild throughout the Midwest. Known as ditchweed, this marijuana now blankets tens of thousands of acres. For years it had a negligible delta-9-THC content and was used mainly as filler by drug dealers, but there is evidence that the ditchweed may be cross-pollinating with the potent marijuana now cultivated outdoors. The same growing conditions and soil that are ideal for corn are also perfect for cannabis. Most local sheriff's departments have three to five men, with more important things to do than hunt for marijuana. And over the past twenty years, a lot of people with strong agricultural skills have needed money badly — or have wanted more of it than almost any other job in the region could provide. A bushel of corn sells for roughly $2, a bushel of manicured marijuana for at least $70,000. White thinks that marijuana is the largest cash crop in the United States and, and if not the largest in Indiana, then right up there with corn and soybeans.

During the 1960s and early 1970s nearly all the marijuana smoked in the United States was imported, mainly from Mexico, Colombia, and Jamaica. Large-scale American production arose in response to a number of events. The aerial spraying of an herbicide, paraquat, over Mexican marijuana fields, begun in 1975, soon created uneasiness about that nation's product. The U.S. Public Health Service warned that smoking marijuana laced with paraquat might lead to irreversible lung damage. In the early 1980s successful interdiction efforts by the U.S. Border Patrol and the Coast Guard made it more difficult to import marijuana. And the tough new federal laws against drug trafficking encouraged some foreign smugglers to switch from marijuana, a bulk agricultural commodity with a strong smell, to cocaine, an illegal substance that is easier to conceal and brings a far higher return per pound. As marijuana prices rose in the United States, American growers responded to consumer demand. Mark A. R. Kleiman, director of the Drug Policy Analysis Program at the University of California at Los Angeles, finds this to be a rare instance in which protectionism actually worked. Import barriers drove prices high enough to make domestic production extremely profitable. Some American marijuana is now worth more per ounce than gold.

The antidrug movement and the burgeoning American marijuana crop led the DEA to devote more of its resources to marijuana investigations. Kleiman estimates that by 1988, federal antimarijuana efforts totaled approximately $970 million — about 20 to 25 percent of all federal drug enforcement expenditures. Today the federal government spends roughly $4 billion a year to fight the war on marijuana. The DEA's Cannabis Eradication/Suppression Program began in 1979 with two states, California and Hawaii. Federal agents now search for marijuana-farming operations — called "grows" or "gardens" by members of the trade — in all fifty states.

No one knows exactly how much marijuana is cultivated in the United States. The numbers published by the government, or by anyone else, are largely speculative. In 2000 the DEA eradicated 2.6 million pounds of domestic marijuana. In the past, the DEA has claimed that its seizures represent more than half the total domestic output. Critics believe that the DEA actually finds only 10 to 20 percent of the marijuana being grown in this country. With prices ranging from $400 a pound, for low-quality New Mexican weed, to more than $7,000 a pound for "boutique" strains like Northern Lights and Afghan Kush, it can be confidently stated that the black market for American marijuana, whatever the actual tonnage, is immense.

Commercial marijuana growers are increasingly moving their crop indoors, using artificial light and hydroponics, to avoid theft, reduce the risk of detection, control the growing process, and profit from up to six harvests a year. Thirty mature plants can easily be grown in an area the size of a bathtub. I asked Steve White to list some of the places where he has discovered indoor grow operations. He laughed. "It would be tough for me to say places we haven't found them." Often a false wall hides a grow room in a house, or the foundation of a house doesn't match its basement, which seems oddly smaller, or there are second stories with no stairwells, or crawl spaces hidden beneath floors.

White once rummaged through a child's closet and found the entrance to a grow room behind the toys. The DEA now employs thermal imaging devices, mounted on helicopters and low-flying airplanes, to detect abnormal heat sources that may indicate the presence of an indoor growing operation — or a pottery kiln, or a Jacuzzi. What is found depends on the skill of the technician. White learned that one of the best ways to find an indoor grow area is with your nose: no matter how well vented the operation, and despite electronic devices than can neutralize odors in the air, marijuana exudes a powerful scent. Not long ago indoor grows were often huge. A group of janitors in Anderson, Indiana, some of whom had traveled to Israel to study hydroponics, were caught with 8,100 plants in a building with walls constructed a foot thick to thwart infrared detection. Nowadays growers rent storage units and apartments, using phony names and paying in cash, and build small grow operations at different locations, with timing devices and automatic controls. The authorities may find one or two — a loss anticipated in the grower's business plan — without being able to trace ownership.

I asked Steve White if a sense of futility ever crept into his work, given the extent of marijuana cultivation in Indiana. "I'm not such a fool as to sit here and tell you that we're going to wipe out marijuana," he replied. But there was no doubt in his mind that the DEA exerts a deterrent effect. "Every time we have a helicopter go up on a mission," White said, "there's someone down below who sees it and thinks, 'Maybe I better not.' "

Ralph Weisheit, a professor of criminal justice at Illinois State University, does not know Steve White but has come to many of the same conclusions about marijuana cultivation in the Midwest. Weisheit first became interested in the subject during the mid-1980s when he saw, on the television news, an old Illinois farmer being arrested for cultivating marijuana. The farmer and his son never smoked pot; they grew it to save their farm from foreclosure. Weisheit was intrigued. With a grant from the research arm of the U.S. Department of Justice, he conducted a two-year study of marijuana cultivation, interviewing law enforcement officials in five states and dozens of Illinois growers who'd been caught and convicted. The book based on that study,

Domestic Marijuana, A Neglected Industry, chronicles the rise of marijuana production in the United States and offers a fascinating portrait of pot growers. Weisheit agrees that most of the marijuana cultivated in the United States probably comes from the nine-state region described by Steve White. He also thinks marijuana is the nation's largest cash crop, by a very wide margin.

Estimates of how many Americans grow marijuana range from one to three million, of which anywhere from 100,000 to 200,000 are commercial growers. Weisheit found that aside from being predominantly white and male, marijuana growers generally do not fit any common stereotypes. Some are pragmatists, growing it purely for the money; during the Farm Crisis of the 1980s many farmers in the Midwest started cultivating marijuana out of desperation. They found it not only easy money, but easy work. As one farmer told Weisheit: "You know, I spent most of my life trying to kill weeds, so trying to keep one alive was hardly a challenge." Other growers are go-getters by nature; they might as well be selling time-shares in a vacation condominium. They try to build marijuana empires. The risks of the trade only add to its appeal. Other growers are less competitive, giving away marijuana to friends or selling it at slightly above cost, sharing their agricultural techniques, and comparing their crops the way suburban neighbors compare homegrown tomatoes.

Marijuana growers are educated and uneducated, liberal and conservative. They are extremely secretive. Few belong to the National Organization for the Reform of Marijuana Laws (NORML), and few read *High Times* magazine or add their names to any list that might arouse suspicion. Indoor growing often attracts people who love gizmos. There are endless contraptions that can be added to a grow room, from computer-controlled watering systems to electric tables that distribute nutrients evenly by tilting back and forth. Some growers become connoisseurs, producing high-quality marijuana in small quantities, manipulating not only the level of delta-9-THC through cross-breeding, but also the proportions of all the other cannabinoids, to subtly—or not so subtly—affect the nature of the high. Weisheit met growers and law enforcement officers alike who were extraordinarily passionate about marijuana, eager to discuss its arcane details for hours. He was surprised, after the publication of his book, by how little controversy it generated in either camp. His mother was disturbed, however, by one of its central findings: "She's very antidrug," Weisheit says, "and her comment was, 'The thing I don't like about this book is that it makes these people seem so normal.' "

Late one night I met a commercial marijuana grower who introduced himself as "Dave." He'd been growing marijuana, on and off, for more than a decade, beginning outdoors and then graduating to a series of increasingly complex indoor systems. Understandably paranoid and suspicious, Dave was also quite proud of his work and regretted being unable to discuss it with friends. His grow operation had to be built surreptitiously, over a period of weeks, like a factory assembled by hand. It used about $50,000 worth of high-tech, hydroponic equipment. When construction was complete, the whole thing looked so beautiful that Dave wanted to throw an opening-night party, but decided that wouldn't be a good idea. Though he'd always hated gardening and never passed a science class in his life, he now possessed a grasp of marijuana botany, plant biology, and advanced greenhouse management techniques that only Special Agent White could fully appreciate. After smoking a joint rolled with some of his latest harvest, Dave spoke about some of the pleasures, risks, rewards, and bizarre phenomena that accompany his profession, a job that he likens to "playing God indoors."

Hidden behind a fake wall, entered through a secret door, in a neighborhood where you would never, ever, expect to find it, Dave's operation was much larger than most. There were hundreds of marijuana plants in long rows, growing from cubes of rock wool connected through an intricate system of white plastic pipes. Suspended above them were extremely bright high-pressure sodium lights, which required a surge of power from special ballasts to start up. On the ceiling was the bluish flame of a carbon dioxide generator burning natural gas. The windows were sealed and blacked out. The room was warm, the air thick and humid, the whole place filled with a pungent smell reminiscent of fresh hay. Like a greenhouse without glass, it felt very still and quiet, except for the sound of water rushing through narrow pipes.

When everything was running smoothly, Dave controlled the basic elements necessary for his plants: air, light, heat, and water. In a closed chamber there is no wind; here, a ventilation system provided it, circulating air rich in carbon dioxide. When outdoor temperatures dropped too low, Dave used the CO_2 generator on the ceiling, in effect, "fertilizing the air." Pumps and timers automatically watered the plants, also delivering nutrients such as nitrogen, phosphorus, and potassium that would normally be derived from soil. One of the critical factors in growing potent marijuana is the proportion of darkness to light. Sometimes Dave's high-pressure sodium lights burned eighteen hours a day, raising the temperature in the grow room to as much as 110 degrees. During the female plant's reproductive stage, there had to be long periods of total, uninterrupted darkness. As little as two footcandles of light could disrupt the delicate process by which delta-9-THC accumulates in the buds. Turning on a flashlight at the wrong moment, Dave said, would be enough to ruin his plants.

Dave was truly a cannabis connoisseur, growing an expensive strain of marijuana from the northern Hindu Kush. As he described how some outdoor growers stuff their marijuana into plastic garbage bags while it's still wet, he grimaced, like a master vintner appalled by the improper handling of grapes. The buds are very fragile, he said: "You're trying to coax this mature flower to retain its essence — and then store it and seal it at that instant in time." His finished product was deep green and aromatic, like some rare, exotic spice.

Growing marijuana indoors requires much more work than cultivating it outdoors. There is also more potential for disaster. A splash of liquid on a hot light will cause it to explode. A broken pipe can flood the room with hundreds of gallons of water. A power outage shuts the whole system down. The nutrient solution, if improperly monitored, can quickly turn too acidic and, as Dave put it, "give the plants a heart attack" — that is, kill them all. Using the wrong jet on the CO_2 generator (as a number of growers have done) can lead to a gas explosion, causing damage that an insurance company is unlikely to reimburse. More common, and yet somehow more surreal, are insect infestations that can harm valuable young plants. Dave had battled spider mites, greenhouse whiteflies, and aphids. Insecticides are not an option in a windowless room, with a crop that will be smoked. Dave used biological controls, relying on hungry young predators to eliminate unwanted bugs. He'd recently unleashed thousands of miniature wasps. This is insanity, he thought—but it worked. Inside a nearby refrigerator, he always kept 500 ladybug eggs, next to the soda, in case of emergency. The day we met, Dave was contending with gnats, who left his plants alone but swarmed him and bit him as he walked about the grow room in the dark.

someone at the door

ON MARCH 18, 1990, a couple of deputy sheriffs in Johnson County, Indiana, spotted a red Jeep being driven erratically and signaled for its driver to pull off the road. Behind the wheel they found Jerry Montgomery, obviously intoxicated; littering the truck were three empty vodka bottles, a five-gallon bucket full of marijuana, and a gray box containing $13,000 in cash. After obtaining a warrant, sheriffs searched Montgomery's house, finding more marijuana and a briefcase hidden beneath his bed. Deputy John Myers pried it open with a screwdriver. In the briefcase were receipts for farm equipment; documents mentioning R.P.Z. Investments, Claude Atkinson, and Ernest Montgomery; an option to buy a property owned by Martha Brummett; and a number of books that suggested that this arrest was the beginning, not the end, of a trail: *Indoor Marijuana Horticulture, The Primo Plant,* and *How to Grow Marijuana Indoors Under Lights.*

The investigation eventually led authorities to a 500-acre farm close to Solsberry, in Greene County, owned by Arno Zepp of Investment Holdings, Inc. On August 22 federal, state, and local law enforcement agents arrested Claude Atkinson, raided the farm, and, with the help of volunteers from the Indiana National Guard, destroyed 10,000 marijuana plants. Atkinson soon began to talk. In May, 1991, Ernest Montgomery was arrested at his Gosport cabin, where 7,000 marijuana seedlings sat in little pots, ready for planting. Early that same morning Mark Young was awakened by someone at the front door. Unlike his former business partners, Young was not growing anything. He and his girlfriend, Patricia, were in the process of moving to Florida. When he saw a man with a badge and a gun, Young had no idea what was happening, but assumed it must have something to do with unpaid taxes.

More than a dozen law enforcement officers surrounded the house. Their commander, a DEA agent, treated Young politely, allowing him to get dressed and agreeing not to handcuff him in front of the neighbors. At the station Young read his indictment. He was being charged, under federal law, not only for his role in distributing 700 pounds of marijuana but also for conspiring to manufacture all 12,500 marijuana plants grown on Martha Brummett's farm. Young was unaware of the punishment he might face until later that day. John Hollywood, a bail bondsman in Indianapolis, arrived in the afternoon to secure his release. But the government refused to set bail. Under Indiana's strict state law, the same charges might bring a maximum sentence of twenty-eight years — at most, fourteen years served in prison, and probably much less. But under federal law, Young's two prior state felony convictions, one of them more than seventeen years old, classified him as a career drug offender. This arrest could prove his third strike. At the U.S. attorney's discretion, he faced a possible mandatory minimum sentence of life imprisonment without parole.

the new rules

THERE HAVE BEEN MANDATORY MINIMUM sentences in the United States since the days of the first Congress, most of them adopted to punish narrowly defined crimes. A number of the old mandatory minimums are still on the books, such as "robbery by pirates" (1790) and "practice of pharmacy and sale of poisons in China" (1915). The overwhelming majority of criminal laws passed by Congress specify only a maximum sentence. It has historically been the role of a federal judge to determine whether a convicted offender deserves that maximum, a lesser sentence, or no prison sentence at all. Until 1987, a federal judge had great leeway in choosing sentences: Congress set only the upper limit, thereby protecting citizens from excessive punishment. Parole boards served as another brake on unduly harsh sentences, deciding when prisoners merited early release.

The first broadly defined mandatory minimums were contained in the Boggs Act, which was passed in 1951, at the height of the McCarthy era, amid the tensions of the Korean War and domestic fears of Communist subversion. There seemed to be an increase in narcotics use among the young, and lenient judges were thought partly to blame. Members of Congress vied to appear tough on drug offenders. Senator Everett Dirksen favored legislation that could impose the death penalty for selling narcotics to minors. Congressman Edwin Arthur Hall advocated giving drug dealers mandatory minimum sentences of one hundred years. Congressman L. Gary Clemente introduced a bill recommending the death penalty for any violation of the Narcotic Drugs Import and Export Act. FBN commissioner Harry J. Anslinger seemed almost moderate in calling for a mandatory minimum of five years for second offenders, which he assured Congress "would just about dry up the [drug] traffic." Congress followed his advice and then lengthened the antidrug mandatory sentences in 1956. One vocal critic of the new sentencing regime was James V. Bennett, director of the U.S. Bureau of Prisons, who attributed the passage of such laws to "hysteria." Thereafter Bennett was secretly followed by FBN agents, who submitted reports on his movements and speeches.

By the late 1960s, a widespread consensus had emerged in both political parties that the antidrug mandatory minimum sentences were a failure. Members of Congress, federal judges, and even prosecutors found them too severe, unjust, and, worst of all, ineffective at preventing narcotics use. The spread of the 1960s drug culture had not been halted by the existence of tough mandatory minimum sentences. In 1970 Congress repealed almost all the mandatory penalties for drug offenders, an act celebrated by Congressman George H. W. Bush, who predicted these "penal reforms" would "result in better justice and more appropriate sentences." A movement arose seeking a new means of determining prison sentences. Allowing judges too little freedom had proved to be unfair, but granting too much could also lead to inequities. A drug dealer in Florida might be given a twenty-year sentence, while a drug dealer in California might get probation for exactly the same sort of crime. Marvin Frankel, a federal judge in New York, outlined a new system of justice that promised to be more impartial at sentencing. A commission of legal experts would set guidelines on how to determine the punishments for various crimes, taking into account both the nature of the offense and the criminal history of the offender.

After long and careful deliberation, the Sentencing Reform Act of 1984 was passed by Congress with overwhelming bipartisan support, creating the U.S. Sentencing Commission. It seemed a triumph of rational jurisprudence over demagoguery, an experiment in social planning that evoked shades of the Progressive Era, when panels of appointed experts were hailed as the ideal form of government. In just eighteen months the commission devised sentences of varying severity for about 2,000 federal crimes. Under the new rules, each federal offense was assigned a numerical value. The judge added or subtracted points in a given case according to various criteria, and punishment was determined by matching the offender's total points with a range of applicable sentences listed on a chart. A judge could depart from these guidelines at sentencing, but had to offer an explanation for doing so. The sentence could later be appealed by the defendant—or by the prosecutor.

The same Congress that passed the Sentencing Reform Act also included, in the very same bill, new mandatory minimum sentences for drug offenses committed near schools. Two years later the Anti–Drug Abuse Act of 1986 moved away from the deliberate calibrations of the sentencing guidelines by endorsing the blunt instrument of mandatory minimum sentences for a wide variety of drug offenses. The University of Maryland basketball star Len Bias had just been killed by crack cocaine, and antidrug sentiment reached new heights. It was an election year, and lawmakers decided once again to send a tough message. Mandatory minimum sentences, based on the amount of drugs involved in an offense, were set at five years, ten years and twenty years. Additional mandatory minimums were added later, including what is now known as a "three strikes, you're out" provision that specified life sentences for repeat drug offenders. During the congressional debates on these mandatory sentences there was little mention of the precedent of failure set by the Boggs Act, or of how the new laws would undermine the sentencing guidelines, or of what the wider effects might be throughout the criminal justice system, from the initial filing of charges to the ultimate rates of imprisonment. According to one survey, the most commonly cited justification for these harsh punishments was a desire for retribution, a legal theory nicknamed "just deserts."

For most of the nation's first 200 years, a convicted man or woman could ask a federal judge for mercy. On the basis of extenuating circumstances, a judge could reduce a prison sentence or waive it altogether. The new mandatory minimum laws took that power from the judge and handed it to the prosecutor. A U.S. attorney now has the sole authority to decide whether a mandatory minimum applies in a particular case — that is, whether to frame a charge under such a statute, or not. The only way a defendant can be sure of avoiding a mandatory minimum sentence is to plead guilty and give "substantial assistance" in the prosecution of someone else. The U.S. attorney, not the judge, decides whether the defendant's cooperation is sufficient to warrant a reduction in sentence. A defendant might cooperate and still not receive a shorter sentence, if the information supplied falls short of expectations. Long mandatory prison terms provide a strong incentive to talk. From the government's point of view, guilty pleas, accompanied by cooperation, avoid expensive trials and supply valuable evidence. From the defendant's point of view, the pressure to name others is enormous.

Some federal judges believe that the quality of much testimony has become unreliable; desperate people will say anything to save themselves. An appeal for compassion is now pointless. All that matters is the demand for cooperation. Under such a system the dilemmas often have an elemental quality. In Kansas City, Tora S. Brown — a nineteen-year-old first offender with an eight-month-old baby daughter — implicated others in a drug case involving PCP, but refused to testify against her own mother. Brown was given a ten-year prison sentence without parole.

a sad day for everybody

ASSISTANT U.S. ATTORNEY DONNA EIDE, in the Southern District of Indiana, offered Mark Young a reduced sentence in return for a guilty plea and his cooperation: forty years without parole. Kevin McShane, Young's attorney, thought the offer was ridiculous; he wouldn't accept forty years as a plea bargain in a first-degree murder case. That remained the government's only offer from May until September of 1991. Meanwhile, one by one, other defendants "flipped," agreeing to cooperate.

Claude Atkinson had been facing a mandatory life sentence; the others, sentences of ten years to life. By offering to cooperate, each had received a "cap" on his sentence, an upper limit of anywhere from eight to thirty-five years. But each could also conceivably walk free, without any prison time. Their sentences would depend on their performances in court, among other things. Young and Ernest Montgomery and his wife, Cindy, were the only remaining defendants who would not plead guilty.

Under the U.S. sentencing guidelines, Mark Young's marijuana offense warranted a prison term of roughly twenty-two to twenty-seven years. The guidelines would apply in his case, unless the U.S. attorney decided to file an enhancement, reflecting Young's criminal history and requiring the mandatory life sentence. Donna Eide made one last offer: eighteen years, pending cooperation. Young refused it. The government filed its enhancement on the Friday before the trial was to begin. The wheels had been set in motion, and Mark Young had a long weekend in which to make his choice: agree to cooperate or risk spending the rest of his life in prison.

Kevin McShane does not believe the government really wanted to give his client a life sentence; that sort of threat is now common in the give-and-take of the plea bargaining process. He does not believe the government really wanted any information from Young. Claude Atkinson, who knew more than anyone else about the marijuana farm, was talking up a storm. The identities of the New York and Florida buyers would have been of interest to federal authorities in other districts, but it was not clear that Young even knew their real names. On the eve of the trial it seemed the government simply wanted to avoid a trial. McShane strongly advised Mark Young to accept the offer of eighteen years; with so many potentially hostile witnesses, his chances in court were uncertain—a roll of the dice. Young's family, which to this point had remained silent on the issue, also urged him to cooperate. His mother visited him in jail and begged. "At the end, when we seen how bad it was, I just really got on him," she recalls. " 'Please, Mark, do it, do like the rest of them are, don't do this, don't end up, you know, with a life sentence, don't do it. Tell whatever you have to tell, like the rest of them are doing, to save yourself.' But no way would he do it. No way."

The day before Young's trial began, Cindy Montgomery agreed to a plea bargain. The trial was notable for the details it revealed about the marijuana growing operation, but the outcome never seemed in doubt. McShane thinks that Young's case was hurt by being tried alongside that of Ernest Montgomery, who had organized the operation. Jerry Montgomery testified against his brother and proved unable, owing to illiteracy, to read his own plea agreement for the jury. Cindy Montgomery testified against her husband. And Claude Atkinson spoke at length about everybody's criminal activities. The atmosphere at the trial was enlivened by jailhouse rumors that Mark Young had not only threatened the lives of Cindy Montgomery and Claude Atkinson and their families but had also slept with one of the jurors, who was going to thwart any guilty verdict. Young called no witnesses in his own defense. There was no physical evidence linking him to the crime, only testimony by Atkinson and Cindy Montgomery. The jury took just two and a quarter hours to render guilty verdicts on all counts. None of the jurors had been informed that a life sentence might apply.

Claude Atkinson was angry to receive a twenty-five-year sentence, despite his cooperation. One of the prosecutors later described him as a "dreamer"; he may have expected to serve only a few years. For a sixty-two-year-old man, a twenty-five-year sentence was tantamount to life in prison. Ernest Montgomery, whose only previous conviction was for disorderly conduct, got thirty-four years, without parole—also, in effect, a life sentence. His brother received eight years, his wife six, and the other defendants sentences ranging from three to ten years in prison. On February 8, 1992, Judge Sarah Evans Barker gave Mark Young a life sentence, as mandated. She also fined him $100, but did not order any of his assets forfeited. He had none, having paid his lawyer with a used car. "Mr. Young, it's a sad day for everybody in the courtroom," she said. "That concludes the matter."

friends in high places

BILL CLINTON'S ELECTION TO THE presidency later that year raised hopes that the war on marijuana might soon come to an end. Clinton was the first baby-boomer to become president, as well as the first commander-in-chief to acknowledge having put a joint in his mouth. During the presidential campaign he'd claimed to have smoked pot as a young man—without violating the drug laws of the United States or getting stoned. "When I was in England I experimented with marijuana a time or two," Clinton said, "and I didn't inhale." His carefully worded, legalistic disclosure prompted a good deal of snickering and disbelief. "I wish I had inhaled," Clinton later told an MTV audience, a remark that implied pot-smoking was a youthful indiscretion, not a mortal sin. As governor of Arkansas, Clinton had once supported the decriminalization of marijuana. As president, however, he never wavered from the tough marijuana policies established by Ronald Reagan. Clinton opposed the use of marijuana as medicine and supported legal punishments for physicians who recommended it to their patients. One of the most liberal members of Clinton's cabinet, Donna E. Shalala, assumed the antidrug role once played by Nancy Reagan. "Marijuana is illegal, dangerous, unhealthy, and wrong," said Shalala, who as secretary of Health and Human Services controlled federal research into the drug's medicinal uses. "It's a one-way ticket to dead-end hopes and dreams."

The number of annual marijuana arrests more than doubled during the Clinton years, reaching their highest level in American history. Far more people were arrested for marijuana during the Clinton presidency than during any other U.S. presidency. Although Richard Nixon often seemed to be the great nemesis of pot smokers, more than three times as many people were arrested for marijuana while Bill Clinton was president.

The huge increase in marijuana arrests during the mid-1990s can be partly explained by heightened police attention to "quality of life" violations. In New York City, Mayor Rudolph Giuliani's "zero tolerance" policy toward marijuana led to a twenty-six-fold increase in pot arrests. But the war on marijuana during the Clinton years was not driven by new strategies of policing in American cities. It was driven by the fear, especially among Democrats, of appearing "soft" on drugs. Condemning marijuana had become an easy way for baby-boomer politicians to distance themselves from the 1960s youth counterculture. It was a way of demonstrating true "Americanism." As a means of enforcing conformity, the war on marijuana increasingly resembled the 1950s anti-Communist crusade. In 1987 one of President Reagan's choices for the U.S. Supreme Court, Douglas H. Ginsburg, had declined the nomination after confessing that he'd smoked marijuana as a young man. Ginsburg's decision to step down set an unfortunate precedent. The defining political question of the McCarthy era — "Are you now, or have you ever been, a member of the Communist party?" — was soon transmuted into a new litmus test for baby-boomers. Every member of Congress and candidate for elected office soon had to answer the question: "Are you now, or have you ever been, a pot smoker?"

In 1981 Congressman Newt Gingrich introduced a bill to legalize the medicinal use of marijuana. Fifteen years later, as Speaker of the House, Gingrich sponsored legislation demanding a life sentence or the death penalty for anyone who brought more than two ounces of marijuana into the United States. Although the Clinton administration opposed that bill, it accepted the basic premises of marijuana prohibition, allowing the heirs of the Reagan revolution to set America's policy on the drug. Senator Mitch McConnell and Congressman Bob Barr emerged as two of pot's fiercest and most outspoken critics. McConnell tried without success to make federal penalties for selling or possessing marijuana equivalent to those for selling or possessing cocaine and heroin. Barr fought hard to prevent any research into the "so-called medicinal use of marijuana" and claimed such attempts were part of a vast conspiracy. "All civilized countries in the world," he said, "are under assault by drug proponents seeking to enslave citizens." He called the effort to reform the nation's marijuana laws a "subversive criminal movement." McConnell and Barr were deeply concerned about the potential harms caused by smoking marijuana; but smoking cigarettes was a different story. Barr opposed lawsuits against tobacco companies, arguing that such efforts were reminiscent of "Soviet rule" and that the product in question was "legal, widely used, profitable, disfavored by the ruling intelligentsia . . . and subject to some colorable claim that it harmed someone, somehow, somewhere." In 2002 McConnell accepted more money from tobacco lobbyists than any other member of Congress. Tobacco use is the leading cause of preventable deaths in the United States, responsible for an estimated 440,000 deaths every year.

Much like the loyalty oaths that became routine in the 1950s, widespread drug testing became a tool for keeping pot smokers out of mainstream society. In the early 1980s about 3 percent of Fortune 200 companies tested their employees and job applicants for illegal drug use. A decade later about 98 percent of these companies demanded such tests. The Drug-Free Workplace Act of 1998 provided federal funds to small businesses that wanted to impose drug testing, too. Because marijuana is the most widely used illegal drug, it is responsible for the vast majority of positive results. The drug tests now being administered by corporations, state governments, and the federal government cannot determine whether a person is stoned. The metabolites of marijuana can remain in a user's body for days or even weeks after pot use; a person who smokes a joint on a Saturday night can easily fail a drug test the following Monday morning. The huge drug-testing system that now governs much of the American workplace cannot reveal if you have ever been stoned on the job. It only reveals whether you are the sort of person who likes to smoke pot. That sort of person can now legally be fired — or prevented from gaining employment in the first place. Meanwhile, someone who downs ten shots of tequila every night does not face the same risk of losing a job. A recent study of 14,000 employees at seven major U.S. corporations found that 8 percent of the hourly workers and 23 percent of the managers regularly consumed alcohol on the job.

The rise in testing for marijuana has been driven not only by drug war ideology but also by economics. The Institute for a Drug-Free Workplace has helped Congress draft new laws to expand testing and has fought against state laws that might restrict an employer's ability to test workers. Two of the four companies represented on the institute's board of directors are pharmaceutical firms that handle drug tests. An industry that hardly existed until the 1980s now has annual revenues of about $740 million. Although common sense suggests that employees who are stoned on the job do not perform as well as employees who come to work sober, the scientific evidence to support such a contention is scarce. A 1999 survey of more than two hundred studies of pot use and the workplace found that "marijuana has no direct, negative effect on workers' productivity." While nobody would dispute the need for routine drug testing of certain workers (such as airline pilots, train operators, and bus drivers), one important group has thus far managed to avoid having to provide their employer with urine samples. Legislation to impose drug testing on members of Congress has repeatedly died in committee and never reached the floor for a vote.

Those who suffer most from the war on marijuana tend to be poor or working-class people. Unlike members of the upper middle class, they cannot avoid prison by hiring costly attorneys or enrolling in private drug treatment programs before trial. They are often devastated by the loss of state or federal benefits that can follow a marijuana arrest. In 1997 Gary Martin was arrested in Manchester, Connecticut, and charged with possession of marijuana. Almost twenty years earlier, he'd been severely beaten in a robbery, resulting in permanent brain damage. After the beating, he endured a series of strokes that left his right side paralyzed. He developed circulatory problems, and his left leg was amputated. Martin began to smoke marijuana to relieve the "phantom pains" from his amputated leg. After being arrested for possessing less than four ounces of pot, he was evicted from his apartment at a special housing complex for the elderly and disabled. None of the doctors or nurses treating Martin were warned that he might be evicted. They would have lobbied the authorities on his behalf. "Kicking this guy out of his apartment for pot," said Tom Condon, a reporter for the *Hartford Courant,* "was just pathetic."

The offspring of important government officials, however, tend to avoid severe punishments for their marijuana crimes. In 1982, the year that President Reagan launched the war on drugs, his chief of staff's son was arrested for selling pot. John C. Baker, the son of future Secretary of State James Baker, sold a small amount of marijuana — around a quarter of an ounce — to an undercover agent near the family's ranch in Texas. Under state law John Baker faced a possible felony charge and a prison term of between two and twenty years. Instead, he was charged with a misdemeanor, pleaded guilty, and was fined $2,000. In 1990 Congressman Dan Burton introduced legislation requiring the death penalty for drug dealers. "We must educate our children about drugs," Burton said, "and impose tough new penalties on dealers." Four years later his son was arrested while transporting nearly eight pounds of marijuana from Texas to Indiana. Burton hired an attorney for his son. While awaiting trial in that case, Danny Burton II was arrested again, only five months later, for growing thirty marijuana plants in his Indianapolis apartment. Police also found a shotgun in the apartment. Under federal law Danny Burton faced a possible mandatory minimum sentence of five years in prison just for the gun, plus up to three years in prison under state law for the pot. Federal charges were never filed against Burton, who wound up receiving a milder sanction: a term of community service, probation, and house arrest. When the son of Richard W. Riley (the former South Carolina governor who became Clinton's secretary of education) was indicted on federal charges of conspiring to sell cocaine and marijuana, he faced ten years to life in prison and a fine of $4 million. Instead, Richard Riley, Jr., received six months of house arrest.

In September, 1996, Congressman Randy "Duke" Cunningham attacked President Clinton for being "cavalier" toward illegal drug use and for appointing too many "soft on crime" liberal judges. "We must get tough on drug dealers," Cunningham argued. "Those who peddle destruction on our children must pay dearly." Four months later, his son Randall Todd Cunningham was arrested by the DEA after helping to transport 400 pounds of marijuana from California to Massachusetts. Although Todd Cunningham confessed to having been part of a smuggling ring that had shipped as much as 30,000 pounds of marijuana throughout the United States—a crime that can lead to a life sentence without parole—he was charged with distributing only 400 pounds of pot. The prosecutor in his case recommended a sentence of fourteen months at a boot camp and a halfway house. Congressman Cunningham begged the judge for mercy. "My son has a good heart," he said, fighting back tears. "He's never been in trouble before." Todd Cunningham was sentenced to two and a half years in prison. He might have received an even shorter sentence had he not tested positive for cocaine three times while out on bail.

the most expensive joint

AMERICA'S MARIJUANA LAWS NOW GIVE the government enormous leeway in choosing to punish some people while affording leniency to others. In the early 1990s a federal judge in Utah, Thomas Green, warned that power over the fate of many drug defendants had shifted from an independent judiciary to the state. By adopting mandatory minimum drug laws, Judge Green said, Congress had curtailed the discretion of federal judges at sentencing, but had placed no similar restrictions on the behavior of law enforcement officers and U.S. attorneys. As a result, the United States now faced "de facto sentencing by police and prosecutors." The Supreme Court has upheld federal mandatory minimums whenever they have been challenged on constitutional grounds, supporting the rise in prosecutorial power.

Today a U.S. attorney wields enormous influence in drug cases by deciding how to frame a charge, what quantity of the drug to include in the charge—and whether to press federal charges at all. A different prosecutor might have charged Mark Young only for drug trafficking, likely bringing him a sentence of about seven years. Young's conviction for "conspiracy to manufacture" all 12,500 plants shows how broadly that crime may be defined. The owners of garden supply stores have been held legally responsible for marijuana cultivated by their customers — an application of conspiracy theory similar to that which once imprisoned people for selling sugar to moonshiners. Gary Tucker, the owner of a garden supply store in suburban Atlanta called Southern Lights and Hydroponics, was sentenced to sixteen and a half years in federal prison for the pot grown by his customers; his wife, Joanne, who worked part-time behind the counter, received ten. Often the most important factor in determining a sentence is the amount of marijuana involved. Mandatory minimums often ignore the defedant's role in the crime: a "mule" driving a truckload of marijuana can be subject to the same penalty as the person financing the shipment. In fact, defendants with the smallest role in conspiracies often serve the longest sentences, because they have so little information to trade.

Drug offenses differ from most crimes in being subject to three jurisdictions: local, state, and federal. A U.S. attorney, simply by deciding to enter a particular case, may greatly skew the range of potential punishments. A person may even be tried twice for the same drug crime. Found innocent by a state jury, a marijuana grower can subsequently be convicted in federal court. In 1985 Donald Clark, a watermelon farmer from Tampa, Florida, was arrested for growing marijuana, convicted under state law, and sentenced to probation. Five years later, the local U.S. attorney decided that Clark had not been punished enough. Clark was indicted under federal law for exactly the same crime, found guilty, and sentenced to life in prison without parole.

There are no established criteria for when a U.S. attorney will enter a marijuana case. The federal government could prosecute any and every marijuana offender in the United States — all 724,000 of them — if it so desired. But in a typical year the federal government charges less than 1 percent of those arrested. In some districts there is a policy that the U.S. attorney will enter cases involving more than a hundred plants or a hundred pounds. In others a federal prosecutor may simply take a special interest in a case. Edward Czuprynski, a liberal activist who had long irritated public officials in Bay City, Michigan, was convicted in federal court for possession of 1.6 grams of marijuana — the amount found in a large joint. Under Michigan law he most likely would have received a $100 fine. But in federal court Czuprynski was sentenced to fourteen months in prison. His license to practice law was suspended. His successful law firm was closed down. "They busted me completely," he says, "and that's what they wanted to do." After spending almost six months in federal prison, Czuprynski was released by order of the Sixth Circuit Court of Appeals. Considering his legal fees of $40,000, his lost income of ten times that amount, and the untold thousands of dollars the federal government spent on his case, Czuprynski said, "That may be the most expensive joint in the nation's history."

More than a decade ago Julie Stewart founded Families Against Mandatory Minimums (FAMM), a grassroots organization with the motto "Let the Punishment Fit the Crime." She had not given much thought to America's drug laws until her older brother was convicted for having grown 375 marijuana seedlings. His sentence was five years. FAMM now has more than 25,000 members, most of them politically active for the first time in their lives. After Mark Young was arrested, his older sister, Andrea Strong, lost two house-cleaning jobs in suburban Indianapolis — a sign of the great stigma that marijuana still carries in many parts of the country. Strong is now FAMM's director of member services, a self-taught expert on federal criminal law and a tireless campaigner for the repeal of mandatory minimums. FAMM lobbies Congress for sentencing reform and compiles case histories of inmates imprisoned under mandatory minimum laws. Among them are Michael T. Irish, a first offender sentenced to twelve years in federal prison for helping unload hashish from a boat; Charles Dunlap, a first offender sentenced to eight years in federal prison for renting a truck used by a friend to import marijuana; and Zodenta McCarter, an elderly woman, a first offender, poor and illiterate, described as "naive, trusting, and childlike in comprehension," who was sentenced to eight years in federal prison for conspiring to sell ditchweed, a strain of wild marijuana that is rarely psychoactive. After being incarcerated, McCarter had a heart attack, endured three operations, and was infected with tuberculosis.

deep in the hole

LEAVENWORTH PENITENTIARY IS THE OLDEST prison in the federal system. It's also one of the most dangerous. A hundred years ago there were no federal prisons. The roughly 2,500 convicts with federal sentences longer than a year served their time in state facilities scattered across the country. In 1896 Congress appropriated funds for construction of the first federal penitentiary, to be located on more than 1,500 acres in rural Kansas, a few miles from the Army base at Fort Leavenworth. The new prison was built by the convicts who would soon occupy it. In its first hundred years or so of operation, only one prisoner has ever escaped from Leavenworth and eluded capture. The red brick walls, with a gun tower at each corner, are thirty-five feet high and extend an equal distance beneath the ground. The main building is massive, ominous, and redolent of power. It was designed to resemble the U.S. Capitol, converting a national symbol of freedom and democracy into one of punishment and obedience. On a bleak winter morning, when the grayness of the sky and that of the neighboring fields seem to merge, Leavenworth looks exactly as an inmate described it more than seven decades ago: like a "giant mausoleum adrift in a great sea of nothingness."

To reach the visiting room, you must state your name and purpose to a corrections officer in a small gun tower and then climb stairs to the front entrance. After passing through two electric doors reinforced with steel bars, you are photographed; stamped with invisible ink; asked to sign a pledge that you are not bearing firearms, explosives, or narcotics; led through a metal detector; and then escorted through another large door with steel bars. The visiting room looks like a Knights of Columbus meeting hall, with blond wood paneling, a row of vending machines, and comfortable chairs separated by small tables. There is no glass between inmates and their guests. Visits are supervised by corrections officers who sit on a platform at one end of the room; surveillance cameras are hidden in the ceiling. As I waited to meet Mark Young, a small boy ran up and down the length of the room playing with his father, a bearded inmate in khaki work clothes.

Jonathan Turley, a professor at George Washington University Law

School, thinks that Leavenworth is a perfect microcosm of the federal prison system: antiquated, overcrowded, and extremely dangerous for both inmates and corrections officers. Leavenworth's rated capacity is about 1,200 prisoners, but at times in the past year it has housed more than 1,700. Overcrowding greatly increases the risk of violence, making prison riots more likely. The federal system as a whole is operating at about 30 percent above capacity. Some facilities now house twice the number of people they were designed to hold, while the federal prison population keeps growing at a rate of more than 10,000 inmates a year.

Tough drug laws, strictly enforced, have fueled this unprecedented growth in the federal prison system. The Boggs Act of the 1950s did not have the same effect, because drug offenses were less common and less vigorously prosecuted. As late as 1967 the Federal Bureau of Narcotics had only 300 agents. Its successor, the DEA, now has 4,600. During the 1980s federal spending to incarcerate drug offenders rose more than 1,300 percent, from $88 million to $1.3 billion. Antidrug mandatory minimum sentences and the guideline sentences formulated to mesh neatly with them have transformed the inmate population. In 1970 there were 3,384 drug offenders in federal prison. Today there are more than 68,000. Many are first offenders, without so much as a previous arrest, who have been imprisoned for low-level drug crimes. Of the more than 7,500 people convicted in 2000 of violating federal marijuana laws, about half had no criminal record deemed relevant at sentencing. State correctional facilities are also being flooded with drug offenders. Violent criminals are sometimes being released early in order to provide prison cells for nonviolent drug offenders whose mandatory sentences do not permit parole. The number of drug offenders imprisoned in America today — more than 330,000 — is much larger than the number of people imprisoned for all crimes in 1970.

Mark Young is big — about six-foot-five, with the build you would expect of an old biker. The day I met him, he had long hair tied in a ponytail. He seemed like a hippie version of the country-and-western star Hank Williams, Jr., with a gravelly drawl and a deadpan sense of humor. Before being sent to Leavenworth, Young married his longtime girlfriend, Patricia Rowland, in a Native American ceremony at the local jail. After the wedding Patricia visited him as much as she could, but it's a nine- or ten-hour drive from Indianapolis to Leavenworth, Kansas. She brought him photographs of changes in their neighborhood: new houses, new stores opening at the mall. They discussed how furniture should be arranged at their rented home. She later moved things around accordingly, and sent him pictures. She didn't want him to forget that a familiar world still existed beyond those red brick walls.

Young had never been in prison before being sent to Leavenworth. A federal marijuana conviction usually leads to incarceration at a minimum-security prison or a prison camp. But Young's life sentence labeled him as a high risk for attempted escape, requiring that he be sent to a maximum-security penitentiary. Young suddenly found himself living among some of the most violent repeat offenders in the federal system: murderers, rapists, armed robbers, international terrorists. His two-man cell was eight feet by ten feet, with a solid metal sliding door and no view of the outdoors, just a window facing the catwalk. A few months after his arrival Young sat in a prison auditorium, packed with inmates, watching *Silence of the Lambs*. A riot suddenly erupted in the darkness. Prisoners divided by race and tore furniture apart to make weapons. Corrections officers were taken hostage. Amid the chaos Young grabbed a piece of a chair and huddled against the theater wall, terrified. Hours later, when officers finally quelled the riot, Young was tear-gassed, handcuffed, and dragged along the floor through a pool of blood.

Because of Young's size, other inmates had left him alone. "But anything can happen to anyone here, at any time," he told me, snapping his fingers. "Just like that." Inmates with life sentences and no chance of parole had nothing to lose. The previous year a good friend of Young's, Clyde Harrison, was stabbed to death in the dining room, in front of hundreds of people, over a $50 debt. The killer politely gave the knife to a corrections officer, handle first. Young had never witnessed anything like it. His friend died instantly, and then "people were stepping over him to get to the salad bar."

Young's trial was such a strange experience that he found it difficult to describe. You'd have to be very stoned, he said, to appreciate how absurd it was. He hardly knew Ernest Montgomery and had met Claude Atkinson only twice, spending a total of less than an hour with him. He had never visited the farm where the marijuana was grown and still didn't know where it was. Most of the people who testified in court were people whom Young had never laid eyes on before. It made no sense to him that the law should give him a life sentence for conspiring to cultivate marijuana. Young was quite candid about a lot of socially unacceptable things he'd done and admitted to finding a buyer for the Indiana group. But he ridiculed Claude Atkinson's efforts during the trial to depict him as a major broker, a PaineWebber of pot. The truth, according to Young, was much less dramatic. He was in Florida, fishing with a buddy and sharing a joint. His friend praised the marijuana, which Montgomery had given to Young as a free sample. A few days later, the friend called Young and asked if there was any more of "that good stuff." Young thought there was. His friend then called a friend, who called another friend: a buyer in New York. Young claimed that he actually received just a fraction of the $70,000 fee alleged in court. He did not really know either the buyer or the seller. Once the two got together, they did the natural thing—eliminate the middle man. "They cheated me!" Young said, laughing hard.

Although he always loved to smoke marijuana, Young never thought much about it until going to prison. Now he's an expert on the subject, a fan of the authors Jack Herer and Chris Conrad, who think that growing hemp can help save the environment. The use of its fibers for paper, Young thinks, could save millions of trees, and its distillation into alcohol-based fuels could end the world's energy shortage. He was busy in prison designing a Harley-Davidson that could run entirely on marijuana—"the Hempster." Much to his family's distress, Young had already been sent to the Hole, Leavenworth's disciplinary building, for smoking marijuana in prison. The pot at Leavenworth was quite good, he said, though expensive. Most illegal drugs were easily obtained at Leavenworth, even hashish, a rarity elsewhere in the Midwest.

I asked Young the question that had been on my mind for weeks: Why didn't he cooperate with the prosecutors, when refusing to talk seemed to guarantee a life sentence? "It crossed through my mind a lot, trying to decide," he said. "But there's two ways I look at it. I feel kind of proud to have principles. And I'm glad I never lost that. But on the other hand, I can't really brag too much, because I didn't have anybody to give them. Who was I going to give them?" I suggested that they only wanted a name, some token of cooperation. The only name Young could provide was that of his fishing buddy—and in the end, he could not do it. "This guy has nothing," he said. "This guy couldn't buy half an ounce of marijuana, okay?" Young understood why the other defendants behaved as they did: "When you're talking the kind of time that they were passing out, you expect anybody to do what they can to fend for themselves." As for him, "No, I wouldn't do it any other way."

The worst thing about Leavenworth, for Young, was the noise, "the constant sound of the roar of hundreds of people talking." His cell offered no escape from it, from voices echoing off the steel and concrete, day and night. Should he ever be released, Young said, the first thing he planned to do was go fishing—"I'm sure now that I'm locked up, the bass have come out." He felt great bitterness toward his prosecutors. "Someone who'd do what they're doing is capable of doing anything . . . They've only proved I'm capable of smoking a joint, or of introducing a guy to another guy who needs some pounds. That's the most they've proved me capable of. What they're doing, they're destroying these families and passing out life sentences, taking people's lives, putting children on the street—I mean horrendous acts." He laughed. "I don't know of anyone that would do anything that malicious for a salary." He had no complaints about the corrections officers—men with families, working toward a pension, who daily walk unarmed amid scores of violent inmates. "I wouldn't take their job for nothing in the world," he said. "Sometimes I wonder if they realize how bad a situation they're in—you know, really." Despite it all, Young expressed a touching faith in the Constitution: "We're just going through a bad period . . . but I believe the Constitution can whip that."

When our time was up, a prison official gave Young a friendly tap on the shoulder and said, "Come on, buddy." Moments later a heavy door shut, and Mark Young was gone.

misery run to waste

TOM DAWSON HAS A FOLKSY, small-town manner and a cluttered, unpretentious office, both of which disguise the fact that he is a very successful criminal attorney who has been admitted to the bar in every federal circuit. Dawson grew up in the town of Leavenworth and has been visiting the penitentiary since 1967. He finds it mind-boggling that Young was imprisoned there for life. "The place is full of nuts," he said. "I mean the place is full of wackos . . . *dangerous* people." Dawson was arguing Mark Young's appeal. The crucial issue before the court was how much marijuana Young could reasonably have foreseen would be produced by the conspiracy. Dawson and Assistant U.S. Attorney Donna Eide found themselves sparring over plants and pounds and the proper equation for turning one into the other. The dispute could have been part of an Abbott & Costello routine, if a man's future didn't depend on the outcome. Dawson is a lifelong Republican who earns a living representing drug offenders, among others. But he has become profoundly disillusioned with the War on Drugs: "It is corrupting everything it touches."

At sentencing, the degree of a defendant's guilt often seems less important than his willingness to hand over assets and name others. "I've had kingpins walk free," Dawson admitted. In a case handled by another lawyer, a major cocaine dealer with a fleet of Learjets testified against "everybody he ever met," Dawson said, and served less than four years in prison, despite being caught with 20,000 kilos of cocaine. "It's just the guy who doesn't cooperate who then gets everybody else's time. It's just the way it works. And they finally will run into some poor guy who says, just like Mark, 'I'm not going to do it. I've got principles.' Well then, fine. You take all their time. And that's really about the way it works." Guilty pleas are what keep a legal system overwhelmed with drug cases functioning. In certain situations, Dawson told me, an innocent person is better off pleading guilty. "If you don't plead and you bet wrong, the sentences are just too high to serve."

The government's financial incentive to seize assets in drug cases has greatly increased the potential for corruption. Dawson said that some plea bargain negotiations turn into haggling sessions worthy of a

Middle Eastern souk. The proceeds from an asset forfeiture are divided among the law enforcement agencies involved in the case. Former Justice Department officials have acknowledged that many forfeitures are driven by the need to meet budget projections. The guilt or innocence of a defendant has sometimes been less important than the availability of his or her assets. In California, thirty-one state and federal agents raided Donald P. Scott's 200-acre ranch on the pretext that marijuana was growing there. Scott was inadvertently killed by a deputy sheriff. No evidence of marijuana cultivation was discovered, and a subsequent investigation by the Ventura County's District Attorney's Office found that the drug agents had been motivated partly by a desire to seize the $5 million ranch. They had obtained an appraisal of the property weeks before the raid.

In New Jersey, Nicholas L. Bissell, Jr., a local prosecutor known as the Forfeiture King, helped an associate buy land seized in a marijuana case for a small fraction of its market value. In Connecticut, Leslie C. Ohta, a federal prosecutor known as the Forfeiture Queen, seized the house of Paul and Ruth Derbacher when their twenty-two-year-old grandson was arrested for selling marijuana. Although the Derbachers were in their eighties, had owned the house for almost forty years, and claimed to have no idea that their grandson kept weapons and drugs in the house, Ohta insisted on forfeiture. People should know, she argued, what goes on in their own home. Not long after, Ohta's eighteen-year-old son was arrested for selling LSD from her Chevrolet Blazer. Allegedly, he had also sold marijuana from her home in Glastonbury. Ohta was quickly transferred out of the U.S. attorney's forfeiture unit—but neither her car nor her house was seized by the government.

A little-known provision of the forfeiture laws rewards confidential informers with up to one-quarter of the assets seized as a result of their testimony. Informing on other people has become a lucrative profession. In major drug cases an informer can earn a million dollars or more. In 1985 the federal government spent about $25 million on its informers. A decade later it spent more than $100 million. This growing reliance on informers has given an unprecedented degree of influence to criminals who have a direct financial interest in gaining convictions. Informers have been caught framing innocent people. Law enforcement agents have been caught using nonexistent informers to justify search warrants. "Criminals are likely to say and do almost anything to get what they want," Stephen S. Trott, a federal judge who was the chief of the Justice Department's Criminal Division during the Reagan years, told the *National Law Journal*. "This willingness to do anything includes not only truthfully spilling the beans on friends and relatives, but also lying, committing perjury, manufacturing evidence, soliciting others to corroborate their lies with more lies, and double-crossing anyone with whom they come into contact, including — and especially — prosecutors."

The legal and monetary rewards for informing on others has even spawned a whole new business: the buying and selling of drug leads. Defendants who hope to avoid a lengthy mandatory minimum sentence but who have no valuable information to give prosecutors can now secretly buy information from vendors on the black market. According to Tom Dawson, some professional informers now offer their services to defendants for fees of up to $250,000.

The workings of the war on drugs have created dissension throughout the federal legal system. Perhaps a hundred senior federal judges currently refuse to hear low-level drug cases prosecuted under mandatory minimum laws. One of them, Jack B. Weinstein of New York's Eastern District, announced his decision with regret, aware that he might be passing the "dirty work" to his colleagues. "I need a rest from the oppressive sense of futility that these drug cases leave," he wrote in his announcement. "I simply cannot sentence another impoverished person whose destruction has no discernible effect on the drug trade." Weinstein believes that imprisonment can serve as a deterrent. It is a question of proportion. In refusing to apply a ten-year mandatory minimum to a poor woman caught smuggling heroin, Weinstein quoted the utilitarian philosopher Jeremy Bentham. "Every particle of real punishment that is produced, more than what is necessary," Bentham wrote, "is just so much misery run to waste."

Deborah Daniels was the U.S. attorney in the Southern District of Indiana from 1988 to 1993. She not only supervised Mark Young's prosecution but also helped set the Justice Department's sentencing policy during the Bush administration. "My position as a prosecutor," she told me, "was not to make the laws." Congress had passed legislation to remove judicial discretion through mandatory minimums and guidelines. The Justice Department decided it would be wrong for prosecutors "to take over that role as judges." The laws were to be fully enforced as written. Daniels acknowledged that in some districts, U.S. attorneys would "work a case backward," deciding what punishment a defendant ought to receive and then finding a way to charge for it. "I don't agree with that. That's cheating. And we didn't cheat in the Southern District of Indiana. We played it straight. And that's how Mark Young got his sentence." She denied that the threat of long sentences was used mainly to induce plea bargains: "We didn't do things like that." The policy of her office was to seek conviction on the most serious readily provable charge — in every case without exception. "The minute you start saying, 'Well, gee, that's kind of severe for this guy and what he did,'" she argued, "then you're deciding what the case is worth."

Daniels thought that Young's sentence is what Congress mandated for that offense. Many people may think it's wrong to give a life sentence when "only marijuana" is involved. Daniels disagreed. The United States can hardly discourage other countries from exporting cocaine, if it is unwilling to fight an illegal drug produced domestically. "Yes, prisons are expensive," she admitted, "but if we are going to crack down on a serious problem . . . we are going to have to bear the brunt of that." She did not think that the pressure to cooperate has diminished the quality of testimony in court. And what most people don't realize about U.S. attorneys, she noted, is that they spend a good deal of their time getting innocent people out of trouble, by declining to file charges. All things considered, Daniels said, in Mark Young's case the system worked exactly as intended.

the most chilling evil

IN A SMALL NEW YORK APARTMENT with Indian bedspreads hung on the walls, I spent a few hours with Ed Rosenthal, America's leading guru of marijuana growing. Rosenthal's books on marijuana have sold more than a million copies. His best-selling titles include *Marijuana Growers Handbook, The Big Book of Buds, Marijuana Beer,* and *Ask Ed: Marijuana Law—Don't Get Busted.* Wherever Rosenthal goes, strangers approach him and offer him free marijuana, hoping to impress. Strangers call him on the phone at night and ask for advice about their grow operations, about how to handle certain insects, how to use computers to regulate lights. Rosenthal, who knows the ins and outs of conspiracy law as well as any legal scholar, politely answers, "I'm sorry," and hangs up. An air of secrecy surrounds him. Downstairs, there was no name beside the buzzer. A friend leaving the building denied knowing him until I identified myself. Balding and yet oddly boyish, Rosenthal is a former philosophy major. He now owns a publishing company that distributes books on cannabis. He also serves as an expert witness at marijuana trials, accompanying his readers at both ends of their journey through the American legal system.

Throughout our discussion, Rosenthal puffed on a pipe of marijuana, like an eminent professor might smoke Prince Albert. His most recent book, *The Closet Cultivator,* had outlined how to build an indoor grow system impossible to detect through any method other than betrayal. I asked Rosenthal, given the current political climate and the severity of the punishments and the number of his friends locked away in prison, whether he despaired of ever seeing marijuana legalized in his lifetime. He shook his head: I had everything wrong. "They've made these laws so brittle," he said, "one day they're going to break." It would happen all at once. The whole edifice of prohibition would come tumbling down, like the fall of the Berlin Wall. Adding millions of new prison cells to the system, Rosenthal said, will never stop people from growing pot. A group of powerful, white, middle-aged men will meet in a room to discuss what to do about marijuana, Rosenthal predicted. And they will reach the only logical conclusion: tax it.

Rosenthal's prediction has not yet come to pass. At the state and local level, however, the war on marijuana is beginning to unravel. In 1996 voters in Arizona approved Proposition 200, a ballot measure that legalized the medicinal use of marijuana and reformed the state's drug laws. Since the early 1980s, Arizona had aggressively pursued a drug strategy of "zero tolerance," administering tough penalties not just for drug trafficking and possession, but also for drug use. Failing a urine test in Arizona was grounds for prosecution: a person could face criminal charges in Phoenix for a joint smoked days or even weeks before in New York City. Arizona's prisons became overcrowded, and tent cities arose in the desert to house inmates. Proposition 200 called for the immediate release of all nonviolent prisoners who'd been convicted of drug possession or use. It called for drug treatment, drug education, and community service instead of prison terms for nonviolent, small-time offenders. And it called for the creation of a state Drug Treatment and Education Fund through an increased tax on alcohol and tobacco. Arizona voters backed Proposition 200 by a margin of two to one. A few years later California voters overwhelmingly supported a similar measure, demanding treatment instead of prison terms for first-time drug offenders.

Given the opportunity at the ballot box, the American people have lately rejected some of the basic premises underlying marijuana prohibition. Since 1996 voters in eight states have supported initiatives permitting the medical use of marijuana. After the Oregon legislature passed three laws recriminalizing marijuana in 1997, a group of activists collected enough signatures to force a public referendum on the issue. The measure to decriminalize marijuana was opposed by the state's Democratic governor and its Republican-dominated legislature. No major political figure from either party would publicly support decriminalization. Nevertheless, the people of Oregon voted to overturn the new criminal sanctions for possessing small amounts of marijuana, defying their own legislators by a margin of two to one. A recent effort to decriminalize marijuana in Nevada, however, was soundly defeated at the polls.

On the whole, conservative Republicans have been more willing than liberal Democrats to criticize the war on marijuana. In addition to former secretary of state George Shultz, economist Milton Friedman, and editor William F. Buckley, the former Republican governor of New Mexico, Gary Johnson, has called for decriminalization. "Drug problems are health problems, not criminal justice problems," Johnson told an audience at the Yale Law School in November, 2001. "The war on drugs is an absolute failure." An opinion poll taken around the same time found that 67 percent of the American people opposed denying marijuana for medical use; 61 percent opposed the arrest and imprisonment of nonviolent pot smokers. The new public mood has greatly minimized the importance of providing a solemn or contrite answer to the key political question of the 1990s. When asked if he'd ever smoked pot, Michael Bloomberg, the Republican mayor of New York City, replied: "You bet I did, and I enjoyed it."

Although President George W. Bush has acknowledged his own struggles with alcohol, he's refused to discuss whether he ever smoked marijuana. Much like the previous baby-boomer who occupied the White House, Bush has taken great care to appear "tough" on drugs. His attorney general, John Ashcroft, has vowed to "escalate the war on drugs." His drug czar, John Walters, previously called for stiffening the criminal penalties for marijuana and has attacked drug treatment in words that bring to mind the late Harry J. Anslinger. Providing treatment to drug users, Walters argued, is "the latest manifestation of the liberals' commitment to a 'therapeutic state' in which government serves as the agent of personal rehabilitation." Instead of expanding drug treatment, the Bush administration plans to expand drug testing. The education bill passed in 2001 provides funds for the widespread testing of schoolchildren. President Bush's choice to head the DEA, former congressman Asa Hutchinson, was one of the House managers of Bill Clinton's impeachment. Hutchinson vehemently opposes the medicinal use of marijuana because "it would send the wrong message to children." In October of 2001 the DEA decided to ban food products containing hemp, even though none of them can get you high. The ban was justified on the grounds that health food products such as Hemp Nuggets may contain minute traces of delta-9-THC. "Many Americans do not know that hemp and marijuana are both parts of the same plant," Hutchinson explained. The DEA has thus far made no effort to ban poppyseed bagels, which contain minute traces of opium.

On February 12, 2002, DEA agents raided a medical marijuana cooperative in San Francisco, confiscating thousands of plants and arresting three people. The raid coincided with an antidrug speech that DEA administrator Hutchinson gave in the city that day. Although the Bush administration champions a states' rights philosophy on most issues, it will not tolerate any challenge to federal supremacy on marijuana drug policy. Under California law, thousands of AIDS patients and cancer patients had been receiving marijuana through a handful of nonprofit cooperatives that worked closely with state law enforcement authorities. One by one, Bush's Justice Department shut them down. With approval from the local city council and sheriff's department, the Los Angeles Cannabis Resource Center had for five years been openly dispensing marijuana to patients whose doctors had prescribed the drug. DEA agents were even given a tour of the facility to demonstrate that recreational drug use was forbidden; nevertheless, the DEA subsequently raided it, removed its marijuana, and confiscated its patient database. John Duran, the center's attorney and a West Hollywood city councilman, described the consequences of the DEA move: "We have 960 patients out in the parks, looking for drug dealers to get their marijuana, which is exactly what the city didn't want."

Among those arrested in the San Francisco raid was Ed Rosenthal, who'd been helping local cooperatives grow marijuana for their patients. Rosenthal had published a book on medical marijuana and had come to believe that different strains of cannabis were useful for alleviating the symptoms of different ailments. One mix of cannabinoids might help AIDS patients regain their appetite; another might reduce the nausea experienced by chemotherapy patients; and Rosenthal was using his expertise in marijuana botany to produce the right plants for sick people. After avoiding legal trouble during more than two decades of marijuana advocacy, Rosenthal was awakened at six in the morning by DEA agents, who arrested him and searched his home. Thousands of plants were seized at a nearby warehouse. Just a few weeks earlier, San Francisco's district attorney, Terrence Hallinan, had been a guest on Rosenthal's monthly radio show and had praised the efforts of the medical marijuana cooperatives. "The government antidrug policy is a big lie that's supported by a thousand other lies," Rosenthal said, after the DEA raid. "My crime is that I'm willing to challenge those lies." On January 31, 2003, he was convicted of growing and conspiring to grow marijuana. He now faces a prison sentence of between five and eighty-five years.

While the Bush administration steps up the war on marijuana, many foreign allies are disavowing it. In Canada, the use of marijuana as medicine was legalized in the summer of 2001, and the government health service is supplying cannabis to patients there on a trial basis. Canada is likely to decriminalize marijuana possession soon, a policy that has been backed by the Canadian Medical Association, the Canadian Association of Chiefs of Police, and the Royal Canadian Mounted Police. Portugal decriminalized the possession of all drugs in 2001. Belgium decriminalized the possession of marijuana for personal use the same year — a policy that Spain and Italy chose in the 1990s. The Netherlands decriminalized marijuana more than twenty-five years ago. Pot for recreational use is sold at government-regulated coffee shops, and the Dutch Office for Medical Cannabis is supporting legislation that would provide "pharmaceutical quality" marijuana, free of cost, through the national health service. After studying the health risks and medical uses of marijuana, the upper house of the Swiss Parliament voted in December of 2001 to legalize it. Switzerland may soon become the first country where the commercial production and distribution of cannabis is regulated by the government.

Even Great Britain, the European country most influenced by the American drug policy, has lately backed away from strict marijuana prohibition. During the 1980s Prime Minister Margaret Thatcher had enthusiastically supported President Reagan's war on drugs, employing similarly tough rhetoric. "We are after you," she warned drug dealers. "The pursuit will be relentless. We shall make your life not worth living." Thatcher promised that her government would "never legalize illicit drugs, hard or soft." Princess Diana joined the antidrug campaign, appearing on a BBC series whose title paid homage to Nancy Reagan's famous advice: "Just Say No." Thatcher's policies were continued by her Tory successor, John Major. The election of a Labour Party prime minister made little difference; Tony Blair seemed greatly influenced by Clinton's tough-on-drugs example. Prime Minister Blair gave Britain its first "drug czar" and scaled the heights of prohibitionist rhetoric in 1999, declaring that the drug trade was "the most chilling, evil industry our modern world has to confront."

Between 1988 and 1998, British arrests for marijuana nearly quadrupled, reaching almost 100,000 a year. As many as 5,600 marijuana offenders were annually imprisoned. And yet British marijuana use during that period continued to rise. Despite having the most punitive marijuana laws in Europe, Great Britain soon had the highest rate of marijuana use among young people. British teenagers were much more likely to smoke pot than their Dutch counterparts, even though the latter could simply walk into a government-approved coffee shop and buy it. As in the United States, a number of prominent conservatives defied conventional wisdom and sought to reform the marijuana laws. Charles Moore, editor of the *Daily Telegraph,* suggested in 2000 that Blair's government should "draw up plans to legalise cannabis." The Police Foundation recommended lowering the penalties for marijuana crimes, and Peter Lilley, a former deputy leader of the Tories, advocated decriminalizing marijuana for personal use. Blair initially resisted making any changes to the law, then agreed to follow the Police Foundation's advice in the spring of 2002. Marijuana was given a lower classification on the list of controlled substances, and police were discouraged from arresting people for small amounts. The possession of cannabis, however, remains a criminal offense in Great Britain, punishable by up to two years in prison.

By refusing to decriminalize marijuana because of its purported health risks, Prime Minister Blair ignored a vast body of British research on the subject. In 1968 a parliamentary committee on cannabis headed by Baroness Wootton of Abinger found that "the long-term consumption of cannabis in *moderate* doses has no harmful effects" and that marijuana is "very much less dangerous than the opiates, amphetamines, and barbiturates, and also less dangerous than alcohol." In 1998 Great Britain's leading medical journal, the *Lancet,* reviewed the scientific literature on marijuana and concluded that "moderate indulgence in cannabis has little ill effect on health." The language of the *Lancet* editorial was remarkably similar to that of the world's first major inquiry into the effects of marijuana use. In 1894 the Indian Hemp Commission concluded, after two years of investigation, that some heavy cannabis users developed bronchitis — but that "moderate use practically produces no ill effects." The British commissioners were surprised that cannabis seemed to pose so little risk to society. On the basis of their seven-volume report, India's colonial rulers decided that marijuana possession should not be made a crime.

some of the costs

ONE OF THE GREAT IRONIES of American drug policy is that anti-drug laws have tended to become most punitive long after the use of a drug has peaked. Dr. David Musto, a professor at Yale Medical School and the preeminent historian of American narcotics policy, explains that when drug use is at its height, so is tolerance. But as drugs recede from middle-class homes, their users are marginalized, scapegoated, and more readily punished. The price that society pays for harsh sanctions becomes invisible to most people. Musto thinks that America's drug laws reflect cultural changes, after the fact. Although extreme punishments may help to limit a drug epidemic, the principal causes of its rise and fall lie elsewhere. This theory is supported by recent history. Marijuana use among the young peaked in 1979. Strict federal laws were passed seven years later, when use had already fallen by about 40 percent; and the explanation most young people gave for quitting marijuana was the perceived health risks, not fear of imprisonment. Tough marijuana laws did not prevent hippies from smoking pot in the 1960s, and three decades later they did not deter the hip-hop generation. During the mid-1990s the rate of teenage marijuana use climbed again, more than doubling in the United States.

Two decades after the latest war on drugs was declared, some rough numbers may hint at its cost: billions of dollars spent so far at the state, federal, and local levels to fight marijuana; ten million Americans arrested for marijuana offenses; about a quarter of a million people convicted of marijuana felonies and sent to prison for at least a year. And after all the time and energy and money that has been spent, and all the personal harm that has been caused, not only has marijuana use among young people increased, but the supply of pot hasn't really been affected. In 1982, when President Reagan launched this war, 88.5 percent of America's high school seniors said that it was "fairly easy" or "very easy" for them to obtain marijuana. In 2000 the proportion of seniors who said they could easily obtain pot was 88.5 percent.

Statistics can only suggest a portion of the truth. Human costs are not so easily measured. Not long after I first wrote about Mark Young's case for the *Atlantic Monthly* in 1994, the 7th U.S. Circuit Court of Appeals vacated his life sentence. The court's reasoning was

somewhat abstruse. It ruled that Young's ignorance of marijuana cultivation meant that his prison sentence had to be determined by the
weight of the pot that he brokered, not by the number of plants that
could produce such a weight of pot (a number that Young could not
have "reasonably foreseen"). The decision sent his case back to the
original court for resentencing. Judge Sarah Evans Barker gave Young a
new prison sentence: twelve and a half years without parole.

Young was transferred from Leavenworth Penitentiary to a medium-security facility. Nevertheless, his time behind bars was never
easy. His wife suddenly stopped visiting, then divorced him. He continued to smoke marijuana in prison and suffered the consequences.
His visiting rights and telephone rights were repeatedly suspended. He
spent months at a time in various disciplinary units, often in isolation.
But he kept smoking pot. It was available throughout the federal system, he later told me, "but you've got to walk through the heroin to
find it." On February 6, 2002, Young was moved to a halfway house in
Indianapolis. He found a job and a new girlfriend. But he kept smoking pot, failed a urine test, and was sent back to federal prison after en-
joying only six weeks of freedom. As of this writing, Mark Young is out
of prison once again, living in Indianapolis, trying to find a new career. The idea of growing or selling marijuana does not appeal to him.
Under the terms of Young's supervised release, for the next eight years
he can't travel outside the Southern District of Indiana, associate with
any felons, or use any illegal drugs. Failing another urine test could
send him back to prison for years. Nevertheless, Young vows to keep
smoking marijuana—because he likes it, he thinks there's nothing
wrong with it, and he's stubborn. "Following the government blindly,"
Young argues, "is more insane than anything I've done."

if you want it

THE CONCLUSIONS OF THE National Commission on Marijuana
and Drug Abuse are as valid today as they were thirty years ago. The
United States should decriminalize marijuana for personal use. Growing or possessing small amounts of pot should no longer be a crime.

Cultivating or selling large amounts of it, using it in public, distributing it to young people, and driving under its influence should remain against the law.

The decriminalization of marijuana should be the first step toward a rational drug policy. The benefits would be felt immediately. Law enforcement resources would be diverted from the apprehension and imprisonment of marijuana offenders to the prevention of much more serious crimes. The huge sums of money that the United States spends each year just to process its marijuana arrests would be available to fund more useful endeavors, such as treatment for substance abusers. Thousands of jail cells would become available to house violent criminals. The profits from selling marijuana on the black market would fall. But the decriminalization of marijuana is only a partial solution to the havoc caused by the war on drugs.

Mandatory minimum sentences for drug offenders should be repealed, allowing judges to regain their traditional powers and ensuring that an individual's punishment fits the crime. The asset-forfeiture laws should be amended so that criminal investigations are never motivated by greed. The use of professional informers should be limited and carefully monitored. Taking these steps would send a clear message to America's youth. The message would not be that smoking marijuana is a wonderful, beautiful thing. It would be something more difficult to say: the United States will no longer pursue a failed policy, waste money, and needlessly ruin lives in order to appear tough.

Decriminalizing marijuana would also help to resolve the current dispute over its medicinal use. Seriously ill patients would no longer risk criminal prosecution while trying to obtain their medicine. Marijuana is less toxic than many common foods. Denying cancer patients, AIDS patients, and paraplegics access to a potentially useful medication that's safer than most legally prescribed drugs is vindictive and inhumane.

Although marijuana does not turn teenagers into serial killers or irreversibly destroy their brains, it is a powerful intoxicant. Its use can diminish academic and athletic performance. Adolescents experience enough social and emotional confusion without the added handicap of constantly being stoned. If smoking marijuana does exert subtly harmful effects on the reproductive and immune systems, teenagers could be at greatest risk. Marijuana use by young people should be strongly discouraged. Lying to kids about marijuana's effects, however, only encourages them to doubt warnings about much more dangerous drugs, such as heroin, cocaine, and methamphetamine. In a nation where both major political parties accept millions of dollars from alcohol and tobacco lobbyists, demands for "zero tolerance" and moral condemnations of marijuana have a hollow ring. According to Michael D. Newcomb, a substance abuse expert at the University of Southern California, "Tobacco and alcohol are the most widely used, abused, and deadly drugs ingested by teenagers." American children aged eleven to thirteen now drink alcohol almost four times as often as they smoke marijuana. Drug education programs should respect the intelligence of young people by promoting healthy lives without scare tactics, lies, and hypocrisy. And drug abuse should be treated like alcoholism or nicotine addiction. These are health problems suffered by Americans of every race, creed, and political affiliation, not grounds for imprisonment or the denial of property rights.

A society that can punish a marijuana offender more severely than a murderer is caught in the grip of a deep psychosis. It has a bad case of reefer madness. For too long the laws regarding marijuana have been based on racial prejudice, irrational fears, metaphors, symbolism, and political expediency. We need a marijuana policy that is calmly based on the facts. An end to the war on marijuana will not come from Congress or the president, from the DEA, the police, the prisons, or the courts. It will come from citizen activism and the ballot box. It will come when ordinary people make their views known. The government's behavior will not withstand public scrutiny for long. This war is over, if you want it.

[2]

IN THE STRAWBERRY
FIELDS

J UST BEFORE SUNRISE farmworkers appear on the streets of Guadalupe, California, emerging from the small houses, backyard sheds, basements, and garages where they spent the night. The men wear straw cowboy hats or baseball caps, windbreakers on this cool morning, sneakers, and ragged work clothes. The women have scarves and bandannas wrapped over their hair, hung around their necks, and tied across their faces, so that only their eyes can be seen. From a distance they seem draped in brightly colored veils. Soon a long line of vehicles is double-parked along Highway 1, awaiting passengers — not the spectacular Highway 1 that hugs the Pacific but a less familiar stretch, four miles inland amid the Santa Maria Valley, halfway between Los Angeles and Salinas. Here Highway 1 becomes Guadalupe's main drag, lined with mom-and-pop stores, Mexican restaurants, boarded-up storefronts, and bars. As dawn approaches, the procession of old Buicks, pickups, ancient school buses towing portable toilets, and beat-up vans heads for the neighboring fields. A handful of workers walk along the shoulder of the road, silhouetted by headlights. Two young men ride bicycles; most likely they slept outdoors. When the sun rises from behind the coastal range, crews of thirty assemble at the edges of huge fields and then start picking strawberries, slowly making their way down the long furrows, hundreds of men and women bent over at the waist, grabbing fruit with both hands. In the early morning light it looks like a scene out of the distant past, the last remnant of a vanishing way of life — and yet nothing could be further from the truth.

In the early 1970s there were about 600 acres of strawberries in the Santa Maria Valley; today there are about six times that amount. The strawberry is one of the most labor-intensive row crops. It's risky and expensive to grow, but it can yield more revenue per acre than virtually any other crop except marijuana. On the same land outside Guadalupe where family farms raised dairy cows not long ago, strawberry farms now employ thousands of migrant workers. Most of them are illegal immigrants from Mexico, a fact that helps explain not only California's recent strawberry boom, but also the quiet, unrelenting transformation of the state's rural landscape and communities.

Agriculture is still California's largest industry. Since the late 1940s California has led America in agricultural output; it now produces more than half the fruits, nuts, and vegetables consumed in the United States. Hundreds of commodities, from the mundane to the exotic, are grown in California, primarily in the Central Valley, an area that contains some of the world's most productive farmland. By some measures, however, California agriculture is in decline. The value of its annual output, adjusted for inflation, has fallen 14 percent over the last two decades. Between 1982 and 1997, roughly 300,000 acres of California farmland were lost each year, mainly to urbanization. Wide-open fields are giving way to subdivisions and strip malls. Water long used for irrigation is being diverted to cities and towns. Improved cooling and transportation systems have opened the American market to overseas competitors. Air pollution has begun to diminish crop yields.

Meanwhile, the fastest-growing and most profitable segment of California's farm economy — the cultivation of high-value specialty crops — has also become the one most dependent on the availability of cheap labor. Nearly every fruit and vegetable found in the diet of health-conscious, often high-minded consumers is still picked by hand: every head of lettuce, every bunch of grapes, every avocado, peach, and plum. As the demand for these foods has risen, so has the number of workers necessary to harvest them. Of the migrants in California today, anywhere from 30 to 60 percent, depending on the crop, are illegal immigrants. Their willingness to work long hours for low wages has enabled California to sustain its agricultural production, despite the loss since 1964 of more than nine million acres of farmland. Fruit and vegetable growers now rely on a thriving black market in labor — and without it even more farms would disappear. Illegal immigrants, widely reviled and often depicted as welfare cheats, are in effect subsidizing the most important sector of the California economy.

The rise in the number of migrant workers in California, along with the growth in the proportion who are illegal immigrants, reflects a national trend that has passed largely unnoticed. During the 1960s it was commonly believed that within a decade there would be no more migrant farmworkers in the United States. Experts predicted that technology would soon render migrants obsolete: if a crop could not be harvested mechanically by 1975, it would not be grown in this country. Census figures lent support to this scenario. Philip L. Martin is a professor of agricultural economics at the University of California at Davis and one of the nation's foremost authorities on farm labor demographics. According to his estimates, during the 1920s there were some two million migrant farmworkers in the United States. During the 1940s there were about one million. And during the 1970s, when Cesar Chavez's labor-organizing drive among migrant workers was at its height, there were only about 200,000. Then the number began to climb. An indigenous agricultural work force was largely replaced by migrants who illegally traveled back and forth to Mexico. Today it is impossible to gauge the size of the migrant work force with any precision, among other reasons because so much of it is composed of illegal immigrants. Martin believes that more than a million migrant farmworkers are now employed in the United States. Not only are there far more migrants today, but they are being paid far less. The hourly wages of some California farmworkers, adjusted for inflation, have dropped more than 50 percent since 1980. Migrants are among the poorest workers in the United States. The average migrant is a twenty-nine-year-old male, born in Mexico, who earns less than $7,500 a year for twenty-five weeks of farmwork. According to one estimate, his life expectancy is forty-nine years.

The rise of the strawberry industry is in many ways emblematic of changes that have swept through California agriculture in recent years. The strawberry has become the focus of a California industry whose annual sales are about $840 million. American farmers now receive more money for fresh strawberries each year than for any other fresh fruit grown in the United States, except apples. And strawberry pickers are not only the poorest migrants but also the ones most likely to be illegal immigrants. During the strawberry harvest, I spent weeks traveling through three regions in California where the fruit is commercially grown, meeting workers, farmers, academics, and farm labor activists. My trip took me through the Santa Maria Valley, where rural poverty has recently become entrenched and where cruel sharecropping arrangements have trapped farmworkers under mountains of debt; through the area around Watsonville and Salinas, where about half the state's strawberries are grown and where the season's heavy rains made many hard lives even harder; and through northern San Diego County, where the forces that threaten California agriculture and those that sustain it are most pronounced, where the needs of farmers and real estate developers increasingly conflict, and where a migrant work force lives in Third World shantytowns within throwing distance of expensive suburban homes. In the strawberry fields of California, I believe, one may find answers to many of the pressing questions raised by illegal immigration, as well as some ethical dilemmas that are much more difficult to resolve.

the industry: a short course

A STRAWBERRY FIELD IS NOT a beautiful sight. It lacks the charm and character of a citrus grove, an apple orchard, or even a field of corn. Strawberries now begin and end in plastic. Before planting, an entire strawberry field is sealed with plastic sheeting and injected with methyl bromide, a chemical brew that kills harmful microbes and nematodes. Then the sheeting is removed and workers install drip irrigation hoses in the beds, cover the beds with new, clear plastic, and insert the plants through the plastic by hand. This plastic helps retain heat, keeps the soil moist, and prevents erosion. At the end of the harvest, workers rip the plants from the ground and throw them away, along with the plastic and the drip irrigation hoses. Second-year plants tend to produce smaller berries.

California did not always dominate American strawberry production. In the early 1950s the state was responsible for only one-third of the nation's strawberry crop. Then California strawberry production began to surge, impelled by new growing techniques, new plant varieties, and an abundance of inexpensive labor. Between 1974 and 1994 California's strawberry output more than tripled; prices fell, and Americans doubled their consumption of fresh strawberries. In 2001 California shipped 91 million boxes of fresh strawberries (a box, also called a flat or a tray, holds a dozen pints and weighs roughly eleven and a half pounds). The state now accounts for more than 80 percent of the strawberries grown in the United States and about one-quarter of the world's commercial strawberries.

In a good year strawberries can be one of the most profitable row crops in California. But they are also one of the riskiest. The fruit attracts a wide variety of pests, including aphids, eelworms, and red spider mites. Even more threatening is the weather. No matter how carefully a grower prepares the field, no matter how well bred the plants, the size of the harvest will in large part be determined by the weather. Ideal growing conditions for strawberries include cool nights and warm, sunny days, with no wind above five miles an hour and no rain once the berries have appeared. Weather that falls short of the ideal may quickly and irreversibly damage the crop. Frost can burn the blooms. A strong wind will rub leaves against the berries, marring their skin with brown streaks. A heat wave will stunt and soften the fruit. Worst of all is heavy rain. Strawberries are so fragile that prolonged rain opens small tears in their skin, and the tears are quickly infected with botrytis, a gray mold. A few days of rain can destroy an entire strawberry harvest.

The market for strawberries can prove just as unpredictable and disastrous as the weather. The perishability of fresh fruit exposes growers to considerable risk. Ten days after a strawberry is picked, it begins to spoil. "I can't stuff my berries into a silo like a wheat farmer does," one grower told me, "and then run computer programs to decide when it's the best time to sell." Wholesale prices for fresh strawberries fluctuate widely, from $3 to $15 a box depending on the quality of the fruit, the supply, the time of year, and all sorts of imponderables. Growers who produce specialty crops do not benefit directly from any government price supports. Although the strawberry plants now grown in California often produce fruit continuously for nine months, one-fourth to one-third of the berries reach maturity at the peak of the harvest—a period that lasts only a few weeks. A grower has little choice but to accept the prevailing market price for those berries. Strawberries for processing, which eventually can be stored, sell for about twenty-five cents a pound.

The most successful growers cultivate a high-quality strawberry, have enough capital to ride out the bad years, and sell their berries through a prominent marketing consortium. Such growers may earn annual profits of $10,000 to $20,000 an acre. But others often find themselves at the mercy of the weather and a volatile market. As in most fruit and vegetable production, the steady profits are usually earned by the middlemen—processors, cooling houses, supermarket chains—and not by the growers. In the strawberry industry, a grower's annual losses can be huge. The cost of production is anywhere from $12,000 to $30,000 an acre. A fifty-acre farm producing high-quality strawberries requires an annual investment of about $1 million. There is very little the grower can do to limit the fixed costs: the payments on the mortgages or the lease, for the plants, the pesticides, and the drip irrigation system. The only cost over which a grower has any real control is the cost of labor.

Many strawberry growers play by the rules and treat their workers well. Indeed, strawberry pickers all aspire to jobs at farms affiliated with Driscoll Associates, where the fields are immaculate and the wages are the highest in the industry. Other organizations—such as Naturipe, Sweet Darling, CalBeri, and Coastal Berry—are also highly regarded. It would be wrong to imply that all strawberry growers routinely mistreat their workers; but some do. Since labor costs constitute between 50 and 70 percent of the total cost in strawberry production, cutting labor costs can sometimes mean the difference between a profit and a loss, or between a bad year and a disastrous one. The temptation to break the law can be great. The punishments for doing so are rarely applied. And in recent years some growers have shown little self-restraint.

One of the easiest ways to reduce labor costs is to keep workers off the books. Growers are often obligated to pay unemployment taxes and workers' compensation premiums for each of their employees, in addition to Social Security and Medicare taxes. Paying an "invisible worker" in cash lowers the cost of that worker by at least 20 percent. Ignoring California's rules about overtime effectively cuts those wages by 50 percent. And failing to pay any wages brings the greatest savings of all. The vast number of illegal immigrants in the migrant work force is an invitation to break the law. They are unlikely to approach authorities about a violation of the labor code.

Sharecropping is the most insidious means by which growers avoid responsibility for their workers. The sharecropper is a straw man, an intermediary, usually a middle-aged farmworker, to whom the grower shifts many of the legal and financial risks. Sharecropping has a long history in the strawberry industry. It is a practice that in the past decade has often resembled not so much a type of agricultural production as an elaborate, well-organized fraud.

the new servitude

WHEN I MET FELIPE (a pseudonym, as are the other names presented without surnames), he seemed in bad shape. His clothes were dirty and torn, his face haggard and unshaven. His strawberry field looked like hell, too. The rows were littered with rotting berries, old boxes, and soda cans. There were broken irrigation hoses; no plastic enclosing the beds. "Too expensive," he told me. "The company doesn't pay me enough." Nearby, his workers picked "cat faces" — small, deformed berries — off second-year plants. Rain had seriously damaged the field. Felipe was selling his fruit for twelve cents a pound. He couldn't understand why the price for strawberries for processing was so low, but the terms of his sharecropping contract required him to accept it. "They use us all year as slaves," he said. "They pay us whatever they want to." He promised to send me legal documents proving his claims. The season was just beginning, and Felipe was already $50,000 in debt—half of that amount rolled over from the year before. He owed the IRS an additional $5,000. "I can't remember any time I've been in good shape," he said. "I'm always down in the hole." Felipe had been a strawberry picker when his grower approached him one day and asked if he'd like to become a "farmer." After sixteen years as a sharecropper, Felipe owned few assets and was ready to quit.

Sharecropping has existed in the California strawberry industry for almost a century, rising and falling in popularity according to changes in the law and the labor supply. At different times, the straw men have been called sharecroppers, sharefarmers, tenant farmers, and "partners." The underlying strategy, of shifting the greatest risks to the farmworker, has only become more refined. During the 1980s sharecropping thrived—not just for strawberries, but also for raspberries, snow peas, and squash. Under a typical arrangement a grower assigned a portion of a strawberry field to a farmworker and his or her family. Instead of paying them wages, the grower promised to split the profits fifty-fifty. The sharecropper became the employer of record, responsible for hiring strawberry pickers, paying their wages, withholding their taxes, and checking their green cards. The grower was responsible for all other production costs and for the overall management of the farm. By setting up farmworkers as supposedly independent operators, growers shielded themselves from labor and immigration laws—and from heavy losses. The sharecropper assumed a large part of the risk. He or she had no way of knowing whether there would be profits in a given year or whether the grower would share them fairly.

A number of hard-working and enterprising sharecroppers managed to succeed under this arrangement, earning enough money to become growers themselves. These farmworkers-turned-farmers are known as *mexicanos*. But many sharecroppers did not fare so well. At the end of the year, they often earned less for their efforts than farmworkers paid minimum wage. And sometimes they earned nothing at all.

The California supreme court ruled in 1989 that similar sharecropping arrangements in the cucumber industry did not permit growers to ignore the workers' compensation laws. Sharecroppers were not independent operators, the court said, and growers could not avoid their legal responsibilities by inventing a new name for their employees. After subsiding briefly, sharecropping reappeared in the strawberry industry during the 1990s. The new version makes the old one seem enlightened and humane. Behind many of the current sharecropping schemes are growers and former growers determined to shield themselves from the financial risks of producing strawberries. Instead of paying the operating costs of a strawberry farm, these growers — now called commission merchants — lend sharecroppers the money for operating costs at interest rates as high as 19 percent. Under the old arrangement, if things went wrong, sharecroppers simply would not be paid for their hard work; under the new one, they are being saddled with thousands of dollars in debt.

Mike Meuter, an attorney at California Rural Legal Assistance (CRLA) in Salinas, thinks that as much as half of the strawberry acreage in his area, which includes Watsonville, is being farmed by sharecroppers. A survey by CRLA staff members in Santa Maria found that between half and three quarters of the acreage in the valley is being sharecropped. Whatever the actual proportion, there is no doubt the practice is once again widespread. Jeannie Barrett, a CRLA attorney who's watched sharecropping arrangements come and go in Santa Maria for almost twenty years, thinks the new version is the worst yet. "It's basically a form of debt peonage," she says.

When I visited Santa Maria one of the largest commission merchants was Kirk Produce (now doing business as Sunrise Growers). The company was founded by a prominent strawberry grower; a number of the other original investors were strawberry growers as well. Kirk's contracts were such works of art that the lawyer who drafted them, Peter M. Gwosdof, also copyrighted them. In order to demonstrate that the sharecropper was not an employee of Kirk's, these contracts stressed that "no partnership, joint venture, co-farming, tenant farming, or other business relation" had been created. But elsewhere they made it clear that when the "Independent Farmer/Grower" leased the land from Kirk and borrowed the money to farm it from Kirk, he or she also had to pay for utilities and irrigation through Kirk, grow berries that satisfied the quality demands of Kirk, and sell all those berries only through Kirk at a price determined solely by Kirk. Moreover, Kirk had the right to retake the land at any time and terminate the lease if the sharecropper's farming practices did not meet with the approval of Kirk. Termination of the lease did not eliminate the debt.

Similar demands are still being made by commission merchants. Most of the sharecroppers who sign this sort of contract—which can be as long as thirteen pages, single-spaced—cannot read them. The contracts are usually in English, whereas the vast majority of sharecroppers are Spanish-speaking farmworkers who have little experience with legal documents. One study suggested that the average sharecropper outside Watsonville had the equivalent of a fifth-grade education. Kirk's contracts recommended that the "Independent Farmer/ Grower" seek "independent legal and/or accounting advice" before signing. But the opportunities for upward mobility are so limited among farmworkers and the desire to have one's own farm is so great, that farmworkers are easily induced to sign such agreements. Only later do they realize the true cost.

Commission merchants have a very good deal. After lending their money to the sharecropper, they get it back in three ways: as payment for services rendered (Kirk often supplied the plants, fertilizer, insecticides, and packing materials), as interest payments, and as repayment of the original loan. In addition, commission merchants charge a fee for every box of strawberries sold and often collect a cooling charge of a dollar or more a box. Many sharecroppers must sell all their berries to their commission merchant, regardless of the price being offered. Sharecroppers often complain that they are not receiving the full value of their fruit. Often they are right. Every sharecropper I met in Santa Maria was receiving $5 a box for fresh berries, though the official market price ranged from $8 to $14 a box at the time.

The documents that Felipe later sent me revealed the kind of bookkeeping that sometimes takes place. They stemmed from an investigation of his case by the Market Enforcement Branch of California's Department of Food and Agriculture. Over the course of eighteen months a commission merchant named Ag-Mart Produce was found to have overcharged or underpaid Felipe by $118,320.62. On days when the market price for strawberries was $8.75 per box, Felipe sometimes received $7, $5, or $1.74 for his boxes. On other days the commission merchant sold hundreds of boxes of Felipe's berries for which Felipe was paid nothing at all. By the time California's Department of Food and Agriculture made these findings, Ag-Mart Produce had stopped doing business in the state.

Some of the worst violations of state and federal labor laws are being committed by sharecroppers overwhelmed by the pressure to repay their debts. Even the most compassionate sharecroppers are in a bind: the workers often have to be paid at the end of each week, but the commission merchant usually pays for the sharecropper's berries every three weeks. The commission merchant also deducts service charges and interest payments directly from the sharecropper's check, so that little money may be left for the workers. As Kirk's attorney, Peter Gwosdof, explained to me, Kirk Produce was not a licensed "finance lender"; it obtained funds through a federal land bank, and was therefore exempt from state usury laws. Kirk could charge whatever interest it liked — though, Gwosdof assured me, Kirk didn't profit from these loans. He said it was in everyone's best interest for the company's "independent growers" to have a good year.

Bill Hoerger, a CRLA senior attorney, thinks that such loans are designed to make the sharecropper appear to be a real businessperson. The commission merchants often don't need the loans to be repaid in order to make a profit. Under the old system, these loans were operating costs; under the new one, bad debts make good tax write-offs at the end of the year. According to Ann Hipshman, assistant chief counsel for the California labor commissioner, the debts leave many sharecroppers trapped in "servitude." One well-established strawberry grower, who finds the new sharecropping arrangements despicable, told me there's nothing new about the scheme. "Read Thomas Hardy's *The Mayor of Casterbridge*," he said, "for the best description of how this whole system works."

Every sharecropper I met was in dire financial straits. A sharecropper often feeds his or her family by listing a phony worker on the payroll and keeping those wages. Visiting sharecropped fields at random, I heard the same story again and again, and I saw the same look of fatigue. Pedro was the only sharecropper I met who didn't seem distraught. He had a soft, round face and a mustache. He was thirty-six, but looked a decade older. He'd picked strawberries for eight years, and then driven a truck. He said one of his acres had flooded and was now lost for the year. The strawberries on his remaining thirty-four acres had been damaged by the rain. After six years of sharecropping, Pedro was $125,000 in debt, most of it rolled over. I asked how he managed to run up so much debt. "I don't know," he said, shrugging. "All I know is I owe it." None of these disasters seemed to have affected his cheerful mood. What mattered most to him was providing work for his migrants and the pride of being his own boss. "I don't care anymore about material things," Pedro said, as he surveyed the workers in his field and plastic torn from beds flapped in the wind. "I'm a Jehovah's Witness."

the search for a peasantry

CALIFORNIA NEVER ENJOYED a period in which family farms dominated the rural economy, employing hired hands who could expect someday to own their own land. Its society never remotely resembled the Jeffersonian ideal. Monopolistic patterns of land ownership established under Spanish and Mexican rule were unaffected by California's admission into the United States. The vast bonanza wheat farms that emerged in California during the mid-nineteenth century offer the earliest example of modern American agribusiness, a model soon emulated by the state's fruit and vegetable growers. California's agricultural potential seemed limitless. The soil was rich, the climate was near perfect, and water for irrigation was abundant. All the state lacked was an army of laborers to harvest its apples, melons, oranges, and dates. The historian Cletus E. Daniel has depicted the initial phase of large-scale agriculture in California as the search for a peasantry. First Chinese and then Japanese immigrants worked the fields, until the Exclusion Act of 1882 and the Gentleman's Agreement of 1907 limited their supply. In the early years of the twentieth century, Mexicans were hailed as the solution to California's perennial farm-labor shortages. The Mexican, it was argued, would not only work hard for low wages whenever needed but also go home when no longer required.

There was complete freedom of movement between California and Mexico until 1929, when undocumented immigration to the United States became a misdemeanor. By then, 70 to 80 percent of the migrant farmworkers in California were Mexicans, and the Mexican population of Los Angeles had grown larger than that of any city except Mexico City. Illegal immigrants from Mexico have long been a mainstay of California's rural economy. Anglo migrant workers, the "Okies" immortalized by John Steinbeck in *The Grapes of Wrath*, were a historical anomaly. For almost a century, the vast majority of California's migrant workers have been Mexican immigrants, legal and illegal. The nationality of these migrants over generations seems as unvarying as the nature of their work. Most of California's produce is harvested today exactly as it was in the days of the eighteenth-century mission fathers — by hand.

Machines have been invented to harvest almost every kind of fruit and vegetable grown in the United States. Such machines are introduced, however, only when the cost of mechanization is lower than the anticipated cost of paying migrants to do the same work. During the 1970s, the United Farm Workers (UFW) achieved great success organizing migrants in the California grape and lettuce industries. The influence of the UFW extended far beyond these crops; simply the threat of unionization persuaded many growers to raise wages, offer benefits, and improve working conditions. At about the same time, California adopted some of the most pro-union legislation in the country, guaranteeing farmworkers the right to collective bargaining, a minimum wage, and unemployment compensation. As labor costs increased, mechanization became a top priority for California growers. But successive Republican governors, George Deukmejian and Pete Wilson, gutted the Agricultural Labor Relations Board and relaxed enforcement of the state's tough labor laws. Union workers were fired; illegal immigrants replaced them; and growers avoided prosecution for workplace violations by hiding behind the legal fiction that labor contractors and sharecroppers were the actual employers of migrants. Hard-won benefits such as sick leave, vacation pay, family housing, and health insurance were eliminated. The living and working conditions of migrants steadily declined.

In the early 1970s, the UFW had perhaps 80,000 members. Today it has about one-third that number. Migrants have become so cheap in California, thanks to illegal immigration, that they are increasingly being used not just to pick fruits and vegetables but to pack them as well, right in the fields. Automated packing houses, employing union workers, are rapidly going out of business. Instead of the mechanization of California agriculture, a prominent labor expert recently observed, we are now witnessing its "Mexicanization."

la fruta del diablo

IT WAS MID-APRIL when I visited Watsonville, and heavy rains had recently flooded hundreds of acres. Bright blue plastic barrels from a Smuckers plant were scattered across local strawberry fields and embedded in the mud. Many fields that hadn't been flooded still had been damaged by the rains. I met with strawberry workers at an old labor camp—a small slum set amid rolling hills and strawberry fields not far from town. For most of the year this bleak collection of gray wooden barracks housed about 350 residents, mainly strawberry workers and their families. But at the peak of the harvest hundreds more crammed into its forty apartments. In the mid-1990s there'd been a major outbreak of tuberculosis at the camp, fueled by its crowded living quarters and poor building design. The bedrooms occupied a central corridor of the barracks; none had a window. The tenants paid $500 a month for their two-bedroom apartments and felt lucky to have a roof over their heads. As I walked around the camp, there were children everywhere, running and playing in the courtyards, oblivious of the squalor.

The sky was overcast, more bad weather was coming, and a year's income for these workers would be determined in the next few months. Half a dozen strawberry pickers, leaning against parked cars, told me that at this point in the season they usually worked in the fields eight or ten hours a day. Only one of them was employed at the moment. Every morning the others visited the strawberry farm on a nearby hillside, inquired about work, and were turned away. The foreman, who had hired them for years, said to try again next week.

Harvest work in the strawberry fields, like most seasonal farmwork in California, is considered "at will." There is no contract, no seniority, no obligation beyond the day-to-day. A grower hires and fires workers as necessary, without need for explanation. It makes no difference whether the migrant has been an employee for six days or for six years. The terms of employment are laid down on a daily basis. If a grower wants slow and careful work, wages are paid by the hour. If a grower wants berries quickly removed from the field, the wages are piece-rate, providing an incentive to move fast. A migrant often does not know how long the workday will last or what the wage rate will be until he or she arrives at the field that morning. There might be two weeks of ten-hour days followed by a week of no work at all, depending upon the weather and the market.

This system did not arise because growers are innately mean and heartless. Harvests are unpredictable from beginning to end. Many growers try to guarantee their workers a certain amount of income each week. Among other things, it makes good business sense to have reliable and capable workers returning each year. And yet there is no denying where the power lies.

The strawberry has long been known to migrants as *la fruta del diablo*—the fruit of the devil. Picking strawberries is some of the lowest-paid, most difficult, and therefore least desirable farmwork in California. Strawberries are fragile and bruise easily. They must be picked with great care, especially the berries that will be sold fresh at the market. Market berries are twisted, not pulled, off the stem to preserve a green cap on top. Workers must select only berries of the proper size, firmness, shape, and color. They must arrange the berries neatly in baskets to catch the shopper's eye. Learning how to pick strawberries correctly can take weeks. The worker is often responsible not only for gathering and packing the fruit but also for tending the plants. The drip irrigation system has to be continually checked. Shoots and runners have to be removed. Rotting berries have to be tossed away, or they will spoil the rest. When a piece-rate wage is being paid, workers must perform these tasks and pick berries as fast as they can. There is a strong undercurrent of anxiety in a field being harvested at piece-rate. Workers move down the furrows pushing small wheelbarrows; they pause, bend over, brush away leaves to their left and right, pick berries, place them in boxes, check the plants, and move on, all in one fluid motion. Once their boxes are filled, they rush to have them tallied at the end of the field, rush back, and begin the process again.

Strawberry plants are four or five inches high and grow from beds eight to twelve inches high. You must bend at the waist to pick the fruit, which explains why the job is so difficult. Bending over that way for an hour can cause a stiff back; doing so for ten to twelve hours a day, weeks at a time, can cause excruciating pain and lifelong disabilities. Most strawberry pickers suffer back pain. As would be expected, the older you get, the more your back hurts. Farmworkers, like athletes, also decline in speed as they age. The fastest strawberry pickers tend to be in their late teens and early twenties. Most migrants quit picking strawberries in their mid-thirties, although some highly skilled women do work longer. Age discrimination is commonplace in the fields — it is purely a question of efficiency.

The hourly wages vary considerably, depending on the grower, the type of strawberry being picked, the time of year, and often, the skill of the worker. Wages are higher in Watsonville and Salinas than in Southern California, because of the greater distance from Mexico. Growers producing top-quality berries for the fresh market may pay as much as $8 or $10 an hour. At the height of the season, when berries are plentiful and growers pay a piece-rate of $1.25 a box, the fastest workers can earn more than $150 a day. But wages at that level only last for a month or so, and even during that period most workers can't attain them. When a crew of thirty picks at a piece-rate, three or four will earn $10 an hour, five or six will earn at or below the state minimum wage, $6.75 an hour, and the rest will earn somewhere in between.

The availability of work, not the pay scale, is of greatest concern to migrants. Despite the hardships that accompany the job, there is an oversupply of people hoping to pick strawberries. The fear of unemployment haunts all farmworkers in California today. Each harvest brings a new struggle to line up enough jobs for a decent income. The average migrant spends half the year working and a few months looking for work.

Another constant worry is finding a place to sleep. Santa Cruz and Monterey counties have some of the highest housing costs in the country. Long popular with tourists and wealthy retirees, the area has also attracted commuters from Silicon Valley. The residents of Watsonville and Salinas are determined to preserve the local farm economy, despite enormous pressure from developers. Agricultural land that currently sells for $40,000 an acre could be sold for many times that amount if it were rezoned; there are strawberry fields overlooking the Pacific Ocean. The determination to preserve agricultural land has not, however, extended to providing shelter for agricultural workers. Since 1980 the acreage around Watsonville and Salinas devoted to strawberries has more than doubled and the tonnage of strawberries produced there has nearly quadrupled. But the huge influx of migrant workers required to pick these berries has been forced to compete for a supply of low-income housing that's been inadequate for decades.

The few remaining labor camps for single men are grim places. I toured one that was a group of whitewashed buildings surrounded by chain-link fences and barbed wire. Desolate except for a rosebush in front of the manager's office, it looked like a holding pen or an old minimum-security prison. A nearby camp was reputed to be one of the best of its kind. Inside the barracks, the walls were freshly painted and the concrete floor was clean. A typical room was roughly twelve feet by ten feet, unheated, and occupied by four men. Sheets of plywood separated the steel cots. For $80 a week, a price far too high for most migrants, you got a bed and two meals a day. I've seen nicer horse barns.

Nevertheless, the labor camps are often preferable to the alternatives. When migrants stay in residential neighborhoods, they must pool their resources. In Watsonville three to four families will share a small house, seven or eight people to a room. Migrants routinely pay $100 to $200 a month to sleep in a garage with anywhere from four to ten other people. A survey of garages in Soledad found 1,500 inhabitants—a number roughly equal to one-eighth of the town's official population. At the peak of the harvest the housing shortage becomes acute. Migrants at the labor camps sometimes pay to sleep in parked cars. The newest migrant workers, who lack family in the area and haven't yet learned the ropes, often sleep outdoors in the wooded sections of Prunedale, trespassing, moving to a different hiding place each night. On hillsides above the Salinas Valley, hundreds of strawberry pickers have been found living in caves.

locked into dependence

THE IMMIGRATION HISTORY OF Guadalupe, California, can be read in the names and faces adorning headstones at its small cemetery. The Swiss and Italian and Portuguese surnames belong to families who settled in the Santa Maria Valley around the turn of the last century, growing beans and sugar beets, running cattle, and raising dairy herds. The Chinese, Japanese, and Filipino names belong to the first wave of farmworkers, some of whom managed to acquire land of their own. Spanish surnames greatly outnumber the rest, marking the recent graves along with plastic flowers and the images of saints. There is a sepulchral custom in Guadalupe, practiced for generations: most of the headstones bear sepia-tinted photographs of the deceased. Walking through the graveyard, one sees at a glance the slightly different ethnic traits and the subtle variations in skin color—long the basis of economic status and rivalry. Now all these faces stare in the same direction from the same place, arranged like crops in long, straight rows.

For most of the twentieth century, the Santa Maria Valley had a diverse farm economy. Although migrants were a large seasonal presence, the area lacked the huge industrial farms that dominated the landscape elsewhere in California. The acreage around Guadalupe was devoted primarily to field crops and irrigated pasture. The cattle ranches and dairy farms were owned and managed by local families. Fruits and vegetables, though an important source of revenue, occupied a small portion of the agricultural land.

Then, from the early 1970s to the late 1980s, the Santa Maria Valley was transformed. As field crops and dairy products became less profitable, farmers either switched to high-value specialty crops or quit farming. Much of the land was bought by outside corporations, such as Mobil and the Bank of America. Irrigated pastures became strawberry fields (dotted with oil wells) on leased land. The number of migrant workers soared. In 1960 Guadalupe's population was 18 percent Latino; today it is about 85 percent Latino. The middle classes fled to the nearby city of Santa Maria, leaving behind a rural underclass.

Juan Vicente Palerm has spent the last two decades studying the social and economic changes in the Santa Maria Valley. The director of the University of California's Institute for Mexico and the United States, Palerm is an anthropologist by training. His early fieldwork traced the lives of Spanish guest workers in northern Europe — migrants imported by treaty to labor in factories and fields. He is an imposing figure, with the graying beard of a patriarch, and has a remarkable grasp not only of labor market dynamics, but also of how every crop in the valley is planted, tended, marketed, and sold. I spent a day with Palerm and one of his graduate students, Manolo Gonzalez (who picked strawberries for a year as part of his research), driving the side streets of Guadalupe, touring the fields, and discussing how the growers of California and the peasants of rural Mexico created an agricultural system that has locked them into mutual dependence.

By relying on poor migrants from Mexico, California growers established a wage structure that discouraged American citizens from seeking farmwork. The wages offered at harvest were too low to sustain a family in the United States, but they were up to ten times as high as any wages Mexican peasants could earn in their native villages. A system evolved in which the cheap labor of Mexican migrants subsidized California agriculture, while remittances from that farmwork preserved rural communities in Mexico that otherwise might have collapsed. For decades the men of Mexican villages have traveled north to the fields of California, leaving behind women, children, and the elderly to look after their small farms. Migrant work in California has long absorbed Mexican surplus labor, while Mexico has in effect paid for the education, health care, and retirement of California's farmworkers.

Whenever migrants decided to settle in California, however, they disrupted the smooth workings of this system, by imposing higher costs on the state — especially if they married and raised children. That is why the Immigration and Naturalization Service (INS) used to round up and deport illegal immigrants in California immediately after the harvest. Nevertheless, millions of Mexican farmworkers have settled in the United States over the years, most of them becoming American citizens. Although agricultural employment has long been a means of entering U.S. society, low wages and poor working conditions have made it an occupation that most immigrants and their children hope to escape. Farm labor is more physically demanding and less financially rewarding than almost any other kind of work. A migrant who finds a job in a factory can triple his or her income. As a result, the whole system now depends upon a steady supply of illegal immigrants to keep farm wages low and to replace migrants who have either retired to Mexico or found better jobs in California.

Juan Vicente Palerm believes that today there are not only more migrants shuttling back and forth from Mexico but also more Mexican farmworkers settling permanently in California. Throughout the state towns like Guadalupe, Calexico, Cutler, and McFarland are becoming enclaves of rural poverty. In the Santa Maria Valley the increased production of fruits and vegetables, higher yields per acre, and an extended growing season have created thousands of full- and part-time jobs for farmworkers. Broccoli fields now occupy more than 20,000 acres, requiring a large supply of resident workers for a staggered harvest that lasts most of the year. Celery and cauliflower production has also increased the number of full-time jobs. Perhaps 40 percent of the farm labor in the valley is currently performed by workers who live there. Many farmworkers now own houses. But the strawberry fields have drawn thousands of poor migrants to the area. Only 12 percent of the work force at a strawberry farm can claim year-round employment. And cultivating the fruit is so labor-intensive — twenty-five times as labor-intensive as cultivating broccoli — that strawberry production now employs more farmworkers than the production of all the vegetables grown in the valley combined. Most strawberry pickers hope to find jobs in the neighboring vegetable fields, where the wages are better and the work is less arduous. Turnover rates are extremely high in the strawberry work force. But there is no impending shortage of potential migrants. The rural population of Mexico has tripled since the 1940s. "In terms of absolute numbers," Palerm says, "there are far more Mexican peasants today than ever before."

Twenty-five years ago academic texts declared that California agriculture — with its large-scale irrigation, sophisticated farming practices, corporate structure, and low-wage, imported labor — was unique. That is no longer true. Southern Spain is fast becoming the "California of Europe," borrowing many of the same techniques to grow the same high-value crops and relying on illegal immigrants from North Africa. Southern Italy and Mediterranean France are adopting the system as well. Mexico, Guatemala, and Chile, with the aid of foreign investors, are recreating California's industrialized agriculture in Latin America, producing some crops that now compete with those grown in the United States. Improvements in transportation systems and cooling technology have created an international market for commodities that until recent years were rarely exported. Juan Vicente Palerm believes that the cultivation of fruits and vegetables for processing will increasingly shift from California to Mexico, where labor costs are much lower. Mexico will produce the frozen vegetables for TV dinners, while California grows artichokes, broccoli, strawberries, and asparagus for the fresh market. The harvest of these specialty crops, however, cannot easily be mechanized: their high value is closely linked to their unblemished appearance. The prosperity of California agriculture increasingly depends on uninterrupted access to Mexico's peasantry.

Most of the strawberry workers in the Santa Maria Valley are Mixtec Indians — some of the poorest and most exploited people in the Western Hemisphere. Soil erosion and declining crop yields in the mountains of western Oaxaca have forced the Mixtecs to become migrant workers. According to Michael Kearney, a professor of anthropology at the University of California at Riverside, their choice is simple: "Migrate or starve." Mixtecs now dominate the lowest-paid jobs in California agriculture. In Tijuana you often see the wives and children of Mixtec farmworkers, small and dark and beautiful, dressed in the bright colors of their native villages, selling Chiclets to tourists on the street.

Until the 1970s almost all the Mexican farmworkers in California were mestizos with strong links to communities already in the state. The new migrants present social workers with unusual challenges. In addition to the ninety-two dialects of Mixtec, there are at least half a dozen other pre-Columbian languages spoken by the indigenous peoples of Oaxaca. Perhaps one-fifth of the Mixtec farmworkers in California speak little English or Spanish. Throughout their migratory route Mixtecs are the victims of robbery and discrimination. In central Mexico they must run a gauntlet of officials demanding bribes. In Tijuana they are preyed upon by smugglers, rapists, and thieves. In the Imperial Desert, east of San Diego, they risk their lives crossing the border. Two or three migrants now die there from exposure every week.

In Guadalupe many of the settled farmworkers resent the new arrivals from Oaxaca. Illegal immigrants often crossed picket lines during the 1980s, helping to drive the UFW from the valley. Adjusted for inflation, the hourly wages have declined, and there is widespread underemployment. Labor contractors now actively recruit illegals, who work for less money and raise fewer objections than legal residents. At harvest time Guadalupe's population of roughly 5,700 swells by as much as one-third, placing great demands on local services. Palerm's researchers once discovered twenty-two people living in a two-bedroom apartment.

Despite the hardships of the long journey, Mixtecs hoping to sustain their native villages have a strong incentive to find work in California. Wages in Oaxaca are about two or three dollars a day. Wages in the strawberry fields of Baja California are about five dollars a day. A Mixtec farmworker in the Santa Maria Valley, making ten dollars an hour at the peak of the strawberry harvest, can earn more in one day than he or she could earn back home in a month.

a reliance on misfortune

IN 1951 THE PRESIDENT'S COMMISSION on Migratory Labor condemned the abysmal living conditions of illegal immigrants employed as migrant workers in the United States. At the time, workers were found living in orchards and irrigation ditches. They lived in constant fear of apprehension, like fugitives, and were routinely exploited by their employers, who could maintain unsafe working conditions, cut wages, or abruptly dismiss them with little worry of reprisal. In many cases, the life of these migrants was, according to the commission, "virtually peonage." The commission estimated that 40 percent of the migrants in the United States — at least 400,000 people — were illegal immigrants. Their presence in such large numbers depressed wages for all farmworkers; that fact was "unquestionable." Indeed, illegal immigrants had begun to displace native-born workers not only in agriculture but in nonfarm occupations such as construction. The commission argued that the only way to stop the flow of illegals was to impose harsh punishments on growers who employed and exploited them. It suggested fines, imprisonment, and a strict prohibition on the shipment in interstate commerce of any goods harvested by illegal immigrants. "We depend on misfortune to build up our force of migratory workers," the commission concluded, "and when the supply is low because there is not enough misfortune at home, we rely on misfortune abroad to replenish the supply."

Congress ignored the commission's recommendations, and for the next two decades it was a crime to be an illegal immigrant in the United States but not a crime to employ one. In 1986 Congress passed the Immigration Reform and Control Act (IRCA), which demanded broad sanctions against the employers of illegal immigrants. But these sanctions have rarely been applied. There are about a million private employers in California — and about 200 federal inspectors to investigate workplace violations of the immigration code. Moreover, the federal penalties for employing an illegal immigrant are rather mild. A first offense may result in a fine of $250, a third offense, in a fine of $3,000.

Instead of stemming illegal immigration, IRCA actually encouraged it. In response to growers' fears that the new sanctions on employers would create a shortage of farmworkers, Congress included in the bill a special amnesty for illegal immigrants who could prove they had done farm work in the previous year. It did not demand much proof. Backed by Congressman Leon Panetta and Senator Pete Wilson, both from California, the Special Agricultural Worker (SAW) program was expected to grant legal status to 350,000 illegal immigrants. Instead, almost 1.3 million illegal immigrants—a number roughly equivalent at the time to one-sixth of the adult male population of rural Mexico—applied for this amnesty, most of them using phony documents in what has been called one of the greatest immigration frauds in American history. More than a million illegal immigrants were eventually granted legal status; many were soon joined illegally by their wives and children. Instead of shrinking the farm-labor force, IRCA guaranteed an oversupply of workers. Counterfeit green cards, Social Security cards, driver's licenses, and SAW work histories—the documents necessary to obtain employment as a farmworker—can be easily obtained in rural California for $50. The process usually takes about an hour.

At the moment an estimated 7 to 8 million illegal immigrants live in the United States. About half of them are Mexican. While some advocates of immigration reform call for another large amnesty, granting green cards or full citizenship to millions, California growers prefer a new guest-worker program. It would recruit migrant workers through an international agreement and would guarantee their wages, their living conditions—and their return to Mexico at the end of the harvest. Vicente Fox, the president of Mexico, also advocates the creation of a formal, well-regulated program to ensure the orderly flow of migrants between the two countries. The United States government operated a similar endeavor, called the Bracero Program, from 1942 to 1964. Migrants who enrolled in the program were shuttled to huge holding pens at the border, forced to await employment with numbers hung around their necks, and then stripped naked and sprayed with a delousing agent before being allowed to enter the United States. Once in this country, the braceros were all but powerless and were bound to a single employer. The Bracero Program was terminated amid revelations that its guest workers were widely being abused. Historians now agree that the program established the social networks and migratory patterns responsible for the subsequent waves of illegal immigration. Indeed, during the program's existence there were often more illegal immigrants than braceros employed in American agriculture.

Despite all these facts, Juan Vicente Palerm does not rule out lending his support to a new guest-worker program. He has no illusions about such arrangements, having witnessed their implementation in Western Europe during the 1960s, their successes and ultimate failure. His willingness to consider a guest-worker program today is based on pragmatism. The living conditions of migrants in California have become so bad, and the dangers they now face crossing the border are so severe, that Palerm feels something must be done at once. A guest-worker program, while no solution, is at least a first step. The North American Free Trade Agreement permits the free movement of American capital across borders without offering any legal protection to Mexican migrant workers. Palerm believes that the terms of a guest-worker program could guarantee migrants some of the basic rights they do not enjoy today. Even if illegal immigration continued alongside the officially approved migration, those farmworkers in the program would no longer have to live underground.

Opponents of guest-worker programs have long based their objections on principle. More than two decades ago, Sidney Weintraub and Stanley R. Ross, then at the University of Texas, suggested that "guest worker" is simply a modern euphemism for an indentured laborer. A guest-worker program legally embraces the concept of second-class citizenship in the United States. It creates a group of people who have limited rights. Aside from the philosophical objections that can be raised, many argue that such programs just don't work. "There's nothing more permanent," one economist has said, "than temporary workers." Guest-worker programs were discontinued in Europe because large numbers of Algerian, Moroccan, and Turkish workers chose to settle instead of returning home.

Mexican farmworkers have long dominated the agricultural labor force in California and the Southwest, but only recently have they begun to migrate throughout the United States. Mexican farmworkers, many of them illegal immigrants, are now picking raspberries in Oregon, detasseling corn in Iowa, harvesting tobacco in Virginia, and tending plants in New Jersey nurseries. Moreover, the same methods long used to employ illegal immigrants in California agriculture — the reliance on intermediaries, such as labor contractors — are being used to employ them in the meatpacking industry, construction work, janitorial service, and the garment industry. The majority of illegal immigrants in California now work in nonfarm occupations and come from regions throughout Mexico, including urban areas such as Mexico City. Michael Kearney thinks that the indigenous people of Chiapas will soon join Mixtecs in the migratory stream. Farm-union organizers strongly oppose a new guest-worker program, while others ask why the government should serve as a labor contractor for agricultural interests. Nonfarm industries are just as eager to hire low-wage workers; hotels, motels, fast-food restaurants, and meatpacking plants would also like to employ guest workers. Such a recruitment program is unnecessary, opponents say, when so many poor Mexican farmworkers already in the United States are struggling to find work.

Philip L. Martin, who served for four years as a member of the Commission on Agricultural Labor, a group mandated by IRCA, believes that the most effective way to improve the lives of farmworkers is simply to enforce the existing labor and immigration laws. Lax federal enforcement has amounted to a tremendous subsidy for fruit and vegetable growers, one that has distorted the economics of those industries. "Cheap labor benefits agriculture in the short run," Martin argues. "But it also helps to blind farmers to the technological changes they will have to make in order to compete with foreign producers, who have access to even cheaper labor." As long as the United States tolerates the employment of illegal immigrants in agriculture, Martin believes, the farm labor market will continue the endless cycle in which farmworkers quit for better jobs and illegals arrive to replace them. "We have essentially privatized the immigration policy of this country," Martin says, "and left it in the hands of California's growers."

Joaquin Avila, a former president of the Mexican-American Legal Defense and Educational Fund, thinks the distinction between legal and illegal farmworkers is less important at this point than the level of wages being paid. The labor market interdependence between the United States and Mexico, a relationship that evolved over decades, cannot be severed overnight. Until economic development in Mexico has diminished the underlying need for migration, he says, the emphasis in the United States should be on making sure that all workers, regardless of their nationality, are paid a decent wage and protected from exploitation.

Despite the many policy options regarding farmworkers, the most likely scenario is that, at the federal level, nothing will be done. The plight of migrants has been deplored by presidential commissions and congressional subcommittees for more than a century, and yet little has fundamentally changed. Growers still exercise a great deal of political influence, while farmworkers possess virtually none. Except for a flurry of attention every few decades, the American people have greeted the whole subject with indifference. The nation's fresh produce is less expensive as a result — but not much. Maintaining the current level of poverty among migrant farmworkers saves the average American household about $50 a year.

During the spring of 1996 the UFW began a major organizing campaign in California's strawberry fields, backed by millions of dollars from the AFL-CIO. A march through Watsonville attracted 12,000 supporters. The strawberry campaign's slogan was "Five Cents for Fairness." If the growers added just a nickel to the price of every pint of strawberries, the UFW argued, and gave that extra nickel to their workers, migrant wages would rise by as much as 50 percent. Growers did not jump at the idea. The previous year, when workers at a strawberry farm in Ventura County overwhelmingly voted to join the UFW, the grower responded by plowing under part of the field immediately and then shutting down the entire operation at the end of the season. The workers were fired and had to sue for back wages. In response to the UFW strawberry campaign, which received nationwide publicity, growers took a more subtle approach. They hired the Dolphin Group, a Los Angeles public relations firm, to present a kinder, gentler view of the industry.

The Dolphin Group had for years worked closely with right-wing Republican candidates and causes. It had produced the infamous Willie Horton ad that helped sink the presidential candidacy of Michael Dukakis. It had created a phony antismoking group, "Californians for Statewide Smoking Restrictions", using money from Philip Morris and the tobacco industry. It had created a phony grape workers group, the "Grape Workers and Farmers Coalition," using money from the California table grape industry. And so in 1996 it created the Strawberry Workers & Farmers Alliance (SW&FA), using money from the strawberry industry. The SW&FA staged its own march in Watsonville, earned the blessing of the local Catholic bishop, and called for "Farm Workers Rights and Human Rights." It also claimed that female UFW organizers were seducing migrant workers to gain support for the union.

Launched with high hopes, the UFW strawberry campaign was soon bogged down in disputes with front organizations backed by growers, such as the SW&FA, the "Strawberry Pro-Workers Committee" and the "Agricultural Workers Committee." Poor migrants who'd never belonged to any union were suddenly confronted by a series of groups claiming to have their best interests at heart. UFW organizers were attacked by anti-union thugs, and many workers feared that showing support for any union might get them fired. The economic benefits a union might bring had to be carefully weighed against the possibility of swiftly becoming unemployed. The UFW managed to win contracts at the state's largest organic strawberry farm and at farms owned by Coastal Berry, the state's largest strawberry grower. UFW workers at those farms gained a pay increase, seniority rights, leaves of absence, paid holidays, and medical insurance for their entire families. Although union organizing continues in the strawberry fields, the effort has proved to be difficult and disappointing. In September, 2002, California's governor, Gray Davis, signed legislation that may strengthen the UFW. The two bills require official mediation whenever contract disputes with growers become stalled. At the moment, perhaps 1,600 of California's roughly 20,000 strawberry workers belong to the UFW.

bowing down to the market

ONE MORNING IN SAN DIEGO COUNTY, I met a strawberry grower named Doug. We sat and talked in a trailer on the edge of his field. Doug's father and his grandfather had both been sent to an internment camp for Japanese Americans during World War II. Upon their release, the grandfather bought a used truck. At first he worked for other farmers, then he leased some land. He spoke no English and so Doug's father, still a teenager, assumed an important role in the business. The two grew vegetables with success and eventually shifted to strawberries, shipping and processing the fruit as well. On the land where their original farm once stood, there are now condominiums, a park, and a school. Doug grows strawberries a few miles inland. His fields are surrounded by chain-link fences topped with barbed wire. An enormous real estate development, with hundreds of Spanish-style condo units, is creeping up the hills toward his farm. Many of the farmers nearby have already sold their land. Doug has spent most of his life in strawberry fields, learning every aspect of the business first-hand, but now isn't sure he wants his children to do the same.

"Farming's not a glamorous business," Doug said. "Farmers don't have a high status in this community. In fact, we're resented by most people." With all the hassles today from the state and from his neighbors, he sometimes asks himself, "Hey, why do this?" Selling the land would make him instantly rich. Instead, he worries about water costs, about theft, about the strawberries from New Zealand he saw in the market the other day. Rain had wiped out a quarter of his early-season berries, just when the market price was at its peak. Doug cannot understand the hostility toward growers in California. After all, agriculture preserves open land. He thinks Americans don't appreciate how lucky they are to have cheap food. He doesn't understand why anyone would impede strawberry production by limiting his access to migrants. "My workers are helping themselves," he said. "I've picked strawberries, and let me tell you, there is no harder work. I respect these people. They work damn hard. And my jobs are open to anyone who wants to apply." Every so often college kids visit the ranch, convinced that picking strawberries would be a nice way to earn some extra money. Doug laughed. "They don't last an hour out here."

We stepped from the trailer into bright sunshine. Workers moved down the furrows under close supervision. Doug takes great pride in being a third-generation grower. He is smart, well educated, meticulous, and it showed in his field. But I wondered if Doug and his workers would still be there in a few years.

Doug picked a berry and handed it to me, a large Chandler that was brilliantly red. I took a bite. The strawberry was warm and sweet and fragrant, with a slightly bitter aftertaste from the soil.

That evening I inadvertently met some of Doug's workers. Ricardo

Soto, a young lawyer at CRLA, had brought me to the edge of an avocado orchard to visit a hidden encampment of migrant workers. Perhaps one-third of the farmworkers in northern San Diego County—about 7,000 people—are now homeless. An additional 9,000 of their family members are homeless, too. Many are living outdoors. The shortage of low-income housing became acute in the early 1980s, and large shantytowns began to appear, some containing hundreds of crude shacks. As suburbs encroached on agricultural land in northern San Diego County, wealthy commuters and strawberry pickers became neighbors. At one large shantytown I visited, women were doing their laundry in a stream not far from a walled compound with tennis courts, a pool, and a sign promising country club living. The suburbanites do not like living beside Mexican farmworkers. Instead of providing low-income housing, local authorities have declared states of emergency, passed laws to forbid curbside hiring, and bulldozed many of the large encampments. San Diego growers appalled by the living conditions of their migrants have tried to build farmworker housing near the fields—only to encounter fierce resistance from neighboring homeowners. Although the shantytowns lower nearby property values, permanent farmworker housing might reduce property values even more. "When people find out you want to build housing for your migrants," one grower told me, "they just go ballistic."

The new encampments are smaller and built to avoid detection. At the end of a driveway, near a chain-link fence, I met a young Mixtec who lived in such an encampment. His name was Francisco, and he was eighteen years old. He looked deeply exhausted. He had just picked strawberries for twelve hours at Doug's farm. I asked what he thought of Doug as a boss. "Not bad," he said politely.

The previous year Francisco had picked strawberries from April until July. He had saved $800 during that period and had wired all of it to his mother and father in the village of San Sebastian Tecomaxtlahuaca. This was Francisco's second season in the fields, but he had not seen much of San Diego County. He was too afraid of getting caught. His days were spent at the farm, his nights at the encampment. He picked strawberries six days a week, sometimes seven, for ten or twelve hours a day. "When there's work," Francisco said, "you have to work."

Each morning he woke up around four-thirty and walked for half an hour to reach Doug's field.

At dusk, thirteen tired men in dirty clothes approached us. They were all from Francisco's village. They worked together at Doug's farm and stayed at the same encampment. They knew one another's families back home and looked after one another here. The oldest was forty-three and the youngest looked about fifteen. All the men were illegals. All were sick with coughs, but none dared to see a doctor. As the sun dropped behind the hills, clouds of mosquitoes descended, and yet the migrants seemed too tired to notice. They lay on their backs, on their sides, resting on the hard ground as though it were a sofa.

Francisco offered to show me their encampment. We squeezed through a hole in the chain-link fence and through gaps in rusting barbed wire, and climbed a winding path enclosed by tall bushes. It felt like a medieval maze. As we neared the camp, I noticed beer cans and food wrappers littering the ground. We came upon the first shack—short and low, more like a tent, just silver trash bags draped over a wooden frame. A little farther up the path stood three more shacks in a small clearing. They were built of plywood and camouflaged. Branches and leaves had been piled on their roofs. The landowner did not know the migrants lived here, and the encampment would be difficult to find. These migrants were hiding out, like criminals or Viet Cong. Garbage was everywhere. Francisco pointed to his shack, which was about five feet high, five feet wide, and seven feet long. He shared it with two other men. He had a good blanket. But when it rained at night the roof leaked, and the men would go to work soaking wet the next day and dry off in the sun. Francisco had never lived this way before coming to San Diego. At home he always slept in a bed.

Beyond the sheds, bushes crowded the path again, and then it reached another clearing, where two battered lawn chairs had been placed at the edge of the hill. There was a wonderful view of strawberry fields, new houses, and the lights of the freeway in the distance.

Driving back to my motel that night, I thought about the people of Orange County, one of the richest counties in the nation—big on family values, yet bankrupt from financial speculation, unwilling to raise taxes to pay for their own children's education, unwilling to pay off their debts, whining about the injustice of it, and blaming all their problems on illegal immigrants. And I thought about Francisco, their bogeyman, their scapegoat, working ten hours a day at one of the hardest jobs imaginable, and sleeping on the ground every night, for months, so that he could save money and send it home to his parents.

We have been told for years to bow down before "the market." We have placed our faith in the laws of supply and demand. What has been forgotten, or ignored, is that the market rewards only efficiency. Every other human value gets in its way. The market will drive wages down like water, until they reach the lowest possible level. Today that level is being set not in Washington or New York or Sacramento but in the fields of Baja California and the mountain villages of Oaxaca. That level is about five dollars a day. No deity that men have ever worshiped is more ruthless and more hollow than the free market unchecked; there is no reason why shantytowns should not appear on the out-skirts of every American city. All those who now consider themselves devotees of the market should take a good look at what is happening in California. Left to its own devices, the free market always seeks a work force that is hungry, desperate, and cheap — a work force that is anything but free.

[3]

AN EMPIRE

OF THE OBSCENE

O N JULY 10, 1986, Attorney General Edwin Meese III's Commission on Pornography issued its *Final Report,* outlining the harmful effects of sexually explicit material and calling for strict enforcement of the federal obscenity laws. The Meese Commission had been surrounded by controversy since its inception. Henry E. Hudson, the commission's chairman, had been criticized for approaching the subject with a bias: as a commonwealth attorney in Virginia, he had rid Arlington County of adult bookstores and prosecuted mainstream video stores for renting X-rated films. Alan E. Sears, the commission's executive director, had sent a letter to the nation's leading drugstore and convenience store chains, warning that any company which sold *Playboy* would be identified in the Meese Commission's report as a distributor of pornography. Another commissioner, Father Bruce Ritter, the founder of a well-known Catholic charity, had tried to broaden the panel's mandate, arguing that homosexuality should be denounced by the U.S. government and classified as abnormal, antisocial behavior.

After half a dozen public hearings and a year-long investigation, the Meese Commission concluded that nearly all hard-core pornography and most soft-core pornography conveyed degrading images of women that encouraged violence against them. Many religious leaders and feminists applauded these findings, while social scientists argued there was hardly any empirical evidence to support such claims. Amid all the debate over the commission's methods and aims and definitions of harm, little attention was paid to a remarkable conclusion no one bothered to dispute. The Meese Commission had found that one man, Reuben Sturman, a resident of Shaker Heights, Ohio, dominated the production and distribution of pornography not only in the United States but also throughout the world.

Reuben Sturman was a former comic book salesman who'd turned a small Cleveland magazine business into an international media conglomerate boasting hundreds of companies in North America, Asia, and Western Europe — a vertically integrated enterprise that produced films, videos, and magazines, that manufactured peep shows and sexual devices, that operated wholesale warehouses and retail stores. A business rival once complained that Reuben Sturman did not simply control the adult entertainment industry; he was the industry. Like another Cleveland native, John D. Rockefeller, Sturman consolidated scores of local businesses into a huge distribution network, building his empire through shrewd marketing, boldness, secret alliances, and a willingness to defy the government. "Every legal subterfuge was used by him with supreme skill," a historian wrote about Rockefeller; much the same could be said of Reuben Sturman, who spent millions of dollars each year on an army of attorneys, who disguised his ownership of various businesses through corporations chartered in Liechtenstein, Panama, and Liberia. Sturman fiercely guarded his privacy, using at least twenty different aliases, rarely speaking to reporters, and frequently hiding his face behind a mask during courtroom appearances. At one point the *Cleveland Free Press* speculated that he might be the wealthiest man in the state of Ohio, though for more than a decade the only photograph of Sturman the newspaper possessed was a mug shot taken in 1964.

To his defenders in the sex industry, Reuben Sturman was a classic American entrepreneur, a self-made man whose toughness, intelligence, hard work, and boundless self-confidence had propelled his rise to the top. But to antipornography activists and Justice Department officials, Sturman was the head of a vast criminal organization, an empire of the obscene whose businesses enjoyed an unfair competitive advantage: protection and support from the highest levels of the Cosa Nostra.

A great deal has been written about pornography, for or against it, from various points of view. But much less attention has been given to the underlying economics, to porn as a commodity, the end product of a modern industry that arose in the United States after the Second World War and has grown to enormous proportions ever since. Critics of the sex industry have long attacked it for being "un-American" — and yet there is something quintessentially American about it, about the heady mix of sex and money, the fortunes quickly made and lost, the new identities assumed and then discarded, the public condemnations so often linked to a private obsession. Largely fueled by loneliness and frustration, the sex industry has never suffered from a shortage of customers. And in recent years it has transformed porn from a minor subculture on the fringes of society into a major component of American popular culture.

Seven months after the Meese Commission released its findings, President Ronald Reagan launched perhaps the most far-reaching assault on sexually explicit material in the nation's history, an anti-pornography campaign that continued under President George H. W. Bush. Hundreds of producers, distributors, and retailers in the sex industry were indicted and convicted. Many of them were driven from the business. The Republican war on pornography, however, coincided with an exponential increase in America's consumption of porn. According to *Adult Video News,* an industry trade publication, from 1985 to 1992 — from the appointment of the Meese Commission to the close of George H. W. Bush's presidency — the number of hard-core video rentals each year in the United States rose from 79 million to 490 million. In 2001, the number climbed to 759 million. Although the revenues of the sex industry are difficult to estimate, Americans now spend as much as $8 billion to $10 billion on "adult entertainment" — on hard-core videos and DVDs, Internet porn, cable and satellite porn, peep shows, phone sex, live sex acts, sexual toys, and sex magazines. That's an amount roughly the same as Hollywood's domestic box office receipts, an amount larger than the revenue generated by rock or country-and-western recordings. Americans now spend more money at strip clubs than at Broadway theaters, regional and nonprofit theaters, and symphony orchestra performances — combined.

Sexually explicit material has become so commonplace that one can easily forget how strictly it was prohibited not long ago. The sociologist Charles Winick has noted that the sexual content of American culture changed more in two decades than it had in the previous two centuries. In 1970 a federal study of pornography estimated that the total retail value of all the hard-core porn in the United States was no more than $10 million, and perhaps less than $5 million.

"Obscenity," "pornography," and "indecency" are terms not easily defined. Each exists in the eyes of the beholder. "Hard-core" and "soft-core" are also terms whose meanings are imprecise, shifting over the years. "Hard-core" now generally refers to porn in which the intercourse or oral sex is vividly and unmistakably real. In soft-core porn these sex acts may be simulated. The U.S. Supreme Court has ruled that obscene speech is not protected by the First Amendment. But for more than a century battles have been fought over what is — and what isn't — obscene. In much the same way that the policies of the Federal Communications Commission have guided the development of the nation's television industry, the Justice Department's shifting enforcement of the obscenity laws has helped determine the structure of the American sex industry. At times strict enforcement has encouraged a long list of illegal activities, from money laundering to extortion. At other times the obscenity conviction of a key industry figure has paved the way for increased competition, prompting the market to operate more efficiently.

During the 1980s the advent of adult movies on videocassette and cable television shifted the consumption of porn from seedy movie theaters and bookstores into the home. As a result, most of the profits generated by porn today are being earned by businesses not traditionally associated with the sex industry — by mom-and-pop video stores in ordinary neighborhoods, leading hotel chains, Fortune 500 satellite and cable companies. In the San Fernando Valley of Southern California, right beside the Hollywood movie industry, a thriving X-rated movie industry has emerged, with its own studios, talent agencies, and stars, its own fan clubs and film critics. America's porn has become one more of its cultural exports, dominating overseas markets. Despite having some of the toughest restrictions on sexually explicit materials of any western industrialized nation, the United States is now by far the world's leading producer of porn, churning out hard-core videos at the astonishing rate of about two hundred and eleven new titles every week.

As pornography left the underground and entered the mainstream, I became curious about who was profiting from this multi-billion-dollar industry. Little had been published about the business of porn — or about the businessmen who ran it. Here was a major industry, a source of tremendous controversy, which seemed to lack a written history. The brief mention of Reuben Sturman in the Meese *Report* caught my attention; nobody I knew had ever heard of him. In the mid-1990s I decided to investigate the origins and the workings of the pornography trade, focusing not on its morality or aesthetics but on its economics. My aim was to follow the money. It led me to interview some of the leading figures in today's sex industry, as well as a few who'd worked in it for decades. I've tried in the following pages to give a sense of how this business evolved and to describe how it now operates, from the industrial parks of Southern California to some unusual buildings in North Carolina. Much of the tale unfolds in the city where today's porn business was born: Cleveland.

The story of Reuben Sturman spans the history of the modern American sex industry, from the distribution of "girlie" magazines under the counter to the sale of adult videos at urban newsstands and suburban malls. Sturman believed there was nothing wrong with what he sold and eagerly battled the federal government for decades. Like Walt Disney, he played a central role in the creation of a whole new industry, one that manufactured profitable fantasies not for children but for adults. Though Reuben Sturman's name remains largely unknown, his influence is now inescapable. The career of this little-known businessman — who thought porn was just another product — sheds light on how an outlaw industry once despised and suppressed came to play such a large role in molding the American imagination.

rise

THE MODERN AMERICAN SEX INDUSTRY began on the kitchen table of a small Chicago apartment, where Hugh Hefner pasted together the first issue of *Playboy* in 1953. There had been successful pin-up magazines during the Second World War, with women posing in swimsuits and names evoking the sensibility of that era: *Flirt, Whisper, Eyeful, Titter,* and *Wink.* There had been nudist magazines, like *Sunshine & Health,* which in purporting to advocate an alternate lifestyle printed photos of naked women playing volleyball. But it was *Playboy* that turned sex into a commodity for mass consumption. Hugh Hefner, only twenty-seven at the time, gave the American public something genuinely new: an idealized midwestern vision of the girl next door, who was wholesome, friendly, interested in hobbies — and willing to take off her shirt. The first issue of *Playboy* featured a color centerfold of Marilyn Monroe and had a press run of 70,000 copies. Within a few years, the magazine's circulation had reached nearly a million.

Reuben Sturman was two years older than Hefner, but of the same ambitious generation, eager for success in business after the Second World War. Sturman's parents were Russian immigrants who ran a small neighborhood grocery shop on Cleveland's East Side. He aimed to do better. After three years in the Army Air Force, Sturman attended Western Reserve University, briefly worked for a candy and tobacco wholesaler, got married, and then decided to start a business of his own. He'd met a man from Owensboro, Kentucky, who somehow had access to remaindered comic books—copies that had gone unsold, that were often returned to the publisher and destroyed. Sturman obtained these remainders at a low cost, two dozen to a package, wrapped in newspaper, and began offering them to local candy stores. He was funny and full of charisma, a good salesman. And his comic books could be sold to the public for a nickel each, half the usual price. Using the garage at his home as a warehouse, Sturman drove through the neighborhoods of Cleveland, visiting mom-and-pop stores, selling bundles of comic books from the trunk of his old Dodge.

The business soon had a name, the Premium Sales Company, and a narrow storefront warehouse. Sturman worked long hours, putting every spare penny back into the business, extending his sales route beyond Cleveland, first to Buffalo, then to Pittsburgh, Detroit, Chicago, and Cincinnati. He eventually opened a wholesale warehouse in each of those cities, supplying them not only with comic books but also with car magazines, movie magazines, crossword puzzle magazines, all bought from the same source in Kentucky. His wife, Esther, joined the company, as did his younger brother, Joseph. By the late 1950s, Reuben Sturman was a rising young businessman with three small children, a house bought through the G.I. Bill, and a wholesale distribution network encompassing eight major American cities.

The huge success of *Playboy* inspired many imitations, cheaply published magazines featuring black-and-white photos of topless women. At about the same time a decades-old literary genre grew in popularity, the "sex-pulp" novel—a paperback with a lurid title, an equally lurid cover, a narrative of little importance, and sex scenes every few pages, described through euphemism and innuendo. Stores usually kept these sex magazines and paperbacks hidden from view, literally under the counter, and most distributors were unwilling to handle them. When an employee at Premium Sales suggested the company should carry a few sex titles, Sturman gave his approval without much thought. It didn't take long for him to notice that there was great demand for such publications and that a sex magazine produced at least twenty times the revenue per copy of a remaindered comic book. Once

Sturman realized these things, he wanted to distribute every sex book and magazine that had ever been printed.

In 1963 Sturman's warehouse in Detroit was raided by the police, who seized 20,000 copies of a nudist magazine. Sturman's response would prove characteristic. He sued the Detroit Police Department for $200,000 in damages, and the case against him was later dropped. In 1964 FBI agents raided his Cleveland warehouse, seizing 590 copies of a paperback called *Sex Life of a Cop*. The FBI also confiscated copies of Jack Kerouac's *The Subterraneans*. Written by Sanford E. Aday, a leading author and publisher of sex pulps based in Fresno, California, *Sex Life of a Cop* was the story of two police officers who seduce most of the young women in their town, including the wives of the mayor and the chief of police. The book angered law enforcement officials across the country and — despite the absence of a single dirty word — was already the focus of obscenity prosecutions in California and Michigan. Henry Miller, whose *Tropic of Cancer* was still banned, thought *Sex Life of a Cop* was offensive, "terrible stuff." It was erotica for the average man.

Sturman's indictment for *Sex Life of a Cop* forced him to consider the larger issues surrounding pornography. Most state obscenity charges were misdemeanors. But under federal law they were felonies and could lead to long prison sentences. Although the political climate was changing, there were still strong limits on sexual expression in American society. Hollywood films did not show any nudity. Married couples on television always slept in separate beds. And in New York State the comedian Lenny Bruce had just been convicted and given a four-month sentence for saying obscene words during his nightclub act. After thinking long and hard, Reuben Sturman came to a conclusion that he would defend at great cost for the next thirty years: Americans should have the freedom to read or to view whatever they wanted, in the privacy of their own homes — and he should have the freedom to sell it. Sturman pleaded not guilty to the obscenity charge. And then he sued J. Edgar Hoover, director of the FBI, for violating his constitutional rights.

infidels, liberals, and free-lovers

OBSCENITY TRIALS POSE AN UNUSUAL CHALLENGE to the courts. A judge or jury must decide not only whether a defendant is guilty but also whether a crime has been committed; that is, whether the material in question is obscene. Unlike murder, whose legal definition doesn't change significantly with each new generation, the crime of obscenity has always reflected the values of the government leveling the charge. The belief that words or images can be obscene has a religious origin closely linked to notions of blasphemy and sacrilege. Although an obscenity offense takes place in a person's mind, the real damage is done to the body and soul.

There were no federal laws against obscenity in the United States until the mid-nineteenth century. After the Civil War, Congress passed legislation banning obscene materials from the mails, an act prompted by the large volume of sexually explicit photographs, known as "French postcards," being circulated within the Union Army. The penalties for violating the new law, however, were rather weak, as was the government's enthusiasm for enforcing it. During the early 1870s these facts inspired Anthony Comstock, a New York grocery clerk in his late twenties, to organize the nation's first anti-pornography campaign. Comstock was a fundamentalist. He believed in the Devil, and he believed that men and women who trafficked in pornography were agents of the "Evil one." As a young boy in New Canaan, Connecticut, Anthony Comstock had been shown obscene material by a group of farmhands, an experience that haunted him for years and provoked his own struggle with sinful behavior, with an overpowering compulsion to masturbate. Comstock's diary reveals a man torn between wild swings of hope and despair, between a longing for purity and fears of defilement. "Like a cancer it fastens itself upon the imagination," he later wrote of obscenity, "defiling the mind, corrupting the thoughts, leading to secret practices of most foul and revolting character, until the victim tires of life, and existence is scarcely endurable." Comstock's mission was to save other young people from that fate, from a lust that "deadens the will . . . and damns the soul."

Outraged by the "obscene literature" and "beastly transparencies" openly sold in New York City, Anthony Comstock rallied the Young Men's Christian Association (YMCA), establishing a New York Society for the Suppression of Vice and taking his crusade to Washington, D.C. In 1873 Congress passed a bill that made it a crime to send "obscene, lewd, or lascivious" materials through the mail and specified punishments of up to ten years in prison at hard labor. The Comstock Law, as it was soon called, also prohibited sending through the mail any information about sexual devices, birth control, or abortion. Comstock was appointed a special agent of the U.S. Post Office Department, authorized to travel the country on postal trains for free and to search through the mails for obscenity. The New York State legislature voted him full police powers and the right to carry a gun.

For the next forty years, Anthony Comstock acted as America's official conscience and censor, opening other people's mail and confiscating whatever offended him. Tall, stocky, and balding, with bushy auburn whiskers, and always dressed in black, Comstock personally arrested hundreds of gamblers, pornographers, strippers, and abortionists. His efforts were supported by a large segment of the public, by reform-minded citizens also seeking the prohibition of alcohol. But many newspapers vilified Comstock, asserting that his actions violated freedom of speech and freedom of the press, that his crusade was an attempt to impose a narrow Christian dogma on the nation. Critics attacked Comstock for using deceit to obtain obscene publications, for staging private exhibits of confiscated material, for paying to attend sex shows and then arresting the performers. He dismissed his opponents, calling them "long-haired men" and "short-haired women" whose lives were hollow and rotten to the core. "*No sect nor class* has ever publicly sided with the smut dealer," Comstock contended, "except the Infidels, the Liberals, and the Free-Lovers."

In addition to seizing marriage manuals, pseudoscientific treatises on sex, and ribald novels like *Fanny Hill,* Anthony Comstock also helped to suppress works by Aristophanes, Voltaire, Walt Whitman, Émile Zola, Honoré Balzac, and Leo Tolstoy. George Bernard Shaw, in Comstock's view, was an "Irish smut dealer." The official seal of Comstock's society showed a publisher being led to a prison cell and a bonfire consuming a large pile of books. Within the first seven years of his reign, Comstock claimed to have destroyed 202,679 obscene pictures and photographs; 12 tons of obscene books; 64,094 rubber articles "for immoral use"; 6,072 indecent playing cards; and 26 obscene pictures that had been hung on the walls of saloons. As Assistant District Attorney William P. Fiero proclaimed, while prosecuting one of Comstock's leading critics: "The United States is one great society for the suppression of vice."

The precedent underpinning Comstock's legislation was an 1868 decision by a high court in Great Britain. The Queens Bench had ruled in *Regina v. Hicklin*—a case involving a pamphlet on the lewd behavior of Catholic priests—that for material to be obscene it must exert the power "to deprave and corrupt those whose minds are open to such immoral influences." In the interest of protecting the young and impressionable, an entire book could be outlawed for the sexual content of a single page. The risk of corruption did not overly concern wealthy Victorian gentlemen, however, who obtained obscene works in expensive, limited editions. Banker J. Pierpont Morgan exemplified the double standard, keeping mistresses and collecting rare erotica while subsidizing Anthony Comstock's work.

The U.S. Supreme Court did not tackle the issue of obscenity until after the Second World War, when novels by William Faulkner, Erskine Caldwell, and Edmund Wilson were accused of being obscene. Under Chief Justice Earl Warren, the court tried to find a definition of the crime that would allow the publication of great literature while keeping a lid on hard-core porn. In 1957 the Supreme Court upheld the obscenity conviction of Samuel Roth—an erudite New York publisher of controversial works—and declared for the first time that obscene speech was not protected by the Constitution. But the court also condemned the practice, followed for almost ninety years, of judging a work on the basis of how an isolated passage might affect a child. The old British standard of obscenity was set aside. The new challenge was how to devise a new standard that could differentiate between the writings of Henry Miller and those of Sanford E. Aday. Justice Potter Stewart later noted the difficulty of the task. Although he could not define obscenity in any intelligible way, Stewart wrote, "I know it when I see it."

In a series of controversial decisions, the Warren Court liberated the novels of one author after another, including those of William Burroughs, Henry Miller — and Sanford E. Aday. As Gay Talese observed in *Thy Neighbor's Wife,* it was the publishers of sex pulps — and not the mainstream literary publishers in New York — who won freedom of expression for America's novelists. By the late 1960s the Supreme Court had evolved a three-part test for obscenity: the dominant theme of the work, taken as whole, had to appeal "to a prurient interest in sex"; the work had to be "patently offensive," according to "contemporary community standards"; and it had to be "utterly without redeeming social value." After a decade of debate among the justices, the Supreme Court had settled upon a definition that raised as many questions as it answered. Why was a work's "prurience," its incitement to sexual cravings or arousal, not an idea worthy of constitutional protection? What were "contemporary community standards" in a nation that encompassed both Haight-Ashbury and Huntsville, Texas? And how worthless did a book have to be in order to be "utterly without redeeming social value"? If a book had consecutive page numbers, one First Amendment attorney joked, then it had *some* social value.

Outside of a religious context, the idea of obscenity began to appear legally indefensible. In 1969, the Supreme Court overturned a Georgia law forbidding the possession of obscene materials. An adult now had the right to own pornography in the United States. The Warren Court's liberal majority seemed on the verge of taking the next step, of affirming an American's right to buy, sell, or produce porn. The spirit of Anthony Comstock, it seemed, was about to be banished from the nation's laws.

adults only

THE FEDERAL OBSCENITY CHARGES against Reuben Sturman were dropped in 1967, when the Supreme Court ruled that *Sex Life of a Cop* did have a social value of some kind. The high court's stance on obscenity, however, was not eagerly embraced by other branches of the government. A federal grand jury in Cleveland issued subpoenas for

Sturman's business records. He refused to supply them. The U.S. District Court ordered Sturman to produce the records, but he appealed that decision all the way to the Supreme Court. Before the Supreme Court could issue a ruling, the term of the Cleveland grand jury expired, as did its subpoenas. The government empaneled a new grand jury, which issued new subpoenas. Sturman ignored them. And so it went, an ongoing cultural war fought with writs and briefs and references to obscure points of law. The suit against J. Edgar Hoover was dismissed by an appeals court, but Sturman had made his point. He was not afraid of the FBI or the federal government, and he would use any legal means to defeat them.

Lawyers became as essential to Sturman's business as the men and women who appeared in its merchandise. Under state laws Sturman faced obscenity indictments in California, Michigan, and Ohio. For his obscenity cases, he recruited two of the most prominent First Amendment lawyers in the country — "the Kings," Sturman called them — Stanley Fleishman and Herald Price Fahringer. Fleishman was a passionate defender of outcasts, nonconformists, and the disabled. Fahringer was a brilliant litigator, a gentleman who looked so distinguished, it seemed hard to believe he would ever shake hands with a pornographer, let alone defend one in court. For most legal matters, Sturman relied upon Bernard Berkman, a Cleveland attorney. Berkman soon became his closest adviser, strategist, and confidant. Among other things, the two men shared a love of chess. They kept matching chess sets in their offices and played against each other for years, announcing their latest moves over the telephone.

Despite the legal difficulties, Sturman's empire continued to expand. He began opening retail stores, first in Cleveland, then in other midwestern cities and Canada. The stores all shared the same basic layout. In the front, there were racks of comic books and general interest magazines, candy, sundries, and tobacco. Toward the back, there was a door marked "Adults Only," and behind it, a huge assortment of sex books and magazines, most of them now published by Sturman. Their content grew more explicit with each new ruling by the Warren Court. The magazines now contained photographs of simulated intercourse and of women in gynecological poses. The paperbacks described orgies, bondage, homosexuality, and incest in greater detail. The sex industry was booming, driven by market forces, responding to consumer demand, and one taboo after another soon fell in the pursuit of commerce.

On September 6, 1968, federal agents arrested Reuben Sturman's wife at their home, handcuffed her in front of their children, and took her to the Cleveland federal building for fingerprinting and a mug shot. She was arraigned on eighteen counts of distributing obscenity through the mail. Sturman's brother was arrested the same day and arraigned on the same charges. The books and magazines named in the indictment for the most part depicted lesbianism. Sturman was out of town when the charges were filed. He and his wife and his brother each faced a possible sentence of ninety years in prison and a $90,000 fine. The arrests were front-page news in Cleveland. "I'm tired of pussy-footing around with smut," said U.S. Attorney Bernard J. Stuplinski.

While the case dragged through the courts, Reuben Sturman's brother quit the business. Sturman and his wife of nineteen years were divorced. As part of the settlement, she relinquished her stake in the company, now called Sovereign News. But Sturman had no intention of quitting. Now that he was the sole owner of Sovereign News, he devoted a great deal of time and energy to concealing that fact. If the authorities could not prove that Reuben Sturman owned the business, they couldn't indict him for anything it sold. Sovereign News was split into hundreds of separate companies, incorporated in Delaware or Nevada. The shares, officers, and board members of these new entities were listed in public documents. And Sturman's name didn't appear on any of them.

Reuben Sturman pioneered new techniques of concealment, recruiting people in Canada with no knowledge of the sex industry, many of them young Americans avoiding the draft, to serve as "nominees" — straw men listed on corporate records as a legal cover for the people actually running the companies. The names of these nominees appeared on public documents, on income tax filings, on the rubber stamps used to sign company checks. Sturman's goal was to confuse the government as much as possible. The nominees were hard to track down in Canada, and their financial stake in various companies was hard to measure, since the IRS did not have access to their tax returns. For example, an investigator trying to learn who ran Sovereign News (the company that still operated Sturman's Cleveland warehouse and headquarters) would find that it was now an asset of "The Bahamian Company," whose shares were controlled by "Wilson and Company," based in Nevada. The president and chief executive of the Bahamian Company, according to the records, was Morton Goss, the owner of a carpet store in Ontario.

Security cameras and heavy steel doors were added to the Sovereign News warehouse, a two-story brick building in the heart of a Cleveland ghetto where Sturman kept his office. Callers who asked for Reuben Sturman were generally told there was no one with that name in the building. Memos to Sturman were addressed to "R and D" or "To whom it may concern." Business letters from him often ended "Best regards," followed by a blank. Sturman offered to pay the legal fees of employees who refused to cooperate with government investigations. He also formed his own company, National Polygraph, to give lie-detector tests and root out informers.

The obscenity charges stemming from his 1968 indictment were eventually dismissed, but Reuben Sturman did plead guilty to a federal offense. During one of the many raids at the Cleveland warehouse, as federal agents searched the building for Sturman, a U.S. marshal approached him in an office and asked, "What's your name?" Sturman replied, "What's *your* name?" When the marshal poked him on the chest and demanded to know his name, Sturman poked the marshal's chest, demanded to know *his* name—and was subsequently indicted for assaulting a federal agent. In order to placate the government, which had been defeated on every obscenity count, Sturman pleaded guilty to the assault charge, a misdemeanor. His punishment was a $300 fine.

By the end of the 1960s, Reuben Sturman was one of the largest publishers, and perhaps the largest distributor, of sex books and magazines in the United States. Two other men joined him at the top. Milton Luros was a former graphic designer who owned adult bookstores and published sex magazines on the West Coast. His printing plant, according to *Forbes* magazine, was the second largest in the state of California, exceeded in capacity only by the print facilities of the *Los Angeles Times*. Michael Thevis, the son of Greek immigrants, dominated the sex industry in the Southeast, operating scores of adult bookstores. At the age of seventeen, Thevis had started out with a single newsstand in Atlanta; his headquarters later occupied a square block of the city's downtown business district. The sex industry, however, was about to undergo a fundamental restructuring, as a product that American men had surreptitiously enjoyed for fifty years appeared on the open market. The porno film brought commercial sex to a much wider audience, heightened the public debate over obscenity, and made Reuben Sturman far wealthier and more powerful than any combination of his rivals.

stags

WITHIN A FEW YEARS of the movie camera's development in 1890, the new technology was being used to film women in various states of undress. By the turn of the century, Argentina had become a center of production for hard-core sex films that were sold to collectors wealthy enough to afford the 35mm projection equipment. The first public exhibitions of hard-core films were staged in the high-priced brothels of Europe, where sex on the screen was provided for the entertainment of waiting customers. The earliest hard-core film made in the United States dates from about 1915. The introduction of affordable 16mm cameras and projectors soon created an underground sex industry that produced and exhibited hard-core films throughout the United States. The popularity of these "stag films," and the tolerance of their display in most communities, reveal the oddly contradictory attitudes toward sex that still permeate American culture.

During the 1920s "stag nights" — gatherings at which hard-core films were shown to an all-male audience — became a familiar, socially acceptable custom. In the United States, hard-core films were not exhibited at brothels or socialist meeting halls; they were shown at politically conservative institutions, at Kiwanis clubs, American Legion halls, and college fraternities. For decades, the operators of stag shows traveled a regional circuit, bringing their own projectors, films, and, sometimes, live entertainment. The cost of hiring a show, which lasted an hour or two, was roughly $50. The people who made stag films and who took them on tour didn't earn great fortunes. It was a subculture often embraced for its own sake. The actresses were paid a modest sum for their work; the men usually worked for free. Many of the performers were pimps and prostitutes. At a time when book publishers were being imprisoned for selling the works of D. H. Lawrence and James Joyce, American law enforcement agencies rarely interfered with stag nights or arrested their promoters. The organizations that sponsored these evenings were likely to be the most respectable in town. So long as stag films were discreetly shown and not made available to women or children, police and prosecutors looked the other way. Indeed, the legislatures of two states, Illinois and North Carolina, exempted stag films from the state obscenity laws, provided the films were not shown in commercial venues.

Stag films depicted a wide range of sexual activities in graphic detail. The basic camera angles, positions, shooting techniques, and themes of hard-core filmmaking were established by the early 1920s and have changed little since then. Although stags were silent films, much of their running time was devoted to plot and dialogue, with the latter displayed on title cards. The films also contained a good deal of humor, featuring the sort of comic situations that would entertain a male audience. The women in stag films were portrayed as creatures eager for sex at the drop of a hat. Given the social stigma still attached to sex work, they often wore masks during their performances.

Between 1920 and the early 1950s perhaps 2,000 hard-core films were made in the United States. One of the nation's largest collections of stag films was assembled by J. Edgar Hoover and maintained at the FBI's Crime Laboratory. Hoover was a leading opponent of vice, obscenity, and the white slave trade, of the "muck merchants" who preyed on America's youth. Less than a year after becoming director of the Bureau of Investigation, as it was called in 1924, Hoover directed his agents across the country to collect obscene material and send it to the bureau's Washington, D.C., headquarters—without informing local U.S. attorneys. This material was placed in a special "Obscene

File" and kept separately from the files holding evidence for official investigations. Its existence was not disclosed until after Hoover's death. For nearly five decades, sexually explicit books, magazines, comics, phonograph records, postcards, and playing cards were added to the FBI's secret collection, which eventually included over a thousand stag films. The only FBI employees authorized to remove items from the Obscene File were J. Edgar Hoover, his personal secretary, and his close assistant, Clyde Tolson.

Seeing an old stag film today can provide a strong initial shock. The images most of us have of America fifty or sixty years ago were gained largely through *Life* magazine photographs, newsreel footage, and Hollywood films. Sex was invisible, rarely mentioned, let alone depicted beyond a passionate kiss. In the popular entertainments of those days, men were honorable, women were chaste until their wedding day, and certain things just weren't done. The reality, of course, differed considerably from the Hollywood version. Private behavior did not conform to the rules being celebrated in public, and mass culture depicted only a small portion of the truth. The grainy black-and-white images of the stag film, so strange and disorienting now—with the familiar trappings of old movies put to an unfamiliar use, the proud display of forbidden acts, the ordinary bodies of the performers, the women in masks and the men naked except for black socks—offer a glimpse of America's secret history.

automated vending

IN A SMALL SHOP ACROSS THE STREET from the Roxy, a burlesque theater in downtown Cleveland, Reuben Sturman saw a stand-up machine, like an arcade game, that showed a film of a naked woman on a small screen when a coin was deposited. Sturman didn't think much of the contraption, which had been around in one form or another, often at carnivals, since the late 1940s. And then Michael Thevis, his friend and valued customer, said that similar "peep" machines were doing terrific business in Atlanta's adult bookstores. Martin J. Hodas, a former jukebox distributor, was installing peeps in stores throughout

New York's Times Square; and Nat Bailen, an inventor who'd hoped his machines would show children's cartoons at shopping malls, now sold them for a more lucrative use in Louisville, Kentucky. Once Reuben Sturman recognized the potential of the peep business, he came up with a simple modification, a way to build a better mouse trap, that soon made peep machines the most profitable sector of the sex trade.

Instead of relying on stand-up machines, Sturman's company placed two coin-operated 8mm projectors in a small booth with a screen and a door that could be locked. A customer deposited a quarter to see one or two minutes of a twelve-minute "loop," a film that could run continuously. Sturman's peep booths were dark and cramped. They turned what had been a communal experience into something quite different — a stag film for an audience of one. And before long they were filled with middle-class American men privately seeking a few moments of pleasure.

The stag circuit had declined during the mid-1950s, as inexpensive 8mm equipment made it easier to shoot hard-core films and to view them with home movie projectors. Stag show operators became unnecessary, and stag films lost most of their plot, characterization, and humor, instead depicting nonstop sexual activity. The producers of these hard-core 8mm films often had trouble finding distributors. Adult bookstore owners were reluctant at first to carry such explicit material, and so a haphazard distribution system evolved. Hard-core films were sold at barber shops, photo stores, bars, gas stations, and truck stops. The widespread introduction of peep machines in the late 1960s gave porn filmmakers access to a vast new market and created an unprecedented demand for new films. Soon there were roughly fifty to seventy-five new peep loops being released every week. What had long been a hobby, or a sideline, or a way to earn a few extra dollars turned into an organized, profit-seeking activity, with investors, processing labs, and full-time employees — an adult film industry.

Reuben Sturman put peep booths into all of his stores. He supplied the booths to other bookstore owners, free of charge, in return for half of the peep receipts. He started a company in Cleveland, Automated Vending, to manufacture peep booths and formed regional companies to service them. In Sturman's bookstores, the booths were put all the way in the back, past the comic books, past the sex pulps and sex magazines. Peep booths were soon the main attraction. Revenue from the sale of paperbacks, magazines, and sexual devices usually covered the operating costs of an adult bookstore. Revenue from the peep machines was sheer profit. The booths cost almost nothing to maintain. New loops cost about $8 each, an expense that could be amortized by the coins of two or three customers. The projectors were durable and cheap. An average-sized store earned at least $2,000 a week from its peep booths, and a large store could easily earn five times that amount. The employees of Sturman's service companies fanned out across the United States on their daily or weekly rounds, visiting hundreds upon hundreds of adult bookstores, checking the coin meters on peep booths, collecting the money, handing store owners or managers their cut, and then heading out, often using dollies to cart off tons of quarters in thousand-dollar bags.

Sturman used the profits from his peep booths to open more stores and warehouses in this country, as well as to enter overseas markets, always working with a foreign partner. In the Netherlands Sturman opened adult bookstores with Charlie Geerts, who became that nation's leading sex merchant. In Great Britain, Sturman formed a joint venture with the Holloway family — Mary, Ben, their daughter, and five sons — who soon dominated the porn business of London. Sturman provided his foreign partners with capital and expertise, while they ran the companies and faced most of the legal risks. He backed partners in France, Germany, and Switzerland. Within a few years of its invention, the peep booth had spread from the major cities of North America to the capitals of Western Europe.

Sturman also used the profits from his booths to diversify. Appalled by the unappealing and unsanitary packaging of most sexual devices, he decided to produce and market his own. Sturman traveled to Hong Kong to arrange the manufacture of plastic goods, of vibrators, and inflatable dolls, then purchased a factory in Los Angeles to make "rubber goods," lifelike facsimiles of male and female genitalia. The new company needed a name, and Sturman wanted one that sounded clean, hygienic, and vaguely Swedish. The "Doc Johnson" line of sexual devices was introduced to adult bookstores on both sides of the Atlantic, neatly packaged and named after Lyndon Baines Johnson, the U.S. president whose Justice Department had given Sturman so much trouble.

The first peep loops were relatively tame, showing naked women who danced or gyrated but rarely engaged in any sexual activity. Film-makers worried that explicit peep loops would be difficult to defend in court. The social value of such films was not readily apparent, since they lacked any plot or dialogue. But as the movies in theaters became more sexually explicit, so did the loops in peep booths. "Sexploitation" films and "skin flicks," the visual equivalent of sex pulp paperbacks, gained in popularity. By the end of the 1960s, such films contained soft-core sex scenes and were shown in rundown movie theaters, while 16mm theaters opened in downtown storefronts, defying authorities, showing newly made hard-core, silent films. In 1970, a documentary on pornography in Denmark received national distribution, present-ing hard-core sex to mainstream American audiences for the first time. Two years later *Deep Throat* opened in Miami, then in New York City. Linda Lovelace, the star of *Deep Throat*, later wrote that her per-formance had been coerced, at gunpoint, by her manager. The director of the film was Gerard Damiano, a former hairdresser from Queens. And the film's financial backers were Anthony Peraino and his two sons, Louis and Joseph, who had close ties to the Colombo family of the Cosa Nostra. *Deep Throat* was essentially a stag film, shot in color, with a soundtrack. Long lines immediately formed at theaters where it was being shown. Men and women from every stratum of American society rushed to see *Deep Throat*, a phenomenon the media labeled "porno chic." Produced for about $22,000, *Deep Throat* earned more than a million dollars at the box office in its first nine months of re-lease and more than $25 million within its first two years.

Although the public exhibition of hard-core films attracted most of the attention in the media, the annual revenues of America's peep booths were much larger—perhaps even four or five times larger—than the annual revenues of its adult theaters. Quietly and without fanfare, Reuben Sturman set up companies to supply films for his booths and subsidized the production of hard-core films in Europe. He dropped by the set of his first feature-length porno film as it was being shot in Holland. The experience was so boring that Sturman never visited another porn set, even though his companies, by his own count, released a new sex film every day for almost twenty years. Reuben Sturman was not obsessed with sex; it was just his business.

citizens for decency

"PORNO CHIC" INSPIRED A BACKLASH, an angry reaction to the adult bookstores and theaters opening all over America, to the nudity and foul language in Hollywood films, to the youth counterculture and the increasingly permissive atmosphere. Many Americans found sexually explicit materials deeply offensive. Regardless of whether it was hard-core or soft-core, they thought that pornography dehumanized women, encouraged promiscuity, spread the myth that sex without love could be fulfilling, disparaged traditional values, and exploited what should remain sacred between a husband and wife. Pornography was held partly responsible for child abuse, incest, the breakdown of the family, and the spread of sexually transmitted diseases. An anti-pornography movement had been building for years, seemingly losing one battle after another, but slowly gaining in force. At the vanguard of the movement was a lawyer from Cincinnati, Charles H. Keating, Jr., whose audacity and ambition equaled, if not surpassed, that of his fellow Ohioan, Reuben Sturman.

Keating was a tall and athletic family man with six children, a former Navy fighter pilot and champion swimmer. Before starting his own law firm, he had tried selling insurance. At a Catholic men's retreat in 1956, Keating was asked to take action against "the filth flooding our newsstands." And so two years later he established the National Organization of Citizens for Decent Literature (CDL), a group that campaigned against obscenity and drew its support from Jewish and Protestant leaders, as well as from the Catholic Church. During the early 1960s Keating traveled throughout the country, giving speeches, attacking indecent literature, such as the bestseller *Peyton Place*, arguing that pornography was "capable of poisoning any mind at any age and of perverting our entire younger generation." Behind the smut peddlers, in Keating's view, lurked the nation's enemies; the rising tide of obscenity was clearly "part of the Communist conspiracy."

In August, 1965, Charles Keating appeared with CDL's chief counsel, James Clancy, before a congressional subcommittee investigating "noxious and obscene matters and materials." The two men had brought with them a group of young CDL supporters, representing the best of America's youth, to lobby Congress for a national commission on pornography. The commission proposed by CDL would study the issue of obscenity, serve as a clearinghouse for law enforcement, and lead the assault on the sex industry. "I positively urge; beg you, if necessary," Keating testified, "that this Commission be created forthwith." Within a decade of its appointment, he promised, the majority of America's pornographers would be rotting in prison — including no doubt, Reuben Sturman, whom Clancy called "most notorious." The peculiar psychology of CDL's leadership surfaced during their testimony. Keating told the subcommittee that he'd toured newsstands near the Capitol the previous night and had bought $45 worth of sexually explicit publications. When he offered to read aloud six pages of *Love's Lash*, Congressman John Dent interrupted and asked him to "spare the committee." Its members were quite familiar with such material and were primarily interested in learning who published "this stuff." Nevertheless, a few minutes later, CDL's chief counsel ignored Dent's request — as well as the presence of Miss Becky Rodenbaugh and all the other young CDL members — and read aloud a lengthy summary of two chapters from *Lust in Leather*. Clancy provided the subcommittee with details of an orgy staged by "sex drugged revelers . . . as music is played in a bolero beat," with descriptions of bondage, lesbianism, adultery, sodomy, and "a naked man in a bull's head mask."

During the next few years, Keating continued to lobby for a national commission on pornography. CDL grew in size and influence, attracting support from four governors, half a dozen U.S. senators, and more than one hundred and twenty congressmen. Senator Karl E. Mundt and Congressman Dominick V. Daniels, both CDL members, introduced legislation to create a National Commission on Pornography and Obscenity. The American Civil Liberties Union (ACLU) expressed strong opposition to the plan, but its protests had little effect. In October, 1967, Congress established the commission long sought by CDL, and President Johnson appointed William Lockhart, dean of the University of Minnesota Law School, to head it. Although Lockhart recognized the threat that obscenity laws posed to great literature, he had argued in a law review article that hard-core pornography was "so foul and revolting that few people can contemplate the absence of laws against it."

As the Commission on Pornography and Obscenity got to work, CDL shifted its attention to the U.S. Supreme Court. In June, 1968, Earl Warren announced his intention to retire as Chief Justice, and President Johnson chose Abe Fortas to replace him. Fortas was already a Supreme Court justice, a moderate on obscenity issues compared to First Amendment absolutists such as justices William O. Douglas and Hugo Black. But Fortas had consistently voted with the liberal majority to redefine obscenity, and as a private attorney he had represented a number of people in the sex industry, including Hugh Hefner.

CDL led the opposition to the appointment of Abe Fortas, putting together "Target Smut," a half-hour presentation of material that had been granted constitutional protection by the Warren Court. While Abe Fortas testified before the Senate Judiciary Committee, CDL staged an exhibition for members of Congress and reporters. Edward De Grazia, in his history of obscenity law, *Girls Lean Back Everywhere*, offers a description of the scene. Two stag films were shown on a wall at the Capitol press room for a male audience that laughed and shouted crude remarks at the screen, while a CDL member, Senator Strom Thurmond, fed quarters into the projector.

After spending two years and almost $2 million on original research, the Commission on Pornography and Obscenity released its report in September, 1970. "There is no warrant," the commission declared, "for continued government interference with the full freedom of adults to read, obtain or view whatever material they wish." The commission had found no evidence that exposure to sexually explicit materials played a significant role in causing "crime, delinquency, deviancy . . . or severe emotional disturbances." Indeed, sex offenders were less likely to have used pornography than the average man and more likely to have been raised in a conservative household. The nation's state, federal, and local obscenity statutes should be repealed, the commission recommended, with tough restrictions on the sale of sexually explicit material to young people and limits on how such material could be publicly advertised or displayed.

Charles Keating had been appointed to the commission by President Richard Nixon to fill a vacancy, and once Keating realized what the commission was going to recommend, he did everything he could to sabotage its work. Keating boycotted the commission's meetings; he demanded that its chairman, William Lockhart, be dismissed; and he filed a lawsuit to prevent the publication of its report. Keating traveled more than 200,000 miles in 1970, giving speeches throughout the country that attacked the Commission on Pornography and Obscenity. When the commission's report was finally released, Keating insisted that it include his own forty-six-page dissent, which was largely written by a young White House aide, Patrick J. Buchanan. In the dissent Keating warned that the commission was advocating "moral anarchy" and "a libertine philosophy!" Presidential commissions were fundamentally undemocratic, Keating now argued, "not a valid part of the American political system." The United States had become more sex-obsessed than Sodom and Gomorrah; American stores were openly displaying "french ticklers, vibrators . . . as well as penis-shaped candy." Obscenity was "intrinsically evil," Keating asserted, and a commission that had been created to solve the problem had instead issued "a blank check for pornographers."

President Nixon had never publicly opposed the Warren Court's decisions on obscenity. In a 1969 speech, Nixon had endorsed the Court's basic stance, arguing that "the ultimate answer lies not with the Government, but the people" and looking forward to the day when porno films "can no longer find an audience." In the fall of 1970, with midterm elections approaching and student demonstrations feeding public anxieties about disorder, Nixon reversed course. He condemned the Commission on Pornography and Obscenity and claimed that overturning the obscenity laws would be tantamount to "condoning anarchy in every other field." The Senate, by a vote of 60 to 5, later censured the commission and rejected its findings, a move applauded by the Reverend Billy Graham, who called the commission's report "diabolical."

Within a three-year period, Nixon appointed four new justices to the Supreme Court: Warren E. Burger, Harry A. Blackmun, Lewis F. Powell, and William Rehnquist. In June, 1973 — as hard-core films like *Deep Throat, The Devil in Miss Jones,* and *Behind the Green Door* played in local theaters, and an X-rated Hollywood film, *Last Tango in Paris,* achieved both critical and financial success — the Supreme Court's new conservative majority expressed its views on obscenity. The Burger Court denied that consenting adults had a right to see whatever they pleased or any right to privacy which might allow the sale of obscene material. And in *Miller v. California,* Chief Justice Burger supplied a new definition of obscenity. The material in question no longer had to be "utterly" without social value to be obscene; it need only lack "serious literary, artistic, political, or scientific value." More importantly, the court said that every community in the nation had the legal right to determine its own standard of obscenity. The underlying aim of obscenity legislation — like that of other limits upon free speech — Burger explained in another case the same year, was "to protect the weak, the uninformed, the unsuspecting, and the gullible." One year after the Miller decision the Supreme Court upheld the Comstock Law, ruling that it did not violate the Constitution.

a piece of the porno

DURING THE FIRST YEAR THAT *Deep Throat* was in general release, it was distributed much like any other movie. Bryanston Distributors Inc., a New York company owned by the Peraino family, shipped prints of *Deep Throat* by mail or by parcel service to theaters around the country. Box office records were maintained, and theater owners paid the Perainos their share of the receipts by check. The Supreme Court's new definition of obscenity, however, inspired an entirely new system of distribution for *Deep Throat.* Now that federal prosecutors could base obscenity indictments on community standards, the risks of transporting hard-core films across state lines had vastly increased. The Perainos immediately stopped using the mails. Copies of the film were given to "checkers," trusted employees who personally delivered the print to the theater, counted the customers at each showing, and then, at the end of the business day, collected the Perainos' share of the box office. It was usually 50 percent, paid in cash. Other Bryanston employees, known as "sweepers," traveled from city to city, gathering the money from checkers, stuffing it into suitcases, and bringing it to the Perainos. The system invited loose accounting and employee theft. But it had the virtue of eliminating any paper trail, and tens of millions of dollars were collected in this way.

The sex industry had always attracted people with criminal backgrounds of some sort. Businessmen concerned about their reputations didn't tend to open adult bookstores with peep booths, and experience defying the law in one form of illicit trade was often useful in another. As the potential risks and profits of the sex industry increased simultaneously, so did the level of criminal activity. Adult bookstore owners in some areas had to pay a "street tax" to local racketeers. Financing for such ventures was often obtained through loan sharks, since banks were reluctant to invest in businesses of questionable legality. Territorial disputes between store owners were not always settled through lawsuits. A particularly bitter feud developed in Pennsylvania between former partners, John Krasner and Allen Charles Morrow, over the locations of their competing adult bookstores. Krasner's wife was kidnapped, his stores were bombed, and one of his employees was arrested outside Harrisburg with eighty-five pounds of explosives, about to destroy one of Morrow's stores. Morrow survived an assassination attempt; Krasner was murdered in the parking lot of a Fort Lauderdale motel.

Violence was by no means the norm in the sex industry—which was peaceful by comparison to numbers-running or the drug trade—although adult filmmakers and store owners were vulnerable to extortion. Their businesses generated a great deal of cash, and they were accustomed to being investigated by the police, not protected. The Los Angeles branch of the Cosa Nostra, led by Dominic Brooklier, worked hard to get "a piece of the porno." But the extortion attempts of the "Mickey Mouse Mafia" proved a failure—among other reasons, because Brooklier's soldiers made arson threats to a phony porn company run by the FBI. More successful were the efforts of various criminal organizations to "dupe" popular hard-core films, to circulate unauthorized prints without paying any royalties. Since the films were of questionable legality, producers were usually reluctant to sue for violations of copyright. *Deep Throat* was widely pirated by small-time hoods unaware of Anthony and Louis Peraino's relationship with the Colombo family. The Perainos turned the practice to their advantage. Representatives of their company would visit theaters where bootleg copies of *Deep Throat* were being shown; theater owners were given the opportunity to continue exhibiting the film in return for half of the box office receipts. Few theater owners refused this offer. As a result, the widespread piracy of *Deep Throat* not only facilitated its nationwide distribution, but also spared the Perainos the cost of making new prints.

Some adult bookstores offered consumers access to a wide variety of illicit goods and services. In his survey of the retail trade in sexually explicit materials, Gary W. Potter, now a professor of criminal justice and police studies at Eastern Kentucky University, found that adult bookstore employees were quite helpful in referring interested customers to local drug dealers, prostitutes, bookies, and fences for stolen goods. Peep booths often provided a cover for men to engage in homosexual activity while ostensibly viewing a "straight" porno film. At bookstores operated by motorcycle gangs such as the Pagans and the Outlaws, methamphetamine was usually for sale. The presence of bikers discouraged extortion, and their girlfriends often worked as "models."

disgusting, nauseating films

ALTHOUGH THE U.S. SUPREME COURT overturned the obscenity conviction of an Albany, Georgia, theater owner who had shown *Carnal Knowledge*—a film directed by Mike Nichols, starring Jack Nicholson, and lacking any explicit sex—the Hollywood film industry became wary, in the new legal climate, of sexual content. Major studios sought to avoid the threat and the controversy of obscenity prosecutions. After 1973, the violence in Hollywood movies became much more graphic, but the sex did not. And a whole new film industry arose in Southern California, separate and distinct from Hollywood, to make porno films.

Six months after the Burger Court announced its position on obscenity, the FBI began another investigation of Reuben Sturman. Agents led by George E. Grotz staked out the Sovereign News warehouse, following the trucks as they made deliveries and tailing porn salesman on their routes. The surveillance continued for a year and a half. With cooperation from a Texas adult bookstore owner, the government induced Sovereign News to ship hard-core films from Cleveland to Fort Worth, Texas, through the mail. On March 19, 1975, federal agents rang the buzzer at Sturman's Cleveland warehouse. They were denied entry, even after holding their search warrant up to the security camera. And so the FBI battered the steel door open with a sledgehammer and entered the building. As roughly two dozen federal agents searched the warehouse, photographing and confiscating materials, they were trailed through the building by Sturman's lawyers, who were photographing them. Six days later, the FBI returned in force for another search of the warehouse. This time, after buzzing, they were simply allowed in the door.

A year later Sturman was indicted under federal law for sending obscenity through the mail. Two months after the federal indictment, he was indicted under state law in Cincinnati for participating in organized crime through the sale of pornography. The state charges were subsequently dismissed when a U.S. district judge declared Ohio's obscenity law unconstitutional. Sturman had yet to be convicted for an obscenity offense; but his attorney, Herald Price Fahringer, was worried about the upcoming federal trial. The material at issue — twenty-four magazines and twelve films — was strong and seriously hard-core. *Cake Orgy*, Fahringer admitted, was "one of the most disgusting, nauseating films you'll ever see. You'll never eat a marshmallow pie again as long as you live." Many of Fahringer's clients were "nervous nellies" as their date in court approached. Reuben Sturman was the exact opposite, seeming never to doubt that he would win.

The trial lasted for a month in the summer of 1978. The prosecution's evidence was introduced by sixteen of the FBI agents who had participated in the raids. After five days of deliberation, the jury returned a verdict, finding Sturman and his six associates not guilty on all counts. Fahringer was stunned. And in a highly unusual move, the jurors sent a two-and-a-half-page note to the judge, William K. Thomas, that criticized the Supreme Court's definition of obscenity. Thomas read the note aloud to the courtroom and promised to send it to Chief Justice Burger. Sturman was delighted, but Special Agent Grotz vowed that the FBI's investigation of Sovereign News would continue, regardless of the verdict.

Every time Reuben Sturman beat the government in an obscenity case, his stature within the sex industry grew — and the government's success in other obscenity prosecutions added new assets to his portfolio. When Milton Luros pleaded guilty to obscenity charges in 1974, as part of a deal in which charges against his wife were dropped, Sturman took over many of Luros's companies in California. When Michael Thevis was imprisoned for obscenity, for arson, for racketeering, and for violating the civil rights of two murdered associates, Sturman moved into the peep business throughout the Southeast. By the end of the 1970s, three other men had gained prominence in the American sex industry. Michael (Mickey) Zaffarano, a former bodyguard for Cosa Nostra figure Joseph Bonnano, subsidized hard-core film production and operated a national chain of Pussycat Theaters. Robert (DiB) DiBernardo, a captain in the Gambino crime family, owned New York's largest distributor of adult materials, Star News, as well as sex shops in Times Square. Harry Virgil Mohney, a secretive businessman based in Durand, Michigan, allegedly controlled adult bookstores and movie theaters across the Midwest, as well as drive-in theaters, massage parlors, strip clubs, and a topless billiard hall. But the empires of these three men, combined, were easily dwarfed in size by that of Reuben Sturman.

In some areas competition at the retail level was fierce; Sturman worried how the advent of peep shows with live performers would affect business in his booths. He did not, however, face much competition at the wholesale level. Through companies with imposing names like Sovereign, Noble, and Majestic News, Sturman sold porn to outlets in all fifty states and in more than forty foreign countries. He also continued to distribute comic books. The scale of Sturman's wholesale network gave him considerable influence over the market. Independent producers of adult material had to deal with Sturman to gain widespread distribution, while independent bookstore owners relied on him for access to new products. Throughout the sex industry, Sturman's economic power was regarded with a mixture of fear, envy, admiration, and respect. The industry's leading figures regularly approached him for investment capital and help in settling disputes.

Reuben Sturman had become an extremely wealthy man, with businesses said to be worth hundreds of millions of dollars. In the quiet Cleveland suburb of Shaker Heights he owned a Tudor mansion filled with antiques and fine art, including a collection of Dutch masters. He owned Cadillacs, Mercedes-Benzes, and a Rolls-Royce. He dressed like a conservative Wall Street banker. He gave money to Jewish charities, the Cleveland Symphony, and the Cleveland Ballet. He was active and fit, leading a daily exercise class at the downtown YMCA, where a brass plaque honored his contributions. He was usually accompanied by James (Diz) Long—a former prizefighter and professional football player as well as an inspector for the Cuyahoga County Board of Elections—who served as his bodyguard, assistant, and chauffeur. There was a sophisticated security system at Sturman's house; in a desk drawer at the office, he kept a gun.

Every year, Sturman threw a lavish Christmas party in the ballroom of a Cleveland hotel, attended by hundreds of porn magnates from all over the world, and then a New Year's Eve party in Las Vegas, where Sturman was well known in the casinos as a high roller at baccarat. He constantly traveled to oversee his business interests, making frequent trips to Chicago, Los Angeles, Hong Kong, Zurich, London, and Amsterdam. He loved to surprise his opponents. When demonstrators picketed his stores, Sturman sent them coffee and donuts. When federal agents staked out his house one night, sitting in a parked car, spying, trying to identify his guests, Sturman walked over to the car and invited the agents to come inside and join the party—which they did, mingling uneasily with adult bookstore owners and hard-core producers. Sturman had every right to feel invincible. He'd attained the sort of control over an entire industry that few men had enjoyed since the age of the robber barons. No one in the sex industry could seriously compete with him. The government could not get a jury to convict him. The demand for his merchandise increased every year. And yet just as his empire reached its peak, a young federal investigator, cocky and somewhat naive, was convinced he'd found a way to bring Reuben Sturman down.

fall

RICHARD N. ROSFELDER, JR., HAD NOT GIVEN much thought to the future, as his college graduation approached in 1970. He was too busy partying. His father, a Cleveland sales manager for Nabisco, was not amused and told him to start looking for work. At a college job fair, Rosfelder stopped at a booth run by the Internal Revenue Service. The recruiter told him the story of how the IRS had nailed Al Capone — who never kept bank accounts or assets in his own name, never signed checks, always paid with cash — after the efforts of the FBI and the Chicago police had repeatedly failed. Rosfelder liked the idea of carrying a badge and a gun in pursuit of white-collar criminals. The whole thing sounded cool. He applied to become an IRS criminal investigator, and his father was later surprised by the news there would soon be a tax collector in the family.

After joining the IRS, Rosfelder was drafted and spent eighteen months in the Army, followed by six months at the Treasury Department's law enforcement training school in Washington, D.C. During his first few years with the IRS Criminal Division in Ohio, he examined the tax returns of organized crime members in Youngstown and drug dealers in Toledo. When Rosfelder was reassigned to the Cleveland office in 1975, he became intrigued with Reuben Sturman. IRS offices across the country were calling with questions about Sturman — and the IRS in Cleveland knew remarkably little about him. The civil division had audited a number of Sturman's companies, but had been unable to track down their officers or directors. IRS agents who visited the Sovereign News warehouse looking for Sturman were turned away at the door, told there was no such company and no such person at this address. IRS audits were concluded without having learned the names of Sovereign's shareholders.

Rosfelder knew that Sturman's organization was doing well. One of its young employees, who lived in the same condominium complex as Rosfelder, owned a pair of brand-new, matching Cadillacs. But it was an exposé of Sturman's empire in *Cleveland* magazine, written by Edward P. Whelan, that made Rosfelder want to investigate Reuben Sturman. Whelan had described Sturman's use of Canadian nominees, beneath the subhead "How to Confuse the Feds." Rosfelder thought the same tactics being used to conceal assets could easily be employed to evade taxes. Sturman seemed to be thumbing his nose at the government, almost issuing a challenge. When Rosfelder asked his supervisor for permission to begin a criminal investigation of Reuben Sturman, the reply was: "You're out of your mind."

Rosfelder was only twenty-seven years old. He had less than four years of experience as an investigator. His intended target owned a multinational conglomerate with hundreds of companies, each filing a separate tax return. His proposal seemed unrealistic and wildly over-ambitious. But it also made a lot of sense. Businesses that conduct transactions largely in cash — such as coin-operated laundries, vending machine companies, some restaurants, discotheques, and bars — provide excellent opportunities for tax evasion, for "skimming" money from the receipts. Even the owners of these businesses often have a hard time keeping track of their money and preventing employee theft. Reuben Sturman's peep booths generated enormous amounts of cash, while offering a service that was difficult to quantify. The peeps were ideal for skimming. It was almost impossible for state or federal authorities to determine how many times a peep loop had been projected in each booth. Rosfelder had a feeling that the temptation to skim was too strong for Sturman to resist.

The easiest part of tax evasion, however, is failing to report income. If you bury the money that's been skimmed in your backyard and never touch it, the odds are you'll never get caught. The hard part, Rosfelder knew, is finding a way to spend that unreported income safely, to launder the money and gain its use without disclosing its origins.

During the 1970s the art of money laundering was being perfected by American drug dealers, their lawyers, and their accountants. One popular method took drug money and added it to the accounts of a legitimate business with a large cash flow, falsely inflating the annual revenue of that business. The disadvantage of this method was that the freshly laundered money became so legitimate that it was now subject to state, local, and federal taxes. A riskier, more complex laundering scheme was developed for dealers who did not want to share any of their profits with the government. Drug money was somehow smuggled out of the United States — no easy feat, since the cash receipts of a drug deal often weighed much more than the drugs — deposited in the offshore accounts of foreign companies, and then returned to the United States as "investments." The IRS had no authority to examine the financial records of foreign corporations, and their American investments could not be taxed.

While working on other assignments, Rosfelder began to collect information on Sturman, hoping to find something that would justify a full-scale investigation. Rosfelder liked to portray himself as just an average Joe, nothing special, not that smart. Behind the self-deprecating façade, there was an extremely bright and self-confident young man. By no means a typical federal agent, he worked hard, played hard, and liked to drive his silver Corvette convertible fast. Reuben Sturman was perhaps the biggest target of federal authorities in Cleveland. An investigation of Sturman promised to be a high-profile case and an interesting challenge. Rosfelder didn't like what Sturman's companies sold, but didn't consider himself an antipornography zealot, either. He had another motive for seeking this case. Reuben Sturman seemed like an arrogant, multimillionaire tax cheat.

Rosfelder approached the Organized Crime Strike Force in Cleveland, a branch of the Justice Department, wondering if its investigators would share any information on Sturman. The strike force was handling the ongoing obscenity investigation of Sovereign News. Although federal law enforcement bureaucracies usually guard their turf fiercely and prefer not to share anything, except blame, David Feldman, the lead prosecutor in the Sturman case, told FBI agent George Grotz to give Rosfelder some help. Everyone on the strike force was confident that Sturman was about to be convicted on obscenity charges; adding an IRS investigation to his troubles seemed like a nice idea. Grotz handed Rosfelder two black three-ring binders that had been discovered in Sturman's office during the March 1975 raids. One binder listed the corporations Sturman owned, the names of their stockholders, officers, and directors, their places of incorporation, their statutory agents. The other contained details of their bank accounts, bank signature stamps, and tax identification numbers. And then Grotz told Rosfelder an interesting story.

Sturman had attempted to open two accounts at the Zurich branch of the Swiss Credit Bank on October 14, 1974, using the name "Paul Bekker" and a fake Dutch passport. Bank officials contacted the police, who immediately sent over four officers. After watching Sturman finish his transactions, Detective Alfred Graf followed him from the bank, stopped him on the street, searched him, found two passports with the same photograph, one real, one fake, and arrested Sturman. Graf asked what he was doing in the bank, suggesting he might be a drug dealer. Sturman denied being a criminal. "I'm here to hide my money in Switzerland," he told the police, "because I don't like to pay the tax." The Swiss did not regard tax evasion as a particularly heinous crime; indeed, their bank secrecy laws specifically protected depositors from foreign tax collectors. Opening an account under a phony name was illegal, but hiding assets in Swiss banks was almost a national pastime. "It's the same for me," Detective Graf reassured Sturman. "I also don't like to pay the tax."

Sturman's arrest in Zurich provided Rosfelder with one of the hardest things to demonstrate in a tax case: proof of criminal intent. Rosfelder now had a solid foundation for his case. All he lacked was evidence of a crime. In November, 1976, he received approval to start an investigation of Sturman. A year later, Rosfelder wrapped up his other cases and began to pursue Sturman, full-time.

Rosfelder chose Thomas N. Ciehanski to be the revenue agent, the numbers man, on the case. The two men decided to inform Sturman, in person, that he was being investigated by the IRS. On a gray, snowy day in the fall of 1977, they drove to the Sovereign News warehouse. In the parking lot a man was clearing snow from the windshield of a Cadillac. Rosfelder thought the man looked like Sturman, but wasn't sure. Sturman was constantly changing his appearance, growing a beard or a mustache and then getting rid of it, wearing eyeglasses on some days and not on others. Rosfelder asked the man where he could find Reuben Sturman. The man told him to ring the buzzer. And then, Sturman drove off in his Cadillac, with a big wave and a smile, as a voice over the intercom told Rosfelder there was no "Reuben Sturman" at this address.

Rosfelder decided to investigate the retail stores first, to figure out how they operated and look for signs of skimming. Rosfelder and Ciehanski followed "Uncle Miltie," one of Sturman's employees, for weeks as he traveled throughout the Cleveland area, visiting dozens of adult bookstores, picking up briefcases full of cash and taking them to the bank. When Rosfelder and Ciehanski examined the tax returns, receipts, and adding machine tapes of Sturman's adult bookstores, all the numbers balanced perfectly, to the penny. The stores were clearly the wrong place to look. When Sturman was tried on obscenity charges in the summer of 1978, Rosfelder and Ciehanski sat in the courtroom every day, listening to testimony, trying to get a sense of the man they were pursuing. Sturman noticed them there and, through his associates, learned who they were. During a recess one day, Sturman passed them in a hallway and said, "You guys look like a couple of dogs waiting for a scrap of meat."

A month after the jury found Sturman not guilty of trafficking in obscene materials, Rosfelder and Ciehanski were invited to join Cleveland's Organized Crime Strike Force. As Richard C. Wassenaar, chief of the IRS criminal division, later acknowledged, the nation's tax laws seemed to offer more promise than its obscenity laws in the war on pornography. Affiliation with the strike force gave Rosfelder added logistical support. He became the case agent, running the Sturman investigation, answering to superiors at both the Treasury Department and the Department of Justice. A grand jury was empaneled to issue subpoenas and help obtain evidence.

Rosfelder decided to bring Sturman to the strike force offices for a handwriting sample. Rosfelder thought a sample might prove useful to the investigation at some point—and it was one of the few things that he could legally compel Sturman to provide. The two men would get a chance to sit in the same office, face to face. Reuben Sturman arrived wearing a cowboy hat and smoking a big cigar. He was in his early fifties. He had already confronted countless FBI agents, U.S. marshals, vice detectives, and prosecutors. This young IRS agent did not faze or intimidate him in the least. Sturman made Rosfelder feel like a flea, a minor irritation, and behaved as though the whole meeting were a joke. He responded to Rosfelder's questions with sarcasm. Although the strike force's forensic experts had assured Rosfelder that a person can never fully disguise his or her handwriting, the samples that Sturman gave were worthless.

The Cleveland grand jury issued subpoenas to Reuben Sturman's employees, to his personal secretary and his ex-wife, but nobody would provide incriminating evidence. Sturman had created a powerful sense of loyalty throughout his organization, urging everyone to remain united against their common enemy, the U.S. government. He paid the legal fees not only of his own employees, but of others in the sex industry indicted for obscenity. No one who worked for Sturman had ever been convicted or sent to prison for distributing his merchandise. After gaining little from the grand jury appearances of Sturman's associates, Rosfelder decided to hunt for the "motherlode"—the Swiss bank accounts. In April, 1979, he and Ciehanski went into the basement of the Capitol National Bank in downtown Cleveland, where they spent the next six months, from morning until night, looking at the bank records of Sturman's companies on microfilm, hoping to find evidence of offshore accounts, going through tens of thousands of canceled checks and deposit slips, without any luck.

skimming the cream

WITHIN DAYS OF THE FBI'S RAID at the Sovereign News warehouse in 1975, Reuben Sturman had begun to change the structure of his corporate holdings. The information in the black binders seized from his office quickly became obsolete, leaving the government with a detailed account of companies that no longer existed. Sturman found a better way to hide his assets, scrapping the system of Canadian nominees for one that was much more impenetrable. With help from Miles Jacobson, an attorney in Garden City, New York, Sturman transferred ownership of his companies to a series of "establishments" chartered in Liechtenstein — the Arandee Investment Establishment, the Eliat Establishment, and others — which maintained their own Swiss bank accounts. Liechtenstein boasted some of the world's strictest corporate secrecy laws. An establishment was an unusual entity, not exactly a corporation, not exactly a trust, run by directors who had to be citizens of Liechtenstein. It issued "bearer shares" with no names on them; whoever had physical possession of these shares owned the establishment. The directors might know the identity of the owner, but if they were unwilling to reveal it, government investigators literally had to find the bearer shares in order to prove ownership. Jacobson also set up companies for Sturman in Panama, where the corporate secrecy laws were even stricter and where businesses could operate tax-free. Even Sturman's home in Shaker Heights became the asset of a foreign corporation.

As early as 1974 Sturman had recognized that technology would soon transform the distribution of sexually explicit materials, telling his employees that "the future lies in audio-visual tape." Three years later, when videocassette players became widely available to American consumers, adult film companies offered their titles on video, while the major Hollywood studios resisted the new medium. As a result, by 1979, 75 percent of all the videotapes sold in the United States were hard-core films. Porn was responsible for the successful launch of the VCR. Sturman released his films on video, opened a chain of mainstream video stores in the Midwest, and established distribution companies, under the name General Video of America, that quickly dominated the wholesale market for hard-core videos in the United States. Intex Nederland, a company he formed with a Dutch partner, became the largest distributor of hard-core videos in Western Europe.

Four months after winning his Cleveland obscenity trial in 1978, Sturman was indicted again for trafficking in obscene materials, this time by a federal grand jury in Pittsburgh. A federal judge later dismissed the charges, ruling that Sturman had been subjected to double jeopardy. And then on February 14, 1980, Sturman was indicted for obscenity yet again, this time by a federal grand jury in Miami, as forty-five of the leading figures in the porn business were rounded up by four hundred FBI agents on the same day. This St. Valentine's Day "massacre" of pornographers was the culmination of a two-and-a-half-year FBI undercover investigation code-named "Miporn." But Sturman's indictment, along with many others, was subsequently thrown out of court—one of the FBI undercover agents had been arrested for shoplifting and had lied about the incident, discrediting his testimony in the porn case. The federal government had now indicted Reuben Sturman for obscenity five times, without gaining a conviction.

In the late 1970s Sturman restructured his holdings once again, ending his relationship with Miles Jacobson. Liechtenstein had amended its corporate laws; the directors of an establishment were now liable for its financial activities; and the lawyers who served in that capacity raised their fees. More importantly, Miles Jacobson's cousin, who was handling some of the offshore accounts, had "borrowed" $592,000 without asking Sturman's permission. After getting his money back, Sturman contacted Edward Coughlin, Jr., an American attorney based in Geneva. Harvard-educated and urbane, Coughlin was an expert at creating unorthodox, international corporate structures. At the time he was also representing Edwin P. Wilson, a rogue CIA agent and gun-runner for Libyan intelligence. Coughlin dissolved all of Sturman's establishments and Panamanian corporations, transferring their assets to newly formed Liberian companies that had bank accounts in Switzerland and names like TransEuropa Films, Amphora Limited, and the Société Financiers et Commerciales, S.A. Liberia's corporate secrecy laws were airtight. A Liberian company needed just one director, not two or three, to issue bearer shares. The nation's currency was the U.S. dollar. And that is why Monrovia, the capital of Liberia, soon became the official headquarters of Reuben Sturman's worldwide pornography empire.

The new corporate structure was well suited to Sturman's needs. He was, in fact, evading taxes on a monumental scale. For years millions of dollars had been skimmed from his peep booths across the United States. Anywhere from 25 to 50 percent of the total peep receipts were sent directly to Reuben Sturman. His employees called it "the cream," which they skimmed from adult bookstores every day or every week, placing the money in safe-deposit boxes or carrying it by hand to Sturman's Cleveland office. Cash was smuggled to Europe in briefcases and suitcases. It was converted into cashier's checks with a face value of less than $10,000, to avoid federal disclosure laws; checks for $9,999 were routinely sent overseas. Once the money arrived in Europe it was used to expand Sturman's foreign empire, or invested, or returned to the United States in a new form. Sturman bought his Rolls-Royce in England with cash and paid many of his lawyers with cash, a practice that on occasion lowered their fees. In addition to the usual motives for tax evasion, such as greed, Reuben Sturman did not want to give the government any money that could be used in the war against him. Paying taxes, in Sturman's mind, was like subsidizing his enemy.

Sturman maintained scores of accounts at the most prestigious banks in Zurich under an assortment of assumed names. At the Union Bank of Switzerland, he was known as "Paul Schuster" and "Roy C. English." At the Swiss Bank Corporation, he was "Robert Butler" and "Robert Stern." A senior vice president of the Swiss Bank Corporation served as his personal banker, meeting regularly with Sturman in a grand office at the bank, managing his investments in foreign currencies and gold. A handful of Sturman's trusted associates had access to these Swiss accounts, also under pseudonyms. Sturman constantly shifted large sums of money between banks in Zurich, London, and Amsterdam. His businesses in Europe were being skimmed, too, producing even more cash in need of laundering. On his 1979 United States Individual Income Tax Return (Form 1040), Reuben Sturman declared a total taxable income, after expenses, of $1,237. And in the space allotted for overseas bank accounts, he listed none.

bingo

A TYPICAL IRS CRIMINAL INVESTIGATION lasts about eighteen months. As Richard Rosfelder's inquiry entered its third year, his supe-

riors at the IRS grew impatient. Although members of the Organized
Crime Strike Force were accustomed to long, complex investigations,
the IRS bureaucracy was geared for quick results. Rosfelder knew he
was on the right track, but still had found nothing concrete to prove
Sturman was breaking the law. Rosfelder's friends and co-workers began
to tease him. They could understand why Sturman worked so hard: he
was earning a fortune. But they wondered why Rosfelder was so gung-
ho, spending his days in a bank basement, staring at microfilm, for an
annual salary that was a small fraction of what Sturman spent on a
Christmas party. Rosfelder trusted his gut and never doubted that his
investigation would prove a success.

Rosfelder was taking a break from the microfilm one day when
Thomas Ciehanski walked into his office, placed a photocopy of a canceled check on his desk, and said, "Bingo." It was a check for $200,000
drawn from the Merchants and Shipowners Bank, chartered on the
Caribbean island of St. Vincent. The check showed that money was
being funneled into one of Sturman's companies from an offshore account, but it did not reveal how or by whom. Rosfelder and Ciehanski
returned to the basement of the Capital National Bank and found
three more deposits from offshore accounts later that afternoon.

The Merchants and Shipowners Bank of St. Vincent, Rosfelder discovered, did not have any offices or branches or safe-deposit boxes.
The bank existed only on paper, with funds in a New York City account.
Money had been transferred to it by something called the Arandee Investment Establishment, through the Union Bank of Switzerland. The
paper trail led Rosfelder to Miles Jacobson. Citing attorney-client privilege, Jacobson refused to answer any questions about the offshore accounts or Reuben Sturman. His refusal could have marked a dead end
for the investigation; indeed, Sturman had anticipated that such a
privilege would block any access to his records. But Rosfelder decided
to apply pressure, warning Jacobson that should evidence of fraud be
uncovered, the lawyers would be joining Sturman as defendants in this
case. Rosfelder had come to believe there was one cardinal rule among
tax attorneys: if someone has to go to jail, it should always be the
client. Jacobson began to talk, describing how he'd helped Sturman
open Swiss bank accounts, form dummy corporations, transfer assets
overseas, and operate a financial system that laundered the same money

twice—first through a Swiss bank, then through the St. Vincent bank—thereby making the money even more difficult to trace. Now that Rosfelder knew the locations of these Swiss bank accounts, he needed to gain access to them, see what they contained, and prove that they belonged to Reuben Sturman.

For decades Switzerland's Banking Secrecy Law made it almost impossible for a criminal investigator to examine the contents of a Swiss bank account. A Swiss bank official who divulged a client's identity could face imprisonment and large fines. The law was justified as part of Switzerland's devotion to neutrality and individual rights, to providing a safe haven for refugees and persecuted minorities. But in reality the law often safeguarded the money of dictators, drug dealers, and wealthy criminals from all over the world. Holocaust survivors were still lobbying the Swiss government, without success, for the return of assets stolen by Nazis and deposited in Swiss banks. In 1973 the United States and the Swiss Confederation signed a Mutual Assistance Treaty that for the first time allowed access to secret bank accounts during the investigation of serious crimes. The Swiss, however, did not regard tax evasion as a serious crime. The treaty didn't permit opening the secret accounts of a tax evader—except when that tax evader was linked to the "upper echelon of an organized criminal group."

As soon as Rosfelder learned about this "organized crime exception" to the Mutual Assistance Treaty, he contacted the Justice Department's Office of International Affairs. Such a loophole did exist, he was told, but the Swiss had never allowed anyone to use it. Gaining access to Sturman's accounts was crucial to Rosfelder's investigation. The accounts could provide irrefutable evidence of tax evasion and of money laundering. Sturman's failure to disclose their existence on his tax returns was in itself a criminal act. With help from the strike force, Rosfelder prepared a dossier on Sturman's alleged ties to the Cosa Nostra. The Justice Department submitted a formal request for information about Sturman's suspected accounts to the Swiss Federal Department of Justice and Police. Sturman wasn't informed that the request had been made.

Meanwhile, Rosfelder enlisted the assistance of Scotland Yard. Margaret Thatcher, the new British prime minister, was starting her own campaign against pornography. Reuben Sturman's investments in London's sex trade were first disclosed in *Private Eye,* after one of his Doc Johnson stores opened beneath the magazine's offices in Soho. The British were appalled by revelations that London's porn business was dominated by an American businessman from Cleveland. When Rosfelder heard that authorities in Great Britain were investigating Sturman's companies, he called Scotland Yard. Commander Len Gillard, the Yard's third-in-command, and Colin Coxall, its head of intelligence, flew to Cleveland for a meeting with Rosfelder. "We have been instructed," Gillard said, "to reduce Mr. Sturman to ground zero in England."

Rosfelder was given access to the bank accounts of Sturman's British companies. Hundreds of thousands of U.S. dollars had been deposited there, in cash — money that had obviously been smuggled into London — but Sturman's name was on none of the accounts. And then Rosfelder gained access to Sturman's Swiss accounts through the treaty's loophole, an unprecedented departure from Switzerland's Banking Secrecy Law. Bank officials were told by the Swiss government not to let Sturman know that his privacy had been breached; any disclosure of that fact would lead to their criminal prosecution, as well. The bank officials felt uneasy. They were violating a Swiss tradition and an important client's trust, not to mention a banking practice responsible for much of their income. They kept opening the accounts that Rosfelder requested — but Reuben Sturman's name did not appear on any of them, nor did it appear on any of the signature cards authorizing withdrawals. Rosfelder was certain that these were the right accounts. He needed a sample of Sturman's handwriting to prove it. Sturman was brought in two more times for a handwriting sample. He was defiant during both visits, cracking jokes, scrawling illegibly for hours, and providing samples that were worthless.

a fear of long prison terms

REUBEN STURMAN DID NOT KNOW that the IRS was examining his bank records in Cleveland, London, and Zurich. But he increasingly felt the pressure of Rosfelder's investigation. Sturman told friends he was planning to retire. He spent more and more time in Southern

California. He fell in love with a beautiful young singer, Naomi Delgado, who had released an album of Spanish hip-hop. They were married and later had a child. Sturman began to sell his companies to his top managers — Majestic News, in Detroit, to James Olsafsky; Capital News, in Chicago, to Paula Lawrence; Sovereign News, in Cleveland, to Mel Kamins (also known as Melvin Kaminsky). But Sturman faced an unusual dilemma: how do you sell something that, technically, you don't own? The problem was resolved, as always, with a clever legal ploy. The ownership of various companies was transferred to Sturman's managers, and then they hired Reuben Sturman to serve as a "consultant." Sturman would fade into the background, hand power to a younger generation, and spend time with his new family.

Government investigators regarded Sturman's talk of retirement as just one more scheme to disguise control of his assets. The consulting agreements seemed like another method of deploying nominees. Sturman's managers were people who owed their success to him, who had followed his directives for years, who were unlikely all of a sudden to disobey the most powerful man in the sex industry. By becoming the legal owners of these companies, the managers now assumed the legal risks. A strike force attorney confronted one of Sturman's managers and told him that the new owners were being used as fall guys. "You idiot, you don't own anything," the attorney said. "You're just a nominee who doesn't even know it." The manager replied with a smile that said, "You idiot, I'm making a couple of million bucks a year, and you're calling me an idiot."

In November, 1981, Scott Dormen — who looked after Sturman's interests in England, collecting his share of the profits from adult bookstores and movie theaters, from Pleasure Publishing, Nightbird Magazines, and a distribution company, Video Blue — was stopped by customs agents at London's Heathrow Airport. Dormen was interrogated for several days, then told to leave Great Britain. He flew to Amsterdam with another Sturman employee and a briefcase crammed with £24,149 in cash, ignoring, as always, the customs form that said any currency with a value of more than £100 sterling had to be declared. Dormen snuck back into England a few months later in order to train his replacement. He was arrested and charged with conspiring to import obscene material. He fled the country, at night, by boat, arriving safely in Holland but forfeiting his bond.

Reuben Sturman was charged in absentia with selling pornography in Great Britain. His British partners were eventually convicted of the same offense. Ben Holloway and four of his children were sent to prison, while his wife, Mary, continued going to work at the family sex shop in Luton.

When Sturman paid a routine visit to the Zurich branch of the Union Bank of Switzerland in 1982, planning to close some accounts, bank officials became nervous, not knowing what to do. They called the Swiss Federal Police, who called Rosfelder in Cleveland. He asked them to try and get a handwriting sample. Sturman was arrested at the bank. He provided a genuine sample. Sturman soon realized that the U.S. government had somehow gotten into his Swiss bank accounts. Associates of his who'd used the accounts were being forced to give handwriting samples. IRS agents were asking them questions about Swiss bank accounts that hadn't been active for years. After making a withdrawal from the Swiss Bank Corporation, Sturman noticed three men were following him. He had no idea how Rosfelder had learned about the Swiss accounts. Sturman knew that the IRS might now have the evidence it needed for a successful prosecution — and yet he was by no means ready to concede defeat.

When the federal grand jury in Cleveland issued subpoenas for Sturman's business records, he began collecting important documents from his files, which had not been stored at his office since the FBI raids in 1975. Sturman's business records were kept in his lawyer's office, in his accountant's mother's garage, in his housekeeper's basement amid paint cans and old clothes. Files that might contain information useful to the government were separated from the rest. "I'll probably regret this," Sturman joked to his secretary, as he started shredding documents. A second round of shredding lasted for three weeks. An entirely new set of business records was created, backdated, and shipped to Sturman's various companies across the United States.

Rosfelder's investigation continued to gain momentum. He traveled to London, Zurich, New York, and Los Angeles, questioning Sturman's associates and receiving invaluable aid from other law enforcement officials, from FBI agents and prosecutors, from vice cops in Boston and in Washington, D.C., from inspectors at Scotland Yard. There was an eagerness in law enforcement circles around the globe to help topple Reuben Sturman, not only because he dominated the international porn trade, but also because he enjoyed thumbing his nose at authority.

One by one, Sturman's trusted aides began to cooperate with the government, as loyalty gave way to a fear of long prison terms. Rosfelder worked his way up the corporate ladder, getting peep show repairmen, store managers, and company accountants to testify against Sturman before the grand jury. A number of these people had been employed by Sturman for decades; some had known him since childhood. Marjorie Rollins, Sturman's personal secretary, offered especially damning testimony. She had attended John Adams High School with Sturman and had become his secretary in 1966. She was a grandmother in her mid-fifties, a dear friend of his family. During her first grand jury appearance, Rollins had refused to cooperate. But she and Sturman later had a falling out. He thought that she had betrayed him. He fired her, and then Rollins gave the government a detailed account of how Sturman conducted business. Amid these defections, Bernard Berkman — Sturman's lawyer and closest confidant — died unexpectedly after a brief illness.

On June 28, 1985, Attorney General Edwin Meese III announced that a Cleveland grand jury had indicted Reuben Sturman on one count of conspiring to defraud the government, one count of obstructing justice, five counts of income tax evasion, five counts of filing false returns, and four counts of currency reporting and foreign bank account violations. Five of Sturman's associates, including his son David, were also indicted. The government accused Sturman of evading more than $3 million in personal income tax between 1978 and 1982, of funneling more than $7 million through foreign bank accounts, and of destroying evidence that had been subpoenaed. He faced a maximum of seventy-five years in prison and large fines. After giving credit to Cleveland's Organized Crime Strike Force and the IRS, Attorney General Meese listed some of the other law enforcement agencies that had aided the investigation of Reuben Sturman: "Scotland Yard, the Swiss Federal Police, Interpol . . . the U.S. Customs Service . . . the Royal Canadian Mounted Police, the Ontario Provincial Police, Revenue Canada, Inland Revenue of Great Britain, the Zurich Police . . . the police departments of Boston . . . San Francisco . . . Los Angeles . . . and Washington, D.C. . . . the Bureau of Alcohol, Tobacco and Firearms, the Federal Bureau of Investigation, the Immigration and Naturalization Service, and [the] Postal Inspection Service."

Richard Rosfelder had no illusions about the Sturman case, doubting that every crime or every offshore bank account had been uncovered. This criminal conspiracy was too big to tackle, or even to comprehend, in its entirety. But Rosfelder felt confident that the government had built a strong case. He thought Sturman had failed to report at least ten times the amount of income specified in the indictment. It was important, however, only to seek charges that could easily be proven. If jurors doubted one accusation, they might begin to doubt the others. He had discovered dozens of Sturman's Swiss bank accounts. Perhaps there were more. Rosfelder didn't mind having missed a few, so long as Reuben Sturman went to prison and couldn't make use of them.

Sturman was arrested in Los Angeles and held on a $3 million cash bond, which he paid with little difficulty. His attorneys, led by J. Michael Murray, immediately attacked the indictment. Over the next few years, hundreds of motions were filed contesting the legality of the government's investigation. Rosfelder's partner, Thomas Ciehanski, retired from the IRS, frustrated by the endless delays in the case, worried that after all their hard work, Sturman would never go on trial. Having learned how Rosfelder had gained access to the Swiss accounts, Sturman's attorneys fought to suppress any evidence obtained from them, filing motions in federal court and in the Swiss court system. They argued that the Mutual Assistance Treaty had been misinterpreted, that Reuben Sturman had a right to know the secret accusations made against him, that his reputation had been unfairly maligned, and that he had no links to the Cosa Nostra which could possibly justify violating the privacy of his accounts. "I am not now and never have been a member of organized crime," Sturman swore in an affidavit. "Nor have I ever taken part in any of the activities of organized crime."

A federal magistrate was given copies of the secret documents that the Justice Department had sent to Switzerland, outlining Sturman's ties to the Cosa Nostra. If the courts ruled that the U.S. government had acted properly, Reuben Sturman was most likely doomed. But if the courts allowed him to examine these documents, and if he could demonstrate that the allegations in them were false, the entire case against Sturman might collapse.

paying tribute to the mob

OPPONENTS OF PORNOGRAPHY HAD LONG ARGUED that the sex industry was "controlled" by the Cosa Nostra. "Combining old-fashioned muscle with sizable payoffs to cops and politicians," *Reader's Digest* asserted in 1973, "Mafia dons from coast to coast make sure that no dirty magazine, hard-core film or peep show machine enters their city without the payment of tribute to the local crime 'family.' " A national pornography consortium, allegedly headed by the five families of the Cosa Nostra, decided not only who could produce porn but also what porn could be released. A 1978 FBI report expressed much the same view, declaring there was "an obvious national control [of the porn business] directly, and indirectly by organized crime figures." The FBI claimed that pornography had become the third largest source of income for the Cosa Nostra, exceeded only by gambling and narcotics.

David Alexander Scott, a Toronto psychologist whose work greatly influenced the Meese Commission, argued that organized crime had entered the porn business in order to market the idea that "deviance is not deviant," thereby increasing demand for other mob rackets, such as drug dealing and prostitution. Scott believed in the existence of a "national pornography consortium," headed by the five families of New York's Cosa Nostra. Top officials in the Los Angeles Police Department (LAPD) endorsed this theory, claiming that Reuben Sturman was merely a front man for the Cosa Nostra. Testifying before the Meese Commission, Daryl Gates, chief of the LAPD, said that as much as 90 percent of the porn industry was in the hands of organized crime.

Experts on the Cosa Nostra, however, tended to minimize its role in the distribution of pornography. The 1986 report by the President's Commission on Organized Crime listed eighteen principal sources of income for the Cosa Nostra—and pornography was not among them. When FBI director William H. Webster surveyed the bureau's field offices at the request of the Meese Commission, three-quarters of them could find no verifiable evidence of extortion or organized crime involvement in the porn trade. Ronald Goldstock—a professor at Cornell University Law School who headed the New York State Organized Crime Task Force during the 1980s—told me that pornography was never among the top dozen sources of income for the Cosa Nostra. James Kossler—who headed the FBI's Organized Crime Squads in New York City during the 1980s and who played a crucial role in the downfall of John Gotti, the head of the Gambino family—agreed with Goldstock's assessment.

Members of the Cosa Nostra were unquestionably involved in the porn industry, subsidizing hard-core film production, operating retail stores, and extorting money from independent businessmen as often as possible. But mob involvement did not necessarily translate into mob control. The sex industry thrived at the margins of legality, attracting a wide variety of men and women, some with shady backgrounds, some without. In New York City, heart of the Cosa Nostra, organized crime families earned most of their income from porn through real estate deals, renting properties to adult bookstores, strip clubs, and massage parlors. Simply doing business with a Cosa Nostra figure did not entail being controlled. All sorts of relationships, from the ordinary to the wildly illegal, were possible. "When a Cosa Nostra member goes and gets a haircut," Ronald Goldstock explained, "it doesn't mean he owns the barber."

Allegations of Sturman's links to the Cosa Nostra were largely based on his relationship with Robert DiBernardo, a member of the Gambino family who eventually became one of John Gotti's top lieutenants. DiBernardo lived a quiet suburban life in Hewlett Harbor, Long Island, doting on his children and coaching Little League. Every weekday morning he commuted to Manhattan, where he owned Star News, New York City's largest wholesale distributor of porn. Star News published its own sex magazines, released a small number of hard-core videos, and operated a giant warehouse on Lafayette Street, near Little Italy. DiBernardo also owned the Show World Center on Forty-second Street, New York's most renowned sex emporium. He wielded considerable influence among other Cosa Nostra figures in the porn trade, resolving disputes over territory. And he earned a great deal of money from labor racketeering, gaining a reputation for violence through his shakedowns of unions in the construction industry. Robert DiBernardo was extremely handsome and polite, always impeccably dressed, and widely feared.

The evidence in the public record linking Reuben Sturman to the Cosa Nostra is inconclusive and largely anecdotal. In 1978 the FBI emphasized the importance of the Cosa Nostra's income from porn and claimed that Sturman had accomplished "almost a total takeover [of the porn business] with the assistance of Robert DiBernardo," relying upon threats and intimidation. One of Sturman's partners in the New England News Company, Boston's leading porn wholesaler, was Joseph Palladino, who had close links with Raymond Patriarca's crime family. But Homer Young, a legendary FBI agent who led obscenity investigations for decades, believed that Sturman had consistently fought to keep organized crime out of the porn industry. In 1979 Sturman testified against Cosa Nostra members in a California extortion trial. He said that two men had approached him in front of the Cleveland YMCA, threatened him with "serious trouble," and demanded payments of $20,000 a month — which Sturman refused to make. His testimony helped destroy the crime family of the Los Angeles don Dominic Brooklier. But Jimmy Fratianno, a high-level member of that crime family who later became an FBI informer, claimed that Reuben Sturman could safely ignore the threats of L.A. mobsters because he was paying hundreds of thousands of dollars to much more powerful New York mobsters for protection.

Based on material in the public record, it is impossible to determine whether Sturman ever made payments to the Cosa Nostra, or what such payments might have obtained. William P. Kelly — a retired FBI agent who investigated obscenity cases for twenty-five years, got to know DiBernardo through the Miporn case, and now advises antipornography groups — does not believe that Sturman served as a front man for the Cosa Nostra. As to whether Sturman made payments to the Gambino family, Kelly said, "I wouldn't be surprised if he did, and I wouldn't be surprised if he didn't." Sturman owned businesses in many cities where the Cosa Nostra was powerful. If he did indeed pay tribute, were favors given in return? Or was he a victim of extortion, like many legitimate businessmen? From all appearances, Robert DiBernardo and Reuben Sturman were on amicable terms. Every year, DiBernardo attended the Sovereign News Christmas party in Cleveland. His presence at this huge annual gathering may have been useful to Sturman, sending a not so subtle message to anyone who might want to make threats.

Perhaps only Sturman and DiBernardo knew the exact nature of their relationship. One of them, however, could no longer disclose it. DiBernardo had made the mistake of telling jokes about John Gotti behind his back. Gotti did not appreciate the humor and ordered a "hit." Robert DiBernardo was shot twice in the back of the head by a friend in May, 1986, while awaiting a cup of coffee. His body was never recovered. According to one federal agent, it was put through a tree-shredder.

a tax case, and nothing more

AFTER STUDYING THE LANGUAGE of the Mutual Assistance Treaty and examining the material submitted to the Swiss, U.S. Magistrate David S. Perelman recommended on August 21, 1986, that Sturman be granted access to the documents alleging his links to the Cosa Nostra. In order to use the loophole in the treaty, the government had to show that the defendant belonged "to an upper echelon of an organized criminal group" or participated "significantly . . . in any important activity of the group" and that the intended prosecution would have a "significant adverse effect" on the group. The magistrate noted that the government's reluctance to release the information on Sturman might cause a reasonable person to doubt its accuracy. "Denying a defendant the right to determine whether the United States Government has complied with an international treaty in seeking evidence against him," Perelman wrote, "is inconsistent with the basic tenets of our jurisprudence."

U.S. District Judge George W. White read the magistrate's report, considered its recommendations, and gave a simple response to Sturman's request: Denied.

Sturman's attorneys were outraged by White's decision and immediately filed an appeal. Members of Cleveland's Organized Crime Strike Force were quite pleased. The Mutual Assistance Treaty did not obligate either government to show a defendant the evidence used to open his or her Swiss bank account. The strike force did not feel like doing Reuben Sturman any favors. The Justice Department felt confident that the information in the dossier was accurate. Giving the material to Sturman could provide the defense with an excuse for more litigation, postponing a trial date even further. The only civil right being violated here, in the view of the strike force attorneys, was the right to keep money in a secret Swiss bank account — and no one at the Justice Department would lose sleep over denying Reuben Sturman that right.

As the various motions and appeals made their way through Swiss and American courts, Sturman was indicted again on federal obscenity charges, this time in Las Vegas. Attorney General Meese announced the indictment in October, 1987, unveiling a new weapon in the war on pornography, charging Sturman under the Racketeer Influenced and Corrupt Organizations (RICO) Act. The RICO Act had been broadened in 1984 to include obscenity violations, increasing the government's power in such cases. If Sturman and his associates were convicted under the RICO statute, the government could seize all the assets connected to their obscenity offense, which in this instance would include: peep machines and the contents of their coin boxes, property at twelve Nevada locations, fourteen corporations, seven retail stores, $162,000 in U.S. currency and checks, two Mercedes-Benzes, three Cadillacs, and a Ford. In addition to the threat of forfeiture, Sturman faced a possible fifty-five-year prison sentence and a $2 million fine. The material at issue in the case was as hard-core as anything on the market — videotapes depicting urination and defecation during sexual activity, depicting torture, depicting men and women having sex with animals.

That same year, Cleveland's Organized Crime Strike Force recruited

Craig S. Morford to help Rosfelder prepare Sturman's tax case for trial. Morford was a twenty-seven-year-old IRS attorney who had not yet worked on a major criminal case. He arrived at the strike force offices and was confronted with hundreds of boxes of documents—business records dating back to the late 1960s, bank records from a multitude of offshore accounts, depositions, seven years' worth of grand jury transcripts, papers recently discovered in Sturman's housekeeper's basement and at his accountant's mother's garage—that had to be read and sorted and analyzed for possible use as evidence in the trial. It took Rosfelder and Morford almost two years to go through all the boxes. They had to decide how to present this extraordinarily complex conspiracy in a form that the jurors could understand. Morford was bright, tough, and very tall. At six-foot-seven, he towered almost a foot above Rosfelder. Though mismatched in size, the two were equally hardworking, disciplined, and determined to win.

Sturman's trial for tax evasion began in September, 1989, more than four years after the original indictment. Stephen H. Jigger, the head of Cleveland's Organized Crime Strike Force, gave the government's opening remarks, telling the jury that the case had nothing to do with obscenity law, pornography, or freedom of speech. It was a tax case, and nothing more. Sturman's attorney, J. Michael Murray, argued that his client's behavior had to be viewed in light of the unrelenting government efforts to destroy an innocent man's livelihood. The concealment of assets was a purely defensive measure, without criminal intent, in the midst of a cultural war. Murray's argument was undercut by the government's first two witnesses, Alfred Graf and Walter Butti, officers with the Zurich police. They described Sturman's 1974 arrest outside the Swiss Credit Bank and read the jury Sturman's own explanation for opening several accounts with a phony passport: "I wanted to bring [money] to Switzerland . . . to avoid taxes."

The prosecution called about ninety witnesses, many of them Sturman's former employees. James Olsafsky—who was Sturman's accountant from 1971 to 1984 and subsequently became the legal owner of his Michigan distribution network—described the challenge of falsifying tax returns as businesses became more profitable. Sturman never wanted to pay any money to the government, and it became a constant struggle to reduce inventory, write off receivables, and invent nonexistent expenses in order to balance the books. Olsafsky also said that transporting the "cream" could be a nerve-racking experience; he had once carried a briefcase filled with $230,000 in cash through airport security on a trip from Cleveland to Chicago. A. Robert Dostal, another Sturman accountant and a graduate of Harvard Business School, revealed his method of finding nominees to list as the officers of Sturman's companies. "My approach," he said, "was to take the white pages of the telephone book and just flip it open." After choosing a name, Dostal would add it to the corporate records, tax returns, and bank accounts, without ever notifying the person in the phone book that he or she had legally become a top executive in Reuben Sturman's porn empire. Marjorie Rollins, Sturman's former secretary, used a more literary approach. She told the court that she selected names for nominees out of her favorite novels. Charles Conway — whose signature often endorsed checks for one of Sturman's companies — shared the surname of *Lost Horizon*'s protagonist.

A number of Sturman's attorneys were granted immunity from prosecution and testified against him. Edward Coughlin cheerfully led the jury through the intricacies of Liberian corporate law and expressed his personal fondness for Sturman. One of the late Bernard Berkman's law partners, Larry A. Gordon, withered under Morford's questioning and reluctantly admitted his role in deceiving the IRS. Miles Jacobson revealed some of the methods used to transfer assets between Swiss banks without leaving a paper trail. On one occasion he and Sturman's elder son had withdrawn approximately $400,000 in cash and gold bars from the Wirtschaft Bank in Zurich, placing the cash in a satchel and the gold bars in a cardboard box. When both the satchel and the box proved too heavy to carry, they were carted out of the bank on a dolly, then transported across town in a taxi to the Union Bank of Switzerland for deposit.

Sturman knew his prospects in the trial were not good, but he didn't act like a beaten man. He often arrived at the courthouse wearing a Groucho Marx disguise — false eyebrows and big eyeglasses and a plastic nose — to hide his face from photographers. His wife provoked comment by wearing a number of suggestive outfits, with low-cut blouses and short skirts, in the courtroom. Sturman seemed to be in high spirits. He was admonished by Judge White for a number of comments to witnesses. "Marjorie, you just forget everything you ever said," Sturman told his former secretary, as she prepared to testify. He assured the judge the remark was a joke, not a threat, and promised to be more careful in the future.

On November 17, 1989, Reuben Sturman was found guilty of every charge in the tax case, as were the other defendants, Ralph Lane (also known as Ralph Levine) and Sturman's son David. Twenty-five years after its first attempt, the government had convicted Sturman for a felony offense. His attorneys immediately appealed the decision. Judge White sentenced Sturman to ten years in prison and imposed $2.5 million in fines, but he allowed Sturman to remain free, pending appeal, on a $1 million cash bond.

At the Las Vegas obscenity trial in October, 1991, J. Michael Murray argued that Reuben Sturman had no idea that such deeply offensive material was being sold at his Nevada stores. These videotapes were an aberration, wholly unrepresentative of Sturman's merchandise. And Murray asked the jury to ponder what the "community standard" of decency—essential to any federal definition of obscenity—might be in a place like Las Vegas. After nine days of deliberation, the jury was still deadlocked, and the judge was forced to declare a mistrial. Two of the jurors who'd voted to acquit Sturman were schoolteachers, both of them women. "The government had no case against me from day one," Sturman told reporters, from behind a surgical mask.

When the government vowed to seek a new obscenity trial, Sturman decided to give up the fight. His initial appeal in the tax case had been rejected, and his case was headed for the Supreme Court. The Swiss courts were ruling against him. A new obscenity trial might end with a different result, only compounding his problems. Sturman agreed to cut a deal with the government, pleading guilty to one RICO violation and seven obscenity offenses, forfeiting assets in San Francisco, Reno, and Las Vegas. In return the government allowed his sentence in the obscenity case to be served concurrently with his sentence in the tax case, should the latter be upheld. Sturman asked to be sent to the federal prison camp near Boron, California, in the Mojave Desert, a few hours from his family in Los Angeles. The government granted the request. Harry Virgil Mohney, probably the second most important figure in the American porn industry, was already imprisoned at Boron. IRS agents in Michigan had caught Mohney skimming cash from his peep machines, too.

On June 10, 1992, Judge Lloyd D. George sentenced Reuben Sturman to four years in prison and fined him $1 million. As Sturman was handcuffed and led away by U.S. marshals, Richard Rosfelder sat in the Las Vegas courtroom, watching. Rosfelder had spent almost fifteen years, full-time, investigating the Sturman empire. He had won a series of battles — exposing the criminal conspiracy, gaining access to the secret accounts, fending off procedural challenges, turning close associates against one another, securing Sturman's conviction — but these victories had somehow felt hollow. Through it all, Sturman had continued to run his business and enjoy his wealth. Nothing seemed to have really changed — until this day. As the king of porn left the courtroom for prison, Rosfelder felt there was finally something tangible about Sturman's defeat.

the new democracy of porn

THE BREAK-UP OF REUBEN STURMAN'S EMPIRE had the same effect as a successful antitrust enforcement, turning the distribution of hard-core material into a fiercely competitive business. The regional branches of Sturman's old company, General Video of America, now separately owned, are still a major force in the industry, with combined revenues exceeding those of any other wholesale distributor. Sturman's son David runs one of the largest porn companies, Sin City. But hundreds of other companies now produce and distribute hard-core videos, often bypassing traditional wholesalers entirely, selling directly to consumers and video stores. Videotape and digital technology have lowered production costs so much, according to one executive, that the only barriers of entry to the porn business today are "a sense of embarrassment and the lack of a good lawyer." The availability of hard-core films on home video forced adult theaters out of business in cities nationwide. Los Angeles once had thirty to forty adult theaters; now it has about half a dozen. The number of adult bookstores in the United States has also declined, though not so precipitously. The bookstores are supported mainly by their peep booths, which at some locations allow a customer to watch five hard-core videos simultaneously on dual television screens, demanding a new quarter every twenty seconds.

Perhaps three-quarters of the hard-core videos made in the United States now come from Los Angeles County. Each year the L.A. County Film Office issues a few thousand permits to X-rated producers who have applied to shoot on location. Countless other filmmakers never bother to ask for permission, shooting sex scenes in motels, condominiums, and suburban homes. The heart of the industry lies in the San Fernando Valley, just a few miles northwest of Universal City, the Warner Brothers lot, and Walt Disney Studios. Hundreds of businesses in the sex trade — sound stages, editing facilities, printing plants, sex toy factories — are tucked into middle-class and working-class neighborhoods, amid a typical Southern California landscape of palm trees, strip malls, car washes, and fast food joints, all bathed in hazy sunshine. You could hardly pick a more mundane spot for the world capital of porn.

The downfall of Reuben Sturman also helped lift the pornography business out of the underground. Most of the revenues now generated by the sale and rental of hard-core videos aren't going to porn companies in Southern California but to mainstream video stores across the United States. The consolidation of the retail video business, marked by the growth of national chains like Blockbuster, put enormous pressure on mom-and-pop stores. Faced with competition from the superstores, which stock a larger variety of tapes and benefit from economies of scale, independent retailers increasingly rely on hard-core porn to attract customers. This marketing strategy has been encouraged by Blockbuster's refusal to carry X-rated material and by the higher profit margins of hard-core videos. A popular Hollywood movie on videotape, such as *Spider-Man,* may cost the retailer $60 per tape and rent for $3 a night. A new hard-core release, by comparison, may cost $20 per tape and rent for $4 a night. Many mom-and-pop video stores now derive a third of their income from porn. According to one industry expert, approximately 25,000 video stores in the United States now rent and sell hard-core films.

The type of hard-core films that were once surreptitiously sold under the counter are now being distributed not only by mom-and-pop video stores, but also by some of America's largest corporations. Pay-per-view porn films run twenty-four hours a day, seven days a week, on cable and satellite networks throughout the country. Soft-core and hard-core movies on pay-per-view have become a major source of profits for these corporations—a "cash cow," one executive told *Variety*. Adult films offer much higher profit margins than conventional fare. When a Hollywood movie is sold to a customer on pay-per-view, the satellite or cable operator usually splits the revenue fifty-fifty with the film's distributor. But when a porn movie is sold on pay-per-view, the satellite or cable operator typically gets to keep 70 percent of the revenue. In 2001, Americans spent about $465 million ordering adult movies on pay-per-view. Most of the money was earned by well-known companies that don't boast about their links with the sex trade, such as EchoStar, DirecTV, AT&T Broadband, and AOL Time Warner. Americans spend an additional $200 million or so on adult films piped into their hotel rooms. Indeed, about half of all the films rented in hotel rooms are porn films. The leading hotel chains—such as Hilton, Holiday Inn, Sheraton, and Marriott International—get a cut of up to 15 percent.

The spread of sex films into mainstream distribution channels has fueled a tremendous rise in the production of porn. Since 1991 the number of new hard-core titles released each year has increased about sevenfold. The falling cost of video equipment has attracted more and more filmmakers to the business. In 1975 perhaps a hundred hard-core feature films were produced, at a typical cost in today's dollars of about $320,000. In 2001 about 11,000 hard-core videos were released, some costing as little as $5,000 to produce. Wholesale prices have been driven down by this flood of new product. As the average revenue earned by each new title has decreased, many porn companies have attempted to maintain their total revenue by increasing their output, only adding to the glut and driving prices down even further.

A market once characterized by a relatively undifferentiated product has segmented into various niches, with material often aimed at narrowly defined audiences. Hard-core videos now cater to almost every conceivable predilection — and to some that are hard to imagine. There are gay videos and straight videos, bondage videos and spanking videos, tickling videos, interracial videos, and videos like *Count Footula,* for people whose fetish is feet. There are "she-male" videos featuring transsexuals and "cat-fighting" videos in which naked women wrestle one another or join forces to beat up naked men. There are companies that produce nothing but cat-fighting videos. There are hard-core videos for senior citizens, for sadomasochists, for people fond of verbal abuse. The sexual fantasies now being sold are far too numerous to list. America's sex industry offers a textbook example of how a free market can efficiently gear production to meet consumer demand.

The uncontrolled, and perhaps uncontrollable, nature of the industry is best illustrated by the thriving trade in homemade, hard-core videos. During the 1980s the camcorders advertised as a means of recording weddings, graduations, and a child's first steps were soon being used to record other kinds of activities. "Swingers" — couples in non-monogamous relationships who seek others so inclined — began making and exchanging tapes of themselves in bed. An underground market arose for these crude but authentic sex tapes, and companies began to distribute them. Today about one-fifth of the hard-core videos and DVDs being sold in the United States are classified as "amateur," featuring to some degree the work of nonprofessionals. Most of the companies that distribute amateur porn are in Southern California. But there are hard-core amateur companies distributing tapes from Vandalia, Ohio, and Shreveport, Louisiana; from Sedona, Arizona, and Liverpool, New York; from Woodridge, Illinois, and Chattanooga, Tennessee. Americans who like to watch and those who like to be watched are now linked in a commerce worth hundreds of millions of dollars.

The oldest, and one of the largest, amateur porn companies is based in La Jolla, California, not far from the Salk Institute. Homegrown Video offers more than a thousand different tapes of ordinary people having sex. The company's current owner, Tim Lake, is thirty-nine years old and could easily pass for a drummer in a Seattle rock band. He has shoulder-length hair and tends to wear baggy shorts, a T-shirt, and a beeper. Lake and his wife, Alyssa, sift through the nine or ten new tapes that arrive at their office each week from around the world. The people who appear in these videos are of every race, size, and shape. Their bodies are different from those seen in mainstream hard-core films, where the performers often look like parodies of the reigning masculine and feminine ideals. The people who send tapes to Homegrown hope to break into the porn business, or earn a little extra money, or just show off. The company pays them $20 for every minute of video it uses.

Tim Lake's real name is Farrell Timlake, and he was raised in Fairfield County, Connecticut. He attended prep schools in New Canaan and Kent, studied literature at Pitzer College, became a performance artist, met his wife at a rock club, and followed the Grateful Dead with her for years. The pair have been together since 1986 and have two children. Lake was a porn star in Los Angeles before buying Homegrown, as was his wife. A number of Homegrown's employees are people Lake got to know on the road with the Grateful Dead. Lake's brother — who attended Exeter and Stanford University, who for a long time disapproved of the porn business — is now Homegrown's chief executive and has performed in one of its films. Running the company has been a real eye-opener for Tim Lake. "The imagination's the only limit on what human beings will do," he says. Lake sees something new just about every day. Homegrown serves as a clearinghouse in America's new democracy of porn, supplying hard-core videos by the people, for the people.

all apologies

IN THE FALL OF 1992 the IRS was having difficulty collecting the back taxes Reuben Sturman owed. But for the first time Sturman seemed remorseful. After spending nearly six months in prison he wrote to Judge George W. White, conceding defeat, apologizing for his actions, and pleading for a reduction in his sentence so that he would not miss his daughter's childhood. "I thought I could outwit the U.S. government," Sturman wrote on December 1, 1992. "That was stupid on my part." A week later, after his request had been denied, Sturman was not present for the 9 P.M. bed check at his federal prison in Boron. Prison authorities searched for him in the Mojave Desert until midnight before alerting U.S. marshals in Los Angeles.

The following day, Richard Rosfelder was having lunch with a couple of reporters at a Cleveland restaurant when his beeper went off. Rosfelder was working on some new criminal cases, having finally closed his file on Sturman. He excused himself from the table, called his office, and was told that Reuben Sturman had escaped from prison. Rosfelder hung up the phone and said to himself, "This guy is amazing."

return

NINE MONTHS BEFORE REUBEN STURMAN escaped from federal prison, four young men had gathered in the desert outside Palmdale, California, about an hour north of Los Angeles, to set off bombs. The four men were friends and rode motorcycles together. Jay Brissette and Donald Mares were carpet-layers. Paul Mahn was a petty thief with a long criminal record. Garth Cohen, a veteran of the Gulf War, had assembled the explosive devices — pipe bombs made of steel and polyvinylchloride, stuffed with black powder. Each bomb had two switches, one to arm it, the other to detonate it by remote control. Cohen had worked with plastic explosives, but had never assembled devices like these before. He used inexpensive radio transmitters, the kind found in radio-controlled toy cars, to activate the bombs from a distance. A small metal pin on the bombs would rotate on command, striking two other pins, completing a circuit, and setting off a powerful explosion. The men tested the bombs, which worked exactly as intended. Each detonation gouged a hole in the desert floor and sent rock and dirt flying into the air. Brissette, the leader of the group, now felt confident about using such devices for their next job. They had been hired to damage adult bookstores in Chicago that once belonged to Reuben Sturman.

Sturman did not want to pay the government any money — and he didn't want his associates paying the government either. As soon as

Sturman realized the IRS had gained access to his Swiss bank accounts, he closed them and opened new Swiss accounts. When the government found Sturman's hidden corporate records, which revealed the elaborate structure of his empire, he responded by discarding that structure and creating a new one, transferring assets to a whole new set of offshore corporations. The evidence that Richard Rosfelder had carefully assembled, that was introduced at the tax evasion trial, only offered a snapshot of Reuben Sturman's empire at a particular moment. By the time Sturman was convicted for tax evasion, the companies Rosfelder had discovered no longer existed, and the millions of dollars in their Swiss bank accounts were gone.

The new system for concealing Sturman's assets was by far the most sophisticated yet. All of his companies and bank accounts were now managed solely by intermediaries, by attorneys and trusted friends. Sturman's name did not appear on any documents, and his signature was not necessary for any transactions. His assets were shifted to Panamanian corporations and trusts that used bank accounts in Switzerland, Luxembourg, the Netherlands, Aruba, and the Cayman Islands.

The IRS was demanding nearly $5 million from Reuben Sturman in back taxes. He was determined to thwart every effort to collect it. Sturman terminated his "consulting" agreements with his former managers, so that the IRS could not get hold of any of the money still owed to him. He directed his managers to pay him the same amounts in cash or—if they were uncomfortable with that arrangement—to assign his consulting contracts to offshore corporations. To hide personal expenditures from the IRS, Sturman made all his purchases with a VISA card issued by a Swiss bank, using funds from a Panamanian company. Despite the tax conviction, his war with the government was far from over. When the IRS seized the contents of his Cleveland home and later seized his house in Van Nuys, Sturman secretly bought them back at government auctions, for a pittance, through foreign corporations.

Sturman's new scheme soon encountered a problem: some of his old associates didn't want to fight the government anymore. They no longer shared his crusading zeal. They now thought that tax cases, not obscenity cases, posed the greatest threat to their livelihood. They could pay the IRS and still earn a fortune. Joining another criminal conspiracy seemed like an unnecessary risk. Even those who wanted to keep paying their old boss were scared, caught between the demands of Reuben Sturman and those of the IRS.

When a number of his old managers stopped paying him — or even worse, gave money they owed him to the government instead — Sturman felt betrayed. These were people he had made rich. Now they were stealing from him, acting like real owners. Mel Kamins, who now controlled the Cleveland operation, had started working at the Sovereign News warehouse as a teenager in 1955, carrying boxes. He'd remained loyal to Sturman during the 1989 tax case, refusing to cooperate with the government and going to prison as a result. But he had stopped making payments to Sturman after being visited by Richard Rosfelder. "Whatever you owed Sturman," Rosfelder told Kamins, "you now owe the U.S. government." Sturman was angered by Mel Kamins' decision. It was not just a betrayal, but an expression of disrespect, an acknowledgement that Reuben Sturman had lost his old power. Sturman wrote letters to Kamins asking for the money, reminding him of their past, saying in effect: "After all I've done for you, how could you abandon me?" When emotional appeals failed to persuade him, Sturman began to make threats.

In December, 1991, Jay Brissette, Donald Mares, and Paul Mahn walked into an adult bookstore in Phoenix, Arizona, told the customers to leave, told the clerk not to move, and then destroyed the peep machines with sledgehammers and baseball bats. Tamara Green, the store's owner, had been paying Sturman only half of what he wanted. After her peep booths were busted up, Green phoned Sturman, said, "I got your message," and then resumed paying him the full amount.

Paula Lawrence May and her husband, Roy, controlled Sturman's former operation in Chicago. They had been warned by the IRS not to pay Sturman so much as a dime. One of Chicago's most prominent tax attorneys met with Sturman and Roy May to find a way of getting around the IRS tax lien. Sturman and his attorney suggested that May could purchase the royalty rights to an assortment of hard-core films for a few million dollars, even though the films had little real value.

Roy May listened carefully to the proposal, then turned it down. His wife had already received a prison sentence for tax evasion. May saw no reason to invite more trouble. The Chicago businesses were now held under his name, and Sturman had no legal right to claim any of their proceeds. May told him, essentially, to get lost.

Reuben Sturman contacted his friend Mickey Fein (also known as Herbert Michael Feinberg) in Los Angeles and told him it was time to damage some more stores, first in Chicago, then in Cleveland. Fein had arranged the job in Phoenix. He was in his early sixties, a bit player in the L.A. porn scene, a hustler who bought and sold other people's hard-core material but who'd never made it big. Fein had met Jay Brissette in a carpet store. Now he called Brissette for another job, giving him the names and addresses of eight adult bookstores in Chicago and promising him $60,000 in cash, with a third of the money up front. Fein wanted the peep machines put out of action.

Brissette and his crew decided to use bombs this time, instead of sledgehammers. They figured that bombs, set off from a distance, were less likely to get them caught. They went into the desert and tested Cohen's devices, with success. And then in April, 1992, Brissette, Mares, Mahn, and Joseph Martinez flew from Los Angeles to Milwaukee on a commercial airliner with eight powerful, radio-controlled bombs packed in their luggage. In Milwaukee they rented a car and headed for Chicago.

None of the men had ever been to Chicago before, and so they spent a day driving around town with a map, getting their bearings and looking for their targets. A couple of the adult bookstores were located in bad neighborhoods. They crossed those stores off their list. The men split into two groups, and on April 15 set out to bomb six stores. The plan was to destroy the electrical boxes behind the stores, cutting off power to the peep machines. One bomb went off as planned, behind a bookstore on South Cicero Avenue. Another bomb, in Chicago's Old Town District, proved to be a dud.

As Paul Mahn and Donald Mares drove along Division Street toward another adult bookstore, a bomb exploded in Mares' lap. The bomb had already been armed, and it was probably detonated by stray radio waves in the area — by a traffic light, a police scanner, or perhaps a child's remote-controlled toy. The explosion set off a second bomb in the rented Chevrolet, which caught on fire.

Paul Mahn climbed from the car first, through a window. His head was on fire. Florence Clanton, a middle-aged woman who'd just stepped out of a clothing store, pulled Mahn's coat over his head, extinguishing the flames, and he ran off. Mares stumbled from the vehicle, on fire from above the waist. Clanton grabbed him and put out the flames, but Mares died moments later on the sidewalk. The fire department arrived, as did members of the Chicago bomb squad. They found two more explosive devices in the burning car. One bomb rolled out of a pair of old pants and landed on a bomb squad officer's foot, without exploding.

Mahn somehow made it to the group's meeting place in a Chicago park, and the three surviving bombers returned safely to Los Angeles. But investigators swiftly tracked them down. Brissette had rented the Chevrolet under his own name. Facing long prison terms, the three men began to talk. None of them had heard of Reuben Sturman, but they led the FBI straight to Mickey Fein. He denied any role in the bombings and refused to implicate Sturman. The government doubted his story. Paula and Roy May told the authorities that Sturman had been threatening them and their Chicago businesses. Roy May phoned Sturman after the bombings and said, "I got your message," as FBI agents recorded the call. "I have no idea what you're talking about," Sturman replied.

A few months later, in June, 1992, Sturman headed to the federal prison in Boron with good reason to worry. He was paying Mickey Fein's legal bills—but if Fein decided to cut a deal with the government, Sturman could face a life sentence without parole for the bombings in Chicago, because one of the bombers had died. On the other hand, Sturman had good reason to believe that his prison sentence in the tax case would soon be reduced. He had recently given a Cleveland attorney more than half a million dollars with which to bribe Judge George W. White. The attorney, Sanford Atkin, was a former Miami policeman and a close friend of the judge's. Sturman had paid Atkin $300,000 in the weeks leading up to his sentencing, and Judge White's ruling on the bond issue—that Sturman could remain free, pending appeal — seemed to be proof that the bribes had worked. Days before reporting to the federal prison at Boron, Sturman paid an additional $250,000 to shorten his sentence.

Sanford Atkin, however, had never given any of the money to the judge. Atkin had kept it for himself, all $550,000 of it, investing in certificates of deposit, paying clients whom he'd bilked, making loans to friends, buying real estate and a Cleveland car wash. Judge White's favorable ruling on the bond issue had been a fluke; no bribery ever took place. One month after arriving at Boron, Sturman applied for a reduction in sentence and wrote Atkin a letter, suggesting that a three-year sentence would be okay. "So do your best," Sturman concluded. "I know that you will, and I love you for it." But the judge denied Sturman's request. He applied again, and the judge denied his request again. Atkin flew to California and met with an irate Reuben Sturman in prison. Atkin said Sturman hadn't waited long enough between requests. In the fall of 1992 Sturman asked Judge White, for the third time, to reduce his sentence, sending the letter full of apology and remorse.

When his third request was denied, Sturman realized he'd been conned. His outlook changed considerably. He was sixty-eight years old and didn't want to die in prison. He would have to serve the full ten years, after all — even longer, if Mickey Fein confessed. Sturman had seen paperwork in an office at Boron that said the government was about to transfer him to a maximum-security prison in Colorado, far away from his family. Now was the time to act.

At 8:45 on the evening of December 7, 1992, Sturman jogged across the prison camp's softball field, climbed over a low fence, and dove into the backseat of a car waiting with an open door. After lying on the seat until the coast was clear, Sturman spotted an In-N-Out hamburger stand in the desert and told the driver to stop. As they waited in the drive-through line, a sheriff pulled up right behind them in a squad car. Sturman's driver began to panic, but Sturman told him to relax. If the sheriff had any idea who they were, he said, they would already have been arrested. Reuben Sturman got his hamburger and was driven off into the night.

getting credits

ALTHOUGH THE RISE OF America's porn industry stemmed mainly from market forces, it also reflected a profound shift in public attitudes toward sex, as religious influences gave way to secular ones. For more than five centuries, radical social movements had embraced pornography. In Renaissance Italy, Giovanni Pico Della Mirandola, author of *The Dignity of Man,* the humanist manifesto, also composed pornographic verse. In Paris during the Enlightenment, Denis Diderot, the compiler of the rationalist *Encyclopedia,* also wrote pornographic novels. Sexual freedom and political liberty have long seemed inextricably linked. A similar pattern can be observed in American history, from the libertine ways of Benjamin Franklin to the mid-nineteenth-century utopian communities that practiced "free love." More recently, the youth counterculture of the 1960s transformed the public discourse about sex in the United States, introducing such phrases as "love-in," "wife-swapping," and "sexual revolution." San Francisco led the way in forging a new morality, and underground newspapers there — like the *Ball,* the *Tribe,* the *Organ, Freedom News,* and *Flash Earth* — routinely published sexually explicit material. The city's hippie filmmakers were among the first to give public exhibitions of hard-core films. Although the profit motive quickly infiltrated the Bay Area's porn community, its leading actors and directors often viewed sex as a means of personal and political liberation.

"Nina Hartley" is the stage name of one of the most famous performers in today's sex industry. Hartley grew up in Berkeley during the height of the counterculture, considers herself a radical feminist, and comes from a long line of American iconoclasts. Her grandfather was a member of the Communist Party during the 1930s, a physics professor at the University of Alabama who was fired for being a "premature anti-Fascist." Her grandmother, an English professor at the university, became a real estate agent to support the family. Hartley's father was also a Communist. When he was fired from his job as a San Francisco radio announcer and then blacklisted during the McCarthy era, Hartley's mother supported the family as a biochemist. Nina Hartley was a bookish teenager who discovered sex at a relatively late age. Raised as a feminist to distrust the male gaze, she secretly fantasized about dancing naked. After graduating magna cum laude from San Francisco State with a nursing degree, Hartley decided to become a porn star. Since the early 1980s she has appeared in more than 650 hard-core films. She is a swinger and a proud exhibitionist. For twenty years she lived in a stable, triangular relationship with her first husband—a former leader of the campus radical group, Students for a Democratic Society (SDS)—and another woman. She is now married to Ernest Greene, the editor of *Hustler's Taboo* magazine. "Nina Hartley" is a deliberate creation, a larger-than-life persona designed to convey the idea that a woman can be healthy, strong, and sexually autonomous.

At a video convention in Atlantic City, I watched a long line of male fans waiting patiently for Hartley's autograph, as she stood in five-inch heels and a mini-dress, with painted fingernails and a big hairdo, exuding movie star glamour. When we met a few weeks later for lunch at a bistro in Marina Del Rey, Hartley arrived wearing a white T-shirt, blue jean shorts, no makeup, and horn-rimmed glasses. She looked like an attractive aerobics instructor or a graduate student in sociology at UCLA. We talked about how the sex industry treats its performers and about American attitudes toward sex. "For all the lip service we give to sex being holy and wonderful and spiritual," Hartley told me, "we let Madison Avenue use it to sell spark plugs and dishwashing detergent—to sell anything *but* sex." A great deal of today's porn is not only misogynist, she argued, but also misanthropic, treating men with disrespect. It's a disposable commodity that reveals the culture's deep fear of sex. "The people who run the porn business are not sex radicals," she said with regret; their sex lives at home are extremely conventional. "You'd be surprised how many of the producers and manufacturers are Republicans."

Some women are drawn to the sex industry because they're exhibitionists who love the sex and the attention. Most are attracted by the money. The highest-paid performers, the actresses with exclusive contracts, earn between $80,000 and $100,000 a year for doing about twenty sex scenes and making a dozen or so personal appearances. Only a handful of actresses, however—perhaps ten or fifteen—are signed to such contracts. Other leading stars are paid roughly $1,000 per scene.

A sex scene usually takes about two hours to shoot but can often require waiting around the set for an entire day. The vast majority of porn actresses are "B girls," who earn about $400 to $800 a scene. Most work two or three times a week, doing one scene a day. At the moment, there is an oversupply of women in Southern California hoping to enter the porn industry. Wages have fallen, and some newcomers will work for $150 a scene.

Hartley says a woman's pay is determined by how closely her appearance fits the dominant standard of beauty, by her willingness to do "nasty things," and most importantly, by her novelty. There is a constant demand for new talent. Few actresses last more than a year or two. Hartley warns new performers to avoid overexposure. Hundreds of women are constantly entering and exiting the industry. As in Hollywood, the demand is greatest for fresh-faced actresses in their late teens and early twenties. Although an eighteen-year-old woman cannot legally purchase a beer in Southern California, she can be paid a few hundred dollars to screw half a dozen men in a porn film without breaking any law.

The actors in porn serve mainly as a prop for the female performers. Leading actors earn less money than the top actresses but enjoy much longer careers. Most enter the business in order to have sex with a large number of women. The men are valued primarily for their ability to perform on cue. Perhaps a dozen men consistently display that skill; some have now appeared in more than a thousand hard-core films.

The fear of AIDS pervades the sex industry today. A number of well-known porn stars have contracted the disease, and rumors circulate about others. All performers are now required to undergo monthly AIDS testing. Their test results serve as a passport for work. Given the long period between an initial infection with HIV and the appearance of antibodies which can be detected, it is remarkable that the porn community has not already been devastated by the disease. Because a widespread outbreak has not yet struck, many performers question the conventional wisdom about AIDS and how it is transmitted. Behind these alternative theories lies a great deal of fear, denial, and wishful thinking. Other sexually transmitted diseases are widespread. Drawing upon her experience as a registered nurse, Nina Hartley has published a set of "Health and Hygiene Tips for Adult Performers."

Attempts to form a union for sex workers have met with little success. Most of the performers, according to Hartley, just want to be rich and pay less in taxes: "Solidarity? Brotherhood? Sisterhood? Ha!" Verbal contracts are routinely made and broken by both producers and performers. Checks sometimes bounce. The borderline legal status of the industry makes performers reluctant to seek redress in court. Hartley said that she and many other porn actresses genuinely love the work. The sex and stardom have a strong intrinsic appeal. For women who lack much education and have few marketable skills, the decision to appear in hard-core films is often based on other needs. Although high-priced call girls generally earn more money than porn actresses, performing in a sex scene can prove less of a risk. "You're not going to be arrested," Hartley explained. "You are not going to be hit. You are not going to end up in a car trunk somewhere." Some women enter the industry with a career plan and stick to it. One famous porn star put herself through law school by acting in hard-core films; others have saved money and then quit. But many are drawn to the sex industry by self-loathing and a drug habit. For these women, hard-core videos often become a permanent record of the lowest, most humiliating moments in their life.

Hartley spends about half the year on the road, dancing in strip clubs four to six nights a week. Like many porn stars, that's how she earns the bulk of her income. The huge growth in the hard-core video business during the Reagan era coincided with the opening of large strip clubs all over the country. Hard-core videos now serve as a promotion for live performances. According to Rob Abner—a former analyst at E. F. Hutton who later published *Stripper* magazine, a trade journal—the number of major strip clubs in the United States roughly doubled between 1987 and 1992. Today there are about 2,300 of these clubs nationwide, with annual revenues ranging from $250,000 at a "dump" to more than $5 million at a well-run "gentleman's club." The salaries of featured dancers rose astronomically during the 1990s. The nation's top five or six porn actresses now earn $15,000 to $20,000 a week to dance at strip clubs, doing four twenty-minute shows each night. Another half-dozen porn actresses earn between $8,000 and $15,000 a week. Featured dancers are now paid, in large part, according to the "credits" they have accumulated—their appearances in hard-core films, on video box covers, in men's magazine photo spreads. The bottom of the pay scale for a featured dancer is about $2,000 a week, while a dancer with some porn credits generally starts at about $4,000 a week. In the hierarchy of sex workers, strippers always used to look down at porn stars, viewing their work with distaste. Now strippers from across America are flocking to Southern California and competing for credits in hard-core films.

A block below the Sunset Strip, at William Margold's small apartment, I met a woman who'd just arrived in Los Angeles, hoping to become a porn star. Margold is quite a character, tall and bushy-haired, with a big mustache and a slouch. He has performed in hundreds of hard-core films since the early 1970s, as well as written them, directed them, produced them, and worked as a porn talent scout and as a spokesman for the industry. He has little money, drives a beat-up old Volkswagen bus, and sounds like a journalist for an underground newspaper, which he sometimes is. Before entering the porn business, he was a probation officer in downtown Los Angeles, who started out clean-cut and neatly pressed and wound up looking like a mess, like his "kids." His father was a federal judge. Margold lives in a state of perpetual rebellion, refusing to act his age, which is somewhere in the late fifties. He runs a hotline for young hard-core actors and actresses in distress. His apartment, nicknamed "the bear cave," had hundreds of teddy bears sitting on shelves, near stacks of hard-core videos and posters from his early porn films.

A young woman who called herself "Rose," on account of a certain tattoo, had flown to L.A. from a town in the Deep South, not knowing a soul. Margold had found her a place to stay. She wanted to become a star, a big porn star. Margold told her that it was unlikely, that at best she would be one of many "B girls" — "a lineman" but never "a quarterback." He told her that she was much more personable with her clothes on. Rose had a lovely face and the signs of a hard life in and around her eyes. She was thirty-three and had worked as a bartender at a strip club, as the manager of an escort service, as a stripper, and as half of a lesbian act that performed for $250 an hour at private parties. She had been a drug dealer and a junkie and had tried every drug you could name. Now that she was clean, she wanted to earn some credits and return home as a featured dancer. Then she would bring all her gorgeous stripper friends to Los Angeles and act as their "mamma," their agent, getting them credits in porn. She had been in L.A. for five weeks, and things were not going well.

On her first day in town, a porn agent told Rose to dye her dark hair blond and get a "boob job." She refused. With nowhere else to stay, she slept at the agent's apartment, which was a mistake. He tried to have sex with her, as did one of his friends. Rose landed a few jobs and performed in a number of sex scenes. But she kept losing roles to other actresses, because she would not give sex to get a part. Rose was angry that producers and film company executives were making such demands. It wasn't right; it wasn't "professional." I said the porn business sounded no different from Hollywood, in that respect, and she let loose a tirade. "It's not just the porn business," Rose said. "It's not just the movie business. It's every business. It's the men on the street. If you want a better job, you're supposed to screw the manager. That's how it is, okay? That's how it is, everywhere."

A few months later, I bumped into Margold and asked him what had happened to Rose. He said they'd had a falling-out and didn't talk anymore. She was still in Los Angeles, someplace, but he didn't know where. She had not become a star.

a simple plan of escape

IN MID-DECEMBER, 1992, Richard Rosfelder and Craig Morford plotted their strategy late into the night at a Washington, D.C., hotel. The next day they were going to meet with staff members from the U.S. Marshals' Fugitive Service and discuss Reuben Sturman's escape. Customs officials at the nation's airports and border crossings had been alerted that Sturman might try to flee the country. But most likely he was already gone. Sturman had associates and bank accounts all over the world. Rosfelder and Morford had worried for years that he might go on the run rather than serve time in prison. Again and again, Sturman had proved them wrong. During the four years between his indictment and his tax evasion trial, Sturman left the United

States twenty-one times, visiting Switzerland, Spain, Egypt, Mexico, and the Netherlands, yet faithfully returning his passport to federal officials at the end of every trip, as required by his bond. Thomas Ciehanski, Rosfelder's old partner, thought that Sturman was now hiding in Spain, where a former business partner lived and where extradition would be difficult to arrange. Given his wealth and connections, Sturman could be anywhere. Rosfelder pictured him on a beach, halfway across the world, sipping a cold drink and smoking a cigar.

It seemed like a waste of time to search for Reuben Sturman. Rosfelder and Morford agreed that it made much more sense to look for his accomplices. On the hotel room's television set, the Discovery Channel was showing a documentary on the Mojave Desert. As Morford looked at the barren landscape surrounding Boron's prison camp, at the sand dunes and scattered Joshua trees, he began to doubt some of the elaborate theories other federal officials were proposing: that Sturman had escaped by foot, by helicopter, or by all-terrain vehicle. The nearest town was a good twelve miles from the prison. Morford thought that a simple plan of escape was the most plausible, that someone had driven up to the prison and met Sturman along the road. The next day, at the U.S. marshals' headquarters, Rosfelder and Morford suggested that the best way to find Sturman's accomplices would be to trace his money. Although Rosfelder usually didn't hunt for fugitives, he was assigned to the case. Rosfelder knew more about Sturman's empire than anyone else in the government. The U.S. Marshals' Fugitive Service made the capture of Reuben Sturman one of its top priorities. Henry E. Hudson, who headed the service, was familiar with Sturman's background. Before taking the post, Hudson had served as the chairman of Attorney General Meese's Commission on Pornography.

While Rosfelder looked through bank records, Tony Olivo, the marshal service's fugitive task force investigator in Cleveland, examined the list of visitors and phone calls that Sturman had received in his six months at Boron. Rosfelder and Olivo kept coming across two unfamiliar names: Stephanie and Douglas Friedman.

adam & eve

HILLSBOROUGH, NORTH CAROLINA, is a charming small town in the countryside near Chapel Hill. Its main street extends for two blocks, lined with old buildings that the local historical societies have fought to preserve. There are antiques stores, bookstores, bronze plaques honoring the fallen heroes of the Civil War, a café, and a hardware store that seems to have changed little in half a century. The roughly 5,000 residents of the town have tried hard to maintain its quiet, rural identity, resisting Chapel Hill's more affluent and cosmopolitan pull. Hillsborough is the county seat of Orange County, and the local newspaper is called the *News of Orange.* The town is an odd setting for the headquarters of America's largest mail-order purveyor of condoms, sexual devices, and hard-core videos. PHE Inc., publisher of the Adam & Eve catalogue, is the largest private employer in Hillsborough. The company occupies a modern, three-story office building and warehouse, next to a nursing home and a veterinarian's office. Inside the huge warehouse, shelves thirty feet high hold sexually explicit material, conveyer belts speed merchandise across the building, and automatic sorting machines drop packages into large bins according to the customer's zip code. The day I visited PHE, its mail-order operation seemed high-tech and impressive but surreal. Dainty, white-haired southern women — ladies you could easily imagine singing hymns in a Baptist church — were smiling and chatting and packing brightly colored dildos into boxes.

Philip Harvey, the owner of PHE, could have stepped out of a play by George Bernard Shaw. Harvey is one of the most influential figures in the American sex industry today. The leading producers of hard-core films trek regularly to North Carolina, to visit Harvey and his staff, promote their latest releases, and seek financing for new productions. Harvey is widely respected not only because of his company's huge buying power but also because of his willingness, like Sturman's, to battle the federal government. Harvey was one of the primary targets of the Justice Department's National Obscenity Enforcement Unit, created after the Meese Commission. His stubbornness helped to derail the war on pornography waged by the Reagan and Bush administrations. Few of his associates in the sex industry are aware, however, that Philip Harvey leads a double life. He spends part of each month in Hillsborough, running PHE, and the rest in Washington, D.C., where he runs a nonprofit corporation devoted to AIDS prevention and family planning.

For more than twenty-five years Harvey has managed family planning programs in developing nations and written dozens of articles on population control for academic journals. He has spent millions of dollars earned in Hillsborough to fund nonprofit programs overseas. Harvey currently supervises projects in India, Ethiopia, Brazil, Vietnam, Malaysia, Indonesia, and the Philippines. This dual life often has its ironies. During the late 1980s, while officials at the Justice Department were doing all they could to put Harvey in prison for obscenity violations, officials at the State Department's Agency for International Development were working closely with him to make contraceptives widely available in the Third World.

Harvey has the bearing of a patrician and the slightly rumpled, tweedy appearance of an Ivy League professor, with reading glasses often perched atop his head. He was born in 1942 and raised outside Peoria, Illinois. His father owned a company that manufactured farm equipment. Harvey attended Exeter and then Harvard University, majoring in Slavic languages and literature. After college and a brief stint in the army, he joined the Cooperative for American Relief Everywhere (CARE). Like many idealistic young people in the 1960s, he wanted to experience a different culture and do something useful. CARE sent him to India, where he spent five years distributing American food to schoolchildren throughout the country. Although the amount of food donated by the U.S. government increased each year, the number of Indian schoolchildren in the program increased even faster. Harvey realized that helping India reduce its population growth was ultimately more important than supplying it with surplus grain. After returning from India in 1969 Harvey received a grant from the Ford Foundation to do graduate work in family planning and population control at the University of North Carolina, in Chapel Hill.

As his graduate thesis Harvey submitted a proposal for the mailorder marketing of condoms. His thesis adviser was unaware that what Harvey proposed was a violation of America's obscenity laws. The Comstock Law still prohibited sending contraceptives, or even information about birth control, through the U.S. mail. Undaunted, Philip Harvey and Timothy Black, a British physician and advocate of family planning, set up a mail-order company in 1970 to sell condoms throughout the United States. The firm's questionable legality prevented it from gaining charitable status, and so the two men created a separate nonprofit corporation, Population Services International (PSI), to distribute contraceptives among the poor overseas. Harvey placed ads in college newspapers across the United States, offering condoms through the mail with the pitch: "Sex Is Your Business (Birth Control Is Ours)." Orders started rolling in, and Black soon left for Africa to manage the foreign operation. With the profits from his domestic condom sales, Harvey became a pioneer in the "social marketing" of contraceptives. Instead of relying on overburdened medical and clinical bureaucracies to provide birth control in developing countries, PSI used the same commercial distribution networks that managed to supply even the most remote villages with brand-name consumer goods. High-quality condoms were provided by PSI at low cost to local entrepreneurs, who sold them at a profit. Harvey came to believe that market forces could distribute birth control products more effectively than any government agency.

The ban on selling condoms through the mail was lifted by President Nixon in 1972, and Harvey's business grew. Condoms were still a product with a bad reputation, kept behind the counter at most drugstores. Even *Playboy* refused to run Harvey's condom ads. He came up with all kinds of promotions to change the condom's tawdry image; once a year he offered a multicolored Christmas sampler. He was sued by the State of New York, where condoms could be sold only at pharmacies. The case reached the U.S. Supreme Court, and Harvey won. Following the advice of Julian Simon's classic text, *How to Start and Operate a Mail-Order Business,* Harvey tried to diversify his product line, offering books on birth control, birth control pills, and pregnancy testing through the mail. None of these products sold well. He tried selling leisurewear, digital clocks, and model airplanes to his condom customers, also without success. But every time a book with erotic pictures appeared in his catalogue, the number of orders soared. Harvey started the Adam & Eve catalogue in 1975, offering sexually explicit materials, lingerie, and massage oils, in addition to condoms. When hard-core videos appeared in the catalogue, it became a multi-million-dollar business.

Philip Harvey thought that mail-order was the most socially responsible way to sell sexually explicit material. A mail-order company had few adverse effects on its community. No customers streamed in and out of its building at odd hours. There was none of the criminal activity that adult bookstores often attracted. Customers could obtain what they wanted discreetly. And people who were offended by sexually explicit material were not confronted with public displays of porn or lurid storefront advertising. Hard-core videos could be shipped throughout the country from North Carolina, unobtrusively, in plain brown envelopes. But the same factors that made Adam & Eve a great success also made it a leading target of President Reagan's campaign against pornography. In the eyes of those who opposed obscenity, there was no proper way to distribute hard-core videos. As Anthony Comstock had warned more than a century before, the mail was "the most powerful agent" for disseminating obscene materials, because "it *goes everywhere* and is *secret*."

By the mid-1980s, Charles H. Keating, Jr., was no longer just a Cincinnati attorney who crusaded against porn. He'd become one of the leading fund-raisers for the Republican party, head of the American Continental Corporation, and owner of the Lincoln Savings & Loan. Keating lobbied President Reagan for another national commission on pornography, one that would reach the correct conclusions this time. Both the Meese Commission and the federal legislation that stemmed from it were greatly influenced by attorneys at Keating's antipornography group, now called Citizens for Decency through Law (CDL). Indeed, the Justice Department's National Obscenity Enforcement Unit had originally been proposed by CDL. When it was formed in 1987, CDL attorneys joined the staff. After more than thirty years of campaigning against pornography, Keating had finally gained the power to get something done. His desire to see the nation's porn merchants "rot in prison" now had the full support of the president, the attorney general, and the Justice Department.

The Supreme Court's ruling on obscenity in 1973, which gave local communities the power to enforce their own standards of decency, had originally been intended to protect conservative districts from the looser morality of liberal ones. The National Obscenity Enforcement Unit tried to use the ruling to achieve a very different aim, attempting to impose the morality of conservative towns on the rest of the nation. The unit commissioned studies to discover where juries in the United States were most likely to vote for obscenity convictions — and then it sought the indictment of national distributors, under federal law, in those districts. H. Robert Showers, the head of the unit, was a former assistant U.S. attorney from North Carolina. He thought *Playboy* fit the legal definition of obscenity, hoped to rid the nation of soft-core porn, as well as hard-core material, and often signed his official correspondence "Yours Truly in Christ."

With Project Wormwood, the Reagan Justice Department targeted Southern California's major producers of hard-core videos. Instead of indicting them in California, where juries were unlikely to convict them, the government sent federal agents from Arkansas, Alabama, Oklahoma, and Florida to a porn industry convention, posing as video store owners. These agents sought out hard-core producers and solicited their products. When hard-core videos arrived by mail at the phony stores in conservative communities — such as Tallahassee, Florida; Tulsa, Oklahoma; and Aberdeen, Mobile, and Birmingham, Alabama — federal prosecutors indicted the California porn companies for interstate transportation of obscene material. Dozens of hard-core producers and distributors were indicted in this way. Wormwood failed, however, to destroy the adult film industry. Through plea bargains and the intervention of sympathetic federal judges, most of the defendants received short sentences and/or large fines. "We always used to worry about being extorted by the mob," one hard-core producer told me, while discussing Wormwood. "Then all of a sudden it was the federal government hitting us up for money."

Project Postporn was aimed at mail-order companies that sold sexually explicit material. The basic strategy was outlined by a CDL attorney in 1983, then described at greater length two years later by Brent Ward, one of Utah's U.S. attorneys, in a memo to Attorney General Meese. Ward argued that mail-order companies should be hit with "multiple prosecutions (either simultaneous or successive) in all levels of government in many locations." He thought that a single company should face as many as thirty-five different criminal prosecutions at once, all over the United States. The idea, as later adopted by the Justice Department, was not to secure a conviction through an obscenity trial, but to mount so many prosecutions at once that a mail-order company would be forced out of business simply by the cost of mounting a defense. The federal government had almost unlimited resources for such a fight; mail-order companies did not. The U.S. Attorney's Manual permitted such multiple-district prosecutions only in unusual situations, but it discouraged the strategy because of its "unfairness" to the defendant. At the direction of Assistant Attorney General William Weld, the Justice Department later rewrote its manual and "encouraged" multiple prosecutions in obscenity cases.

On May 29, 1986, Philip Harvey's warehouse in North Carolina was raided by approximately thirty federal and state law enforcement agents, including at least one federal agent from Utah. PHE's employees were kept in the building all day for questioning, and their personal belongings were searched. Harvey was caught completely by surprise. Members of the Christian Action League of North Carolina had been ordering Adam & Eve catalogues for years and then complaining to federal officials. But the FBI had investigated Harvey's company in 1984 and had determined that nothing it sold was obscene. Indeed, local FBI agents refused to participate in the raid on Harvey's warehouse. U.S. postal inspectors were recruited instead, some of them joining the investigation with reluctance.

When Harvey's attorneys, John Mintz and Wade Smith (a former FBI administrator), met with federal prosecutors from Utah and North Carolina to explore a possible plea bargain, they were told that as part of any deal, Harvey would have to stop selling hard-core and soft-core videos. He would have to stop selling books like *The Joy of Sex*. Although financially secure and engaged in meaningful, nonprofit work, Harvey wouldn't accept that sort of deal. He refused to be bullied by the government. "There comes a point in life," Harvey later recalled, "when you simply have to say *enough is enough.*"

Carl Fox, the district attorney in Orange County, North Carolina, thought that prosecuting Philip Harvey for obscenity would be a waste of time and taxpayer money. But George Hunt, the district attorney in neighboring Alamance County, disagreed and indicted Harvey on eight counts of disseminating obscene material under state law. Federal prosecutors assisted Hunt's prosecution. If Hunt could prove that Harvey's merchandise violated the community standards of his own state, obscenity convictions might be easier to obtain elsewhere. In March, 1987, Harvey went on trial in Alamance County. Half of the jurors were born-again Christians, and one was a minister's son. The prosecution showed hard-core videos in the courtroom, including a lengthy orgy scene that featured porn star Vanessa Del Rio. Harvey's attorney argued that this material appealed to a healthy, not a prurient, interest in sex. He introduced no evidence in Harvey's defense. The jury deliberated for five minutes and then found Harvey not guilty on all counts. "It just seems like the government is trying too hard to regulate what we look at," Robert West, the foreman of the jury, told the *Greensboro News and Record*. Support from the local community gave Harvey a tremendous boost, but his troubles were far from over. "We must regain momentum after the Adam & Eve verdict," one U.S. attorney in North Carolina wrote to his staff, "and come with as many indictments as possible."

The multiple prosecutions of Project Postporn were coordinated by a dozen attorneys at the National Obscenity Enforcement Unit. H. Robert Showers selected the mail-order companies to be targeted, chose the districts in which to prosecute them, set the timetables for prosecution, and demanded approval of all search warrants, indictments, and plea bargains. Postporn was a centrally organized, nationwide effort by the federal government to stop the distribution of all sexually explicit materials through the mail. It achieved a good deal of success. Karl Brussel, his wife, and his son, the operators of a mail-order company called Brussel/Pak Ventures, were indicted in four different districts, with trials set to begin at intervals of two weeks or less. Brussel accepted a plea bargain in which he promised to shut down his business, never sell sexually explicit materials again, and serve a year in federal prison. Avram C. Freedberg, the owner of a Connecticut mail-order company, faced pending indictments in Connecticut, Mississippi, Indiana, and Delaware. When he challenged the Justice Department's tactics, the obscenity unit threatened to indict his wife as well. Freedberg accepted a plea bargain, dissolved his company, and promised never to promote, sell, or distribute predominantly sexual material again. Five other mail-order companies were driven out of business through similar plea bargains — without any judicial ruling that what they sold was obscene.

Aware that federal grand juries in Utah, Kentucky, and North Carolina were investigating Adam & Eve, Philip Harvey struck back. He sued the Justice Department, asserting that its threat of multiple prosecutions abridged his First Amendment rights. In July, 1990, U.S. District Court Judge Joyce Hens Green ruled that the government was indeed trying to suppress "constitutionally protected activities through the use of harassment." Judge Green issued a preliminary injunction that prevented the Justice Department from prosecuting Harvey in more than one district at a time. The Justice Department responded a few weeks later, indicting Harvey on obscenity charges in Utah — even though his company had not sent any catalogues or merchandise to Utah in more than four years. Harvey challenged the indictment in federal court. On May 26, 1992, the Tenth Circuit Court of Appeals dismissed Harvey's Utah obscenity indictment, declaring that there was "substantial evidence" that the Justice Department had used "repeated criminal prosecutions to chill the exercise of First Amendment rights." Harvey had forced the government to abandon its threats of multiple prosecutions, and he had avoided an obscenity conviction. But his victory was not complete. The Justice Department attacked on a new front, one month before President George H. W. Bush left office, raiding Harvey's warehouse again and seizing a list of his Alabama customers. In a plea bargain with federal prosecutors in Alabama, Harvey later confessed to having violated U.S. postal regulations by using the wrong-sized typeface on his envelopes in 1985, a misdemeanor punished with a $250,000 fine.

Although battling the Reagan and Bush administrations cost Harvey more than $3 million in legal fees, Project Postporn actually helped his company. It wiped out many of his mail-order competitors and dissuaded others from entering the business. About 30 million copies of the Adam & Eve catalogue are now distributed each year in the United States, attracting more than 2 million customers. Most of these customers are white, middle class, married, and suburban. Adam & Eve no longer sends catalogues to the rural areas of some southern states. Customers from those areas have complained, but Harvey isn't seeking another fight with the government. Before including any new product in his catalogue, he now submits it to a group of consultants who belong to the American Association of Sex Educators, Counselors and Therapists. An independent reviewer must conclude that a product is not harmful before Adam & Eve will sell it. Harvey considers the review process valuable not only from a legal point of view but also for his company's morale: three-quarters of PHE's employees are women.

In 1990 Harvey began to produce sex education videos, and his company has become the leader in that field, advertising in mainstream magazines such as *Rolling Stone* and the *Atlantic Monthly*. Harvey feels grateful to have survived an assault by groups who claimed to have "the righteousness of the Lord and the might of the U.S. government" on their side. He still travels regularly to developing nations to meet with the administrators of his family planning projects. One of our conversations was interrupted by a call from Addis Ababa. Harvey now distributes oral rehydration salts in Ethiopia, for children with severe diarrhea, as part of his overseas social marketing program. And he recently added "The Nina Hartley Collection," a line of products endorsed by the star, to his catalogue. The Nina Hartley Love Doll sells for $149.95, batteries not included.

bribery and extortion

ON FEBRUARY 9, 1993, AT 7:30 A.M., three U.S. marshals entered a small apartment in Anaheim, California, with a pass key. "Hey, Rube!" one of the marshals yelled, startling Reuben Sturman, who was alone and asleep in bed. On a nearby dresser, there was a loaded .38-caliber revolver in an open briefcase. Sturman raised his hands and did not resist arrest. For the previous five weeks, he'd been living at this rented, furnished apartment under the name Abe Levine. The neighbors had assumed he was a retiree. Instead of fleeing the country, Sturman chose to hide out a few miles from Disneyland.

The government has never revealed exactly how it found Sturman. Richard Rosfelder and Craig Morford told me about searching through bank records and phone logs, about a hidden camera aimed at a Los Angeles post office box, about old-fashioned detective work and tips from unnamed sources. Sturman thought he'd been betrayed by his new secretary, Stephanie Friedman, who was at the Cleveland offices of the Organized Crime Strike Force on the morning he was captured.

Stephanie Friedman was the daughter of Mickey ("the Dwarf") Friedman, the owner of an adult movie theater in Ohio. After her father died, she'd called Reuben Sturman in the spring of 1991. She was in her mid-twenties. Sturman invited her and her brother Douglas to California, bought them airplane tickets, and put them up at his home in Van Nuys. Sturman found Stephanie Friedman a job in the art department at Doc Johnson, where she worked for a couple of months before becoming his personal assistant. Soon she was keeping track of his complicated financial arrangements. Checks arrived from all over the United States, made out to various foreign corporations — to Amphora Ltd., the Fima Finance and Management Corporation, Concorde Development, the Hispano American Finance and Holding Company. Friedman noted the arrival of these checks in a green ledger book, photocopied them, endorsed them with a signature stamp, and then mailed them to Switzerland, Luxembourg, and the Netherlands, for deposit in various bank accounts. Sturman explained to her that the U.S. government was his enemy, that this system was designed to lead investigators into dead ends, that finding one account would not reveal the existence of the others.

During a three-month period in 1992, $445,000 was sent overseas by Friedman, then wired back to the United States, often into the trust account of Sturman's Beverly Hills law firm — another innovative method of money laundering. These payments continued after Sturman went to prison. He called Friedman at least once a day from Boron, and she visited him every other week. In November, 1992, she helped open a bank account in Los Angeles for a company called Escape Inc. Her brother Douglas picked Sturman up on the road outside the prison, drove him to the In-N-Out burger stand, and later dropped him off, around midnight, at an intersection in Encino, a wealthy suburb in the San Fernando Valley. Stephanie Friedman cooked meals for Sturman while he was on the run and did his laundry. Her brother gave Sturman rides and placed bets for him.

When Stephanie and Douglas Friedman were subpoenaed to appear before a Cleveland grand jury, Sturman's wife, Naomi Delgado, drove them to the L.A. airport and told them to lie. If reporters ask where you're headed after your testimony, Delgado joked, tell them you're going to Disneyland. According to Rosfelder and Morford, the Friedmans were prepared to lie before the grand jury when Reuben Sturman was captured. After hearing the news, the two became white as a ghost, consulted with their attorney, and then agreed to cooperate. Stephanie Friedman told Rosfelder and Morford about the new set of offshore corporations and bank accounts, about the payments made in defiance of the IRS, about the escape, about the attempt to bribe Judge White. And while Rosfelder and Morford were still reeling from these revelations, she told them that Sturman and his wife had tampered with the jury during the tax evasion trial. The suggestive outfits that Naomi Delgado had worn to court were part of an attempt to seduce a juror.

For days in that Cleveland courtroom, Delgado had smiled and winked at one of the male jurors, an auto mechanic in his early twenties. The juror had no idea that this beautiful admirer was the lead defendant's wife. During a recess, as the juror called his girlfriend on a pay phone, someone handed him a note. On it there was the address of a restaurant, an appointed time, and a lipstick kiss. While the case was still under deliberation, the juror met Sturman's wife for dinner at the restaurant, thinking that life was too good to be true. He became uncomfortable, however, as Delgado began to discuss the case, suggesting that Sturman was innocent. After the meal, the juror grew even more uneasy, as Delgado flirted with him in the backseat of a Mercedes driven by Sturman's bodyguard. Delgado later told a friend she would have done anything to help her husband; but that did not prove necessary. The juror accepted only a kiss on the cheek before getting out of the car at his parents' house, where he still lived. He refused to meet

Delgado again, tried to avoid her subsequent phone calls, and voted to convict on all counts.

Hearing about the jury-tampering scheme made Richard Rosfelder feel slightly ill. While Rosfelder had sat in the courtroom, confident about the evidence he'd painstakingly assembled for years, Reuben Sturman had managed to get to one of the jurors, during deliberations, without the government finding out. More than three years had passed since the tax trial, yet the young juror had never said a word to authorities about his dinner and his phone conversations with Sturman's wife. The plan was so crazy, Rosfelder thought, it could have worked. A hung jury would have been a disaster for the government — and a different juror might have eagerly accepted sex or money in exchange for a vote of not guilty.

Stephanie and Douglas Friedman cooperated fully with the government, testifying before a grand jury and leading investigators to a storage unit in Van Nuys where Sturman's latest financial records were hidden. In return for their testimony, the government did not file any charges against them. The Friedmans were later given new identities and relocated through the Justice Department's Witness Protection Program.

Rosfelder soon found himself immersed once again in the minutiae of bearer bonds, Liberian corporations, and Swiss bank accounts. One of the documents that Stephanie Friedman provided was a six-page list of the people who were still sending money to Reuben Sturman, despite the IRS tax lien. The list was in Sturman's own handwriting, and it included some of the most prominent names in the sex industry. While sitting in prison, Sturman had secretly earned at least $150,000 a month. Within weeks of his capture, the IRS raised the amount of the back taxes that Sturman owed from $4.9 million to more than $29 million — making him perhaps the largest individual tax evader in American history. Rosfelder went down the list, contacting Sturman's associates, making it clear that their checks should now be made out to the Internal Revenue Service. And the "cream" that had been skimmed for years from Sturman's peep machines started flowing into the U.S. Treasury.

Hoping to avoid a prison term, Naomi Delgado agreed to help the government's investigation of the attempt to bribe Judge White. Federal officials had no reason to believe that White was involved in the scheme, but they needed to make sure. Not long after escaping from Boron, Sturman had called Sanford Atkin on a cell phone, furious about the half a million dollars that Atkin had clearly stolen from him. Delgado arranged to meet Atkin, wearing a hidden microphone. Atkin, no doubt relieved that her husband was behind bars again, spoke freely to Delgado about the plan to bribe the judge. Their conversation provided strong evidence that Atkin had received money from Sturman to pay for a reduced sentence. An extensive investigation subsequently found that Judge White had no role in the crime and no knowledge of the promises being made by Sanford Atkin.

On March 10, 1993, Reuben Sturman was indicted in Chicago on ten counts of extortion and conspiracy. Under federal law, he faced a possible life sentence, without parole, because of the bomber's death. Prosecutors had offered Sturman a reduced sentence in return for a guilty plea and information about his ties to the Cosa Nostra. Sturman dismissed the offer, saying there were no mob ties to discuss. When the trial began in August, 1993, Naomi Delgado was one of the prosecution's key witnesses. Sturman had threatened to harm Roy and Paula May's children, Delgado testified, and to burn down their house, if the Mays did not pay him what they owed. But Delgado became distraught during cross-examination, breaking down in tears and claiming that the prosecutors in Cleveland had pressured her to implicate Sturman. "I've known Reuben for fourteen years," she said, "and I've never known him to hurt anybody."

After two days of deliberation the jury convicted Sturman of conspiring to commit extortion but found him innocent of direct involvement in the bombings. The jurors believed that Sturman had hired men to destroy peep booths; the evidence that he knew explosives would be used was less convincing. Six weeks later, on October 26, 1993, Naomi Delgado was indicted for tampering with a juror and for instructing the Friedmans to mislead the grand jury. Her lawyer accused the government of bad faith, asserting that her cooperation had been given with the expectation that she would not face charges. Attorneys at Cleveland's Organized Crime Strike Force were less than pleased with Delgado's testimony; they had never committed to any deal and suspected that Delgado was still concealing some of Sturman's assets. Jury tampering was a serious crime, and the government decided to punish her for it. Sturman was enraged by his wife's indictment. "They want me and everyone around me," he later told a reporter for Cleveland's *Plain Dealer.* "I'm surprised they didn't indict my six-year-old kid."

Sturman was also indicted for jury tampering and for telling the Friedmans to lie. At a hearing before a federal magistrate, he requested a court-appointed attorney. Adam Bourgeois, an old friend, had represented him for free during the trial in Chicago. Sturman now claimed to be broke, saying that legal fees and the IRS tax lien had completely wiped him out. In a financial statement submitted to the court, Reuben Sturman declared that the total value of his liquid assets was roughly $10. The federal magistrate granted Sturman's request, appointing a public defender to represent him.

On June 17, 1994, Sturman appeared before U.S. District Judge Paul Plunkett for sentencing in the Chicago extortion case. Plunkett gave him the minimum sentence recommended by the federal guidelines — nineteen years and five months in prison, without parole. Sturman was almost seventy at the time. The judge refused to impose a large fine, as demanded by the government. Sturman told the court that he was penniless. "All I've got is my prison commissary account," he said, "and I defy anybody to prove otherwise."

a smut-peddler who cares

LARRY FLYNT HAS LONG PERSONIFIED, to a great many people, everything that is evil about the American sex industry. Flynt is just the sort of man the obscenity laws were meant to convict. For almost thirty years his flagship publication, *Hustler* magazine, has defied authority and good taste, setting out to offend as many Americans as possible, publishing scatological humor that demeans Christians, Jews, Muslims, Asian Americans, women, and homosexuals. An infamous *Hustler* cover showed a woman being fed into a meat grinder, above the caption "Grade A Pink." Flynt has relished playing the infidel, the nation's id unleashed, arriving at one court appearance in a diaper made out of the American flag, serving five months in federal prison for shouting obscenities at the justices of the U.S. Supreme Court, running for president as a Republican in 1984 with the campaign slogan "A Smut-Peddler Who Cares." Organized religion — and evangelical Christianity, in particular — has been the target of some of Flynt's harshest attacks. For a number of years, Jesus Christ was listed on *Hustler*'s masthead as publisher of the magazine. During the 1980s the Reverend Jerry Falwell sued Flynt for $45 million in damages after a *Hustler* parody suggested that Falwell had committed incest in an outhouse with his mother. The case eventually reached the Supreme Court, and Flynt won with a ruling that afforded constitutional protection for satire.

Flynt's office is on the top floor of a modern building, sheathed in black glass, overlooking Beverly Hills. The office is huge and dimly lit, filled with antiques, oil paintings, bronze sculptures, and Tiffany lamps. It feels like the lair of a Victorian railway magnate. When I visited, Flynt sat behind a massive desk, on which the latest issues of his various magazines were carefully arranged in rows. He wore a dark three-piece suit. His auburn hair was slicked back. He was courteous, reflective, and perfectly lucid. On the basis of his looks and his manner, he could have been the president of the Cincinnati Rotary Club. When we began our conversation, his voice was weak, and his hand shook as he raised a cup of water to his mouth. But as we spoke about some of his old friends and enemies, Flynt's voice grew stronger and the fire returned to his eyes.

Larry Flynt had known Sturman for decades, considered him a good man and a dear friend. He could not understand why Sturman had remained in California after his escape instead of fleeing the country. Nobody could; it just didn't make sense. Sturman's downfall saddened Flynt. His imprisonment was a victory for the wrong side and, given Flynt's many brushes with the law, had an added chill — like a bad accident narrowly avoided. Charles Keating's fate, on the other hand, brought a smile to Larry Flynt's face. Keating had tried to get Flynt thrown in prison for years, using all his influence with Ohio prosecutors to have *Hustler* banned in Cincinnati and its owner indicted for obscenity. The two men had battled often, each embodying what the other despised most. Flynt had always thought Keating was a liar and a fraud—and now the government agreed.

When Keating's Lincoln Savings & Loan crashed, becoming the largest bank failure in American history and leaving taxpayers with a debt of $2.6 billion, his antipornography organization was engulfed in the scandal. During a three-year period in the mid-1980s, Keating had shifted $840,000 from Lincoln Savings & Loan and its holding company to Citizens for Decency through Law, as the savings bank teetered on the verge of collapse. CDL became defunct in 1989. The following year Father Bruce Ritter—an influential member of the Meese Commission and winner of the first annual "Charles H. Keating, Jr., Award" for promoting decency—resigned from his position at Covenant House, a New York shelter for homeless teens, amid accusations of financial and sexual impropriety. Father Ritter, who'd urged the Meese Commission and the U.S. government to condemn homosexuality, had allegedly used Covenant House funds to have sex with young male prostitutes. Keating was now in federal prison; Ritter had retired to a monastery in disgrace; and Flynt was in a big new office, feeling vindicated and delighted and ready to send *Hustler* into cyberspace.

Larry Flynt imagines a future in which the television set and the personal computer have merged. Americans will soon lie in bed, he told me, cruising the Internet with their remote controls and ordering hard-core films at the push of a button. Flynt had recently started a new magazine called *Hustler Hard Drive.* He thought hard-core videos would soon become obsolete, replaced first by DVDs and, ultimately, by porn on the World Wide Web. Every new delivery system for adult material offered the consumer greater anonymity during the transaction. In Flynt's view, the Internet would combine the video store's diversity of choice with the privacy of buying through the mail.

The distribution of pornography through the Internet has indeed soared in recent years. Porn has once again been at the forefront of technological innovation, pioneering the use of streaming video, Java-based methods of transmitting footage, and encryption for secure credit card purchases via the Internet. Americans now spend about $1 billion a year for online pornography. Surfing the Web to view explicit images or to chat about sex with strangers has become a daily routine for millions. In 2000 a survey found that 31.9 percent of the nation's men and 10.5 percent of its women had visited a sexually oriented Web site. That same year, a poll conducted by *Christianity Today* magazine found that 27 percent of America's pastors sought out porn on the Internet anywhere from "a few times a year" to "a couple of times a month or more."

Easy and discreet access to pornography online has accelerated the decline of sex magazines. Nude photographs on the printed page now seem woefully obsolete. *Penthouse* is teetering on the verge of bankruptcy. *Playboy* is losing money, and *Hustler*'s circulation dropped steadily in the 1990s. Larry Flynt has diversified the holdings of his company, introducing consumer magazines, producing and distributing hard-core videos, and earning revenue from a *Hustler* Web site. But Flynt's brave new world of porn may eventually obviate the need for pornographers. In 1997 perhaps 22,000 Web sites offered sexually explicit images for free; today the number is closer to 300,000. Hardcore professionals are rapidly being displaced by amateurs. It has become increasingly difficult to earn money from pornography on the Internet—and almost impossible to control what is being posted. Flynt told me that he was shocked by some of the material he'd downloaded. "Some of the stuff on there," he said, "I mean, even I wouldn't publish it."

As of this writing, every legal effort to restrict pornography on the Internet has failed. The Communication Decency Act was ruled unconstitutional by the Supreme Court in 1997; five years later the court struck down the Child Online Protection Act. Both measures were deemed too broad in scope, potentially limiting access to material that is sexually explicit but not obscene. The regulatory scheme proposed by President Nixon's Commission on Pornography and Obscenity more than three decades ago—a proposal vehemently attacked by antipornography groups—would have imposed much tougher restrictions on the distribution of hard-core material than those in place today. The commission argued that adults should be allowed to buy porn, but that strict limits should be placed on how it could be marketed and where it could be sold. In some American cities hard-core videos are now openly displayed at newsstands, beside copies of *Teen People* and *Popular Mechanics*.

The Clinton administration largely abandoned efforts to enforce the obscenity laws, discontinuing the policies of the Reagan and Bush administrations. The National Obscenity Enforcement Unit had already been renamed the Child Exploitation and Obscenity Unit, reflecting a change in emphasis. Child pornography cases were given a high priority, while mainstream porn distributors were mostly left alone. The election of George W. Bush to the presidency, however, has raised fears in the sex industry that the Justice Department may launch a new crackdown. During the 2000 campaign Bush said he would "insist on vigorously enforcing federal antipornography laws." Attorney General John Ashcroft invited prominent opponents of pornography to his office not long after taking the job. The Comstock Law remains on the books, and obscene speech is still not protected by the First Amendment. Under the RICO statutes the government can seize an entire video store when a single video is ruled obscene.

Paul Cambria, one of the sex industry's leading attorneys, recently composed a list of things that hard-core producers and distributors might want to avoid in the current legal climate. "Do not include any of the following," Cambria's list begins, spelling out some new rules of porn etiquette. "No bukkake . . . No food used as sex object. No peeing unless in a natural setting . . . No coffins. No blindfolds. No wax dripping . . . Toys are OK if shot is not nasty . . . No black men–white women themes."

Larry Flynt thinks children should be strictly denied access to sexually explicit material. But he believes that adults can safely read any book or see any movie without risk of being corrupted, and that the obscenity laws are an insult to the intelligence of the American people. Flynt says that if the nation's obscenity laws were ever rescinded, the amount of hard-core material in the United States would skyrocket — but not for long. Once the taboo is finally lifted, once porn loses the aura of a forbidden vice, people will gradually lose interest in it. After a huge rise in popularity, Flynt argues, "the whole bottom would drop out of the porn market." Within a decade of overturning the obscenity laws, he claims, the size of the American sex industry would decline to a fraction of what it is today.

Bruce A. Taylor is president and chief counsel of the National Law Center for Children and Families. Taylor's experience with obscenity cases dates back to 1973, when he was a volunteer law clerk at the Cleveland prosecutor's office, helping to investigate Reuben Sturman. Taylor served as the general counsel for the CDL in the early 1980s and later became a senior trial attorney at the Justice Department's obscenity unit. He prosecuted Sturman in the Las Vegas obscenity trial. The National Law Center for Children and Families strongly supports keeping children away from sexually explicit material on the Internet. Taylor thinks that Larry Flynt's predictions are absurd, that eliminating the nation's obscenity laws would be an unmitigated disaster. Taylor opposes hard-core porn because, among other reasons, it depends upon prostitution. After almost thirty years of fighting obscenity, he still can't believe what some people will do for money. No matter how well meaning Philip Harvey may seem to be, Taylor considers him a "pimp for the porn industry." Bruce Taylor warned me not to be fooled by Flynt: "Of course people in the business want to see it legalized!"

Larry Flynt's theory—that legalizing porn will eventually reduce the demand for porn—is not as outlandish as it may seem. That is exactly what happened in Denmark a generation ago. In 1969 Denmark became the first nation in the world to rescind its obscenity laws, an act taken after much deliberation and study. According to Vagn Greve, a former director of the Institute of Criminal Law and Criminology at the University of Copenhagen, when Denmark's obscenity laws were overturned, there was a steep rise in the consumption of porn, followed by a long, steady decline. "Ever since then," Greve told me, "the market for pornography has been shrinking." Porn sales remain high in Copenhagen mainly because of purchases by foreigners. Greve's colleague at the institute, the late Berl Kutchinsky, studied the effects of legalized pornography in Denmark for more than twenty-five years. In a survey of Copenhagen residents a few years after the "porno wave" had peaked, Kutchinsky found that most Danes regarded porn as "uninteresting" and "repulsive." Subsequent research confirmed these findings. "The most common immediate reaction to a one-hour pornography stimulation," Kutchinsky concluded, "was *boredom*."

what mobsters do

REUBEN STURMAN SPENT A YEAR at a maximum-security prison in Lompoc, California, before being transferred to F.C.I. Manchester, a medium-security prison located in a remote part of Kentucky. Few of his old friends from the sex industry bothered to visit him. As porn companies signed distribution deals with well-known, publicly traded corporations, Sturman increasingly seemed like a relic from a shady era that most industry figures wanted to forget. On October 27, 1997, Sturman died alone at a prison hospital in Lexington, Kentucky. A spokeswoman said the cause of death was "heart and kidney failure." Although the *Washington Post* ran a brief obituary, neither the *New York Times* nor any of the major television networks reported Sturman's death. The most heartfelt epitaph was offered by the *Chattanooga Free Press*. "The smut lord is dead," the paper noted on its editorial page. "But the evil he and his court-coddled colleagues have done—the degradation of our nation's culture and the corruption of our youth—lives on." After a funeral service in San Francisco, attended by a handful of family members, Reuben Sturman's remains were cremated and scattered over the Pacific Ocean.

The Justice Department still won't reveal what was in the secret dossier submitted to the Swiss government or in the documents outlining Sturman's ties to the "upper echelons" of organized crime. When I pushed Craig Morford for details of Sturman's relationship with the Cosa Nostra, suggesting that the government's refusal to disclose that information raised doubts about its accuracy, Morford said the evidence of organized crime links was irrefutable. And he suggested that I was missing the point. "Why do we target organized crime?" he asked. "What is it that mobsters do? Well, they extort money. They resort to violence when they don't get their way. They corrupt the system by trying to bribe judges, by trying to fix juries. That is why we go after the mob." In Morford's opinion, whatever Reuben Sturman may have been in the beginning of his career, by the end he'd turned into exactly what the government always said he was.

Richard Rosfelder retired from the IRS in 1996, having spent two decades on the Sturman case. He is now a private investigator in Cleveland, specializing in white-collar crime and working again with his former IRS partner, Thomas Ciehanski, among others. "Sturman created an illusion about what this was all about," Rosfelder says, "that he was a great businessman, that he was a real intelligent guy, that he was surrounded at his big parties by friends. Well, there was none of that happening. When it became beneficial for people to dump on him, they did. It was all about the money." Rosfelder would like to think that Sturman died broke. There is evidence that, before heading to prison, Sturman found it increasingly difficult to get hold of whatever wealth he still possessed. He borrowed money from family members and associates to buy back his Van Nuys home at a government auction. He borrowed $100,000 for one of the payoffs intended to bribe Judge White. His lifestyle following the escape was hardly extravagant. But the question of whether Reuben Sturman died a wealthy man or a pauper remains unanswered.

Rosfelder concedes that Sturman may have stashed millions of dollars in overseas accounts that the IRS never found. The Swiss bank accounts that Rosfelder discovered were accounts regularly being used to launder money. There may have been other accounts, many others, in which Sturman simply parked his money. Rosfelder prefers not to dwell on the possibility that large amounts of Sturman's money or gold are still hidden away in foreign banks. "That would make my investigation seem like it didn't really get to the heart of the matter," Rosfelder says. "And I don't want that to be the case."

just a harmless old man

WHEN I VISITED F.C.I. MANCHESTER IN 1996, the place looked more like a corporate headquarters than a penitentiary, with cheery postmodern architecture, atriums, skylights, and white walls. The prison is set amid lush green hills in the heart of the Daniel Boone National Forest. The nearest town of any real size is London, Kentucky, about thirty miles to the west, home of the World Chicken Festival. It feels a long way from Cleveland, Zurich, or Southern California. For miles in every direction, there are hills and trees and not much else. The facility is surrounded by two chain-link fences topped by large rolls of razor wire. A corrections officer in a pickup truck slowly cruises the perimeter, day and night, holding a shotgun.

Reuben Sturman was seventy-one years old but seemed much younger. He arrived promptly for our meeting, crossing the prison grounds with a jauntiness in his step, wearing khaki work clothes and new sneakers. His hair was gray and cropped short, as was his beard, though his eyebrows were dark brown. He had a firm handshake and a strong air of authority, like a proud, recently deposed head of state. He was charming and funny, full of life, undimmed. But once or twice, when I asked a question that he didn't like, Sturman gave me a steely look that I will not soon forget.

Sturman's anger at the U.S. government was palpable and intense. He thought the government had treated his wife "abominably," sending her to a medium-security prison, not a prison camp, for two years, leaving their young daughter in the care of grandparents. The government also wanted to seize his wife's house and her car. It had always tried to do that sort of thing, and now it had the power. Whenever federal agents raided his Cleveland warehouse, they came en masse, dozens of them, trying to intimidate his employees. They would take things and mess the place up. The government had behaved that way from the very beginning, with *Sex Life of a Cop*. "They were scum," he said of the federal agents. "They really were, and still are, a terrible bunch of people. But that's the way life is. I wasn't going to cry over that. As bad as they were, I was going to beat them every time."

Fifteen years after the IRS gained access to his Swiss accounts, Sturman still felt indignant about the entire episode, as though he had been cheated out of a victory, out of something that was rightfully his. "Rosfelder's a horrible man," Sturman said. He leaned over the conference table in the small room where we met, as a prison official sat outside the door. "Rosfelder lied to the federal government. He lied to the Swiss government. He lied to everybody." The information Rosfelder submitted to the Swiss was "nonsense." Even the Meese Commission had acknowledged that Reuben Sturman was not a member of the Cosa Nostra. Accusations of organized crime links were much easier to make than to refute. The LAPD had good reason to raise the specter of "organized crime" involvement in the sex industry. "They could never bring anyone to trial [for obscenity] and win in Los Angeles," Sturman explained, pounding the table. "And they tried every way from Sunday." The government had seized his bank records and business records dating back to the late 1960s, it had persuaded many of his top managers to talk—where was the evidence that he had made payments to the Gambino family? There was no evidence, because he had never paid the Gambino family "any money in any way, shape, or form." Rosfelder had made the whole thing up "out of whole cloth."

I brought up Robert DiBernardo. "He was one of my customers," Sturman said. "Not one of the bigger ones at all. I knew DiBernardo as a business acquaintance, not as a friend. He seemed to be a nice fellow. I didn't know he was in organized crime for the first ten years we did business. His two partners were Jewish. His first wife was Jewish. His second wife was Jewish. His kids went to Hebrew school. I thought DiBernardo was Jewish. I really thought he was Jewish—until I had my eyes opened. But that had nothing to do with me, anyway. Gotti's people shot him, and he disappeared from the face of the earth." Sturman claimed that his own life had been threatened many times by hoodlums and that he always told them the same thing: "Do whatever you have to. But get out of my sight."

We talked for a couple of hours, and he described in great detail how he had formed various companies, fought numerous obscenity battles, and expanded his empire overseas. As for tax evasion, Sturman said he felt under no obligation to give the government any money that might be used to attack him. He seemed to enjoy discussing the early days of the sex industry. Lately, the business had gone to hell. There was too much product on the market, too much price competition. Only the retailers were doing well. "We used to spend $400,000 on a film," he said. "Now you can make a film for $5,000 or $8,000—junk, real junk. I always told my people, don't lower your price, no matter what. Keep your quality up and keep your price up."

Sturman's mood sank as the conversation turned to more recent events. Bribery and extortion did not seem to fit his own self-image, that of a brilliant strategist, always a step ahead. When I asked for some explanation of the bombings, his answer was brief and matter-of-fact: "Those people owed me money. They refused to pay me. And so we went into one of their stores and we broke up the store, to send them a message. Sure enough, they started paying me again." He laughed. "I thought it was very nice of them."

Sturman anticipated the question that I most wanted to ask — why didn't he skip the country? — and started to reply before I could finish my sentence. "That was stupidity on my part," he said. "I thought being in a big city was the easiest way to get lost. And I would've been free and clear if I'd just kept my mouth shut and not gone to see my family. I love my wife and I love my child . . . And I just couldn't see myself leaving for Europe or Asia . . . I wouldn't want them to be on the run with me. I figured if I stayed in L.A. and stayed away from everybody I knew there, I'd be fine. But I couldn't stay away from my wife and child."

Sturman had offered to give the government an additional $12 million, as part of a deal. But the government didn't seem interested. "Oh, they hate my guts. I'm a public enemy." Aside from this money, apparently owed to him by various associates, Sturman swore to me that he was dead broke. He spent most of his time in prison reading fiction. Few of the other inmates had any idea who he was or how he came to be there. From all appearances, he was just a harmless old man.

"You wanted to know how the industry started," Sturman said, toward the end of our interview. "Well, you're looking at the person who started it."

When our time was up, I walked with Sturman and a prison official into a large courtyard, with footpaths and a lawn, that seemed to belong on a college campus. There was brilliant sunshine, and it took my eyes a moment to adjust. Sturman shook my hand, said to the prison official, "Show this young fellow to the door," as though the official was his personal assistant, and, without waiting for a response, turned and briskly walked away. Watching Sturman head across the courtyard toward a group of inmates in the distance, I pictured him as a young man, selling comic books from the trunk of his old car, getting to know the owners of Cleveland candy stores—and the power he later wielded, the wealth he made and lost, the businesses around the world, the houses, the Rolls-Royce, the millions of dollars in coins flowing through his peep machines, the millions spent to lay him low, all because of sex. And as he disappeared into the crowd, becoming indistinguishable from any other man in khaki, I wondered if Reuben Sturman still had a trick or two up his sleeve.

pagan and christian views

IN THE SATYR PLAYS of ancient Rome, the sex and violence were often real. The wealthy citizens who staged these spectacles put condemned criminals in the fatal roles, recreating for an audience the rapes and murders of familiar myths. The destruction of the performers was a byproduct of the entertainment. Many historians now believe that the sexual promiscuity of imperial Rome was greatly exaggerated by later commentators. Nevertheless, sex inhabited Rome's public spaces in a manner quite alien to that of the modern world. At hippodromes throughout the Roman Empire, teams of women posed as Nereiads, swimming naked in enormous, man-made pools before large crowds. The mystery cults and the Saturnalia encouraged citizens of all ranks to surrender their individuality briefly and give themselves over to their passions. Sexually explicit murals were painted, not only on the walls of brothels, but also on the walls of bedrooms and living rooms in private homes. Household objects were decorated with lewd scenes. Statues of Priapus were set in formal gardens, and stone carvings of erect phalluses were commonly placed on doorways and at street corners for good luck, to ward off the evil eye.

Peter Brown, a professor of history at Princeton University, argues in *The Body and Society* that Christianity marked a fundamental change in attitudes toward the human person. The pagans had imagined a chain of being in which men and women were linked to the gods by their spirits and to the animal world by their bodies. Saint Paul popularized the notion of a fundamental antithesis between the spirit and the flesh. "I see another law in my members," Paul wrote, "warring against the law of my mind." The body became "a temple of the Holy Ghost," and certain bodily practices became tantamount to pollution. The early Christians were both ridiculed and admired for their sexual abstinence. It set them apart. In a world haunted by death and corruption, a person could at least exert control over his or her own body, achieve a physical purity, and thereby attain salvation. In one of Paul's epistles, the implications of this doctrine were made clear — "Be not deceived: neither fornicators, nor idolaters, nor adulterers, nor effeminate, nor abusers of themselves . . . shall inherit the Kingdom of God."

For almost two millennia, pagan and Christian views of the body have remained in conflict, their rivalry expressed in various forms. But the old systems of moral authority have lately been replaced by a new one. The rules that govern sexual behavior are no longer determined by the pronouncements of Stoic philosophers, high priests, martyrs, and saints. Democracy has increasingly granted freedom of choice in matters of sexuality, while the free market ministers to consumer tastes. Although I have described some of the leading figures in the American sex industry, I don't mean to imply that a handful of people are somehow responsible for today's porn. On the contrary, that responsibility extends far and wide, to men and women all across America, the movers of the invisible hand, to leading citizens in every state, to people whom you know well and would never suspect. The content of America's porn says a lot about the state of the nation. Like the rest of popular culture, it serves as a mirror. The critics of porn may not like what they see, but must confront an awkward, underlying truth: sometimes the price of freedom is what freedom brings.

OUT OF THE
UNDERGROUND

T HE CHIEF BUSINESS OF THE AMERICAN PEOPLE is business,"
President Calvin Coolidge once said. The quote succinctly expressed his worldview. Coolidge believed that factories were temples where workers must worship, that small government was always the best government, that corporations should remain unfettered by regulation, that taxes should always be low. His presidency lasted from 1923 until 1929, a period of alcohol prohibition, rapid economic growth, and middle-class prosperity. It was an era in which free market values reigned supreme. The Great Depression left Coolidge's reputation in tatters. He became a figure of ridicule, his policies abandoned by the New Deal, his outlook derided as narrow, conformist, simplistic, and cold. "How can they tell?" Dorothy Parker said, after being informed of Coolidge's death. He was widely remembered as one of America's worst presidents—until January of 1981. That month a portrait of Thomas Jefferson was removed from the Cabinet Room at the White House and replaced by a portrait of Calvin Coolidge. The newly elected president, Ronald Reagan, considered him a personal hero, and ever since, the number of Coolidge fans has grown.

The business philosophy espoused by Coolidge and revived by Reagan has the marketplace at its core. In such a scheme, any constraints placed upon businessmen are denounced as limitations of freedom. Antitrust laws, worker safety laws, environmental laws, and minimum-wage laws are considered impediments to the necessary workings of the market. They stand in the way of efficiency. They pose a fundamental threat to society — and yet concentrated economic power does not. "There is nothing written in the sky," declared William Baxter, head of the Justice Department's Antitrust Division during the Reagan years, "that says the world would not be a perfectly satisfactory place if there were only a hundred companies." So long as these multinationals competed with each other, Baxter thought that having all economic activity controlled by a hundred chief executives shouldn't be a problem. This unwillingness to limit corporate behavior on moral grounds has been accompanied, however, by a government crusade to judge, condemn, and punish individuals for their alleged moral failings. The freedom to buy and sell goes only so far. Certain things cannot be sold because they are immoral, while other things — such as the exploitation of illegal immigrants, their poverty and poor health — hardly raise a moral qualm.

Many of the social and economic trends of the past two decades seem remarkably similar to those described in Frederick Lewis Allen's classic history of the 1920s, *Only Yesterday*. The sex scandals, stock swindles, and celebrity murder trials, the youthful hedonism and religious fundamentalism, the Big Bull Market, thriving black markets, fondness for literary irony, and political apathy of that era have strong contemporary echoes. The names and details may have changed, but the headlines seem uncannily familiar. These two periods are linked, not only by their ideologies, but also by an underlying spirit. Widespread illusions about endless prosperity managed to thrive amid disillusionment about almost everything else. And both periods ended abruptly: one on October 24, 1929, Black Thursday, when the stock market crashed; the other on September 11, 2001, amid the brilliant blue skies of a Tuesday morning.

underground influences

"THE ERA OF BIG GOVERNMENT is over," Bill Clinton said in 1996 — another memorable presidential quote. While the federal regulatory apparatus has indeed shrunk over the past twenty-five years, the criminal justice system has attained an unprecedented size and scale. More prisons were built during Clinton's two terms in office than during any other American presidency. The philosophy of small government championed by Coolidge, Reagan, Clinton, and both Bushes applies only to business regulations. The war on drugs and the current war on terrorism now confront ordinary Americans with a government that wields extraordinary power over their daily lives. This reality can hardly be denied. Like it or not, the era of big government is back, and bigger than ever.

The shifting relationship between the mainstream and the underground illustrates how our notions of freedom are by no means fixed; how the legality of a transaction determines its modes of production and consumption; how the workings of a market are ultimately subject to human, not divine, intervention. Consider the fate of Reuben Sturman. The commodity for which he was repeatedly indicted is now widely distributed by some of the largest corporations in the United States. Something that society long considered immoral is now ubiquitous and banal. Moreover, corporate America has embraced not only the products once distributed by Sturman but also some of his attitudes toward taxation. Business practices once confined mainly to the underground have gradually infiltrated the mainstream economy.

Before the Enron Corporation collapsed, it had created almost 900 subsidiaries overseas, including 692 in the Cayman Islands, 119 in the Turks and Caicos islands, and 43 in Mauritius. Tens of millions of dollars were routinely shifted among these offshore accounts to hide profits and evade taxes. During four of the five years from 1996 to 2000 Enron paid no income tax to the federal government—and collected nearly $400 million in tax refunds. Sturman's tax-dodging schemes, by comparison, now seem quaint and old-fashioned.

Over the past decade hundreds of American companies—including some of the nation's major insurance and accounting firms—have reincorporated overseas to avoid paying taxes. These offshore corporate moves are called "inversion transactions," despite the sexual connotation ("inversion" was a Victorian term for sodomy). Corporate inversions now cost the federal government an estimated $4 billion a year in lost tax revenue. Bermuda has profited enormously from such relocations, but many other small countries have benefited, too. The Cayman Islands currently have a population of 35,000—and 45,000 offshore corporations, and bank assets that approach $700 billion.

The art of money laundering has also advanced greatly since the days when Sturman's employees hauled sacks of quarters, suitcases of cash, and boxes of gold bars. Michel Camdessus, managing director of the International Monetary Fund, has estimated that the annual revenues from money laundering are now about 2 to 5 percent of the world's GDP—about $800 billion to $2 trillion a year. The South Pacific islands of Niue, Nauru, and Vanuatu have replaced Liberia as popular offshore havens. In 1998 alone an estimated $70 billion was shifted from Russian banks to accounts in Nauru, giving the barren little island a banking system with deposits worth about $7 million per person.

In addition to influencing the accounting practices of corporate America, the underground has subsumed a wide range of economic activities that used to occur in the mainstream. The sort of black market labor once narrowly confined to California agriculture is now widespread in meatpacking, construction, and garment manufacturing. The growth of the underground has lowered wages, eliminated benefits, and reduced job security in these industries. Until the late 1970s meatpacking was one of the highest-paid industrial jobs in the United States, with one of the lowest turnover rates. Today it is one of the lowest-paid, with one of the highest turnover rates. For more than a century Mexico has supplied the United States with migrant farmworkers; now it also supplies a migrant industrial work force that's almost as poor and just as easily exploited.

Important sectors of the American economy are starting to resemble those of lesser developed countries. Nowhere is this transformation more apparent than in Los Angeles County, where illegal immigration has soared and an estimated 28 percent of the workers are now paid in cash. A 2002 study by the Economic Roundtable estimated that the growing underground economy in Los Angeles is responsible for between 9 and 29 percent of the city's economic activity. Cutbacks in the aerospace industry, the loss of manufacturing jobs, and the influx of poor immigrants have created an L.A. economy that's increasingly dependent on low-wage, labor-intensive industries. As a result, personal income is falling; the gap between rich and poor is widening; social security and payroll taxes are going unpaid; and the new work force may limit future prospects for economic development. Workers in Los Angeles today have less education than workers in any other American metropolitan area. Roughly 11 percent of the working-age population in L.A. has less than a sixth-grade education. During the 1950s Los Angeles loomed as an American city of the future, a utopian vision of suburban paradise. Today it portends a much darker future: a return to the chaotic and exploitative economic relationships of the past, a triumph of underground practices and values.

Illegal immigration has been responsible for many of these changes, yet debate on the subject is too often framed in ethnic or cultural terms. At heart it is an economic question. Huge disparities of wealth have long existed between developed and developing nations. The huge migrations of the past two decades have been fueled in large part not by a shift in the inequality between nations, but by the ability of employers to make use of black market labor. In many respects illegal immigration is a symptom of market failure. Companies that are willing to break the law gain a competitive advantage over those that employ legal residents, that pay good wages and fully pay their taxes. Dipping into the underground rewards employers who cheat.

The passage and enforcement of strict labor laws could do more to solve the problems caused by illegal immigration than any crackdown on the border between Mexico and the United States. Adjusted for inflation, the value of the U.S. minimum wage has declined by about 37 percent since 1968. A significant increase in the minimum wage, combined with tough penalties for companies that violate labor laws, would greatly improve the lives of the poorest Americans. Shifting the punishment from undocumented workers to their employers is bound to have a noticeable effect. The former have every incentive to break the law; the latter have much more to lose. The legal status of workers is not of central importance—wages and working conditions are. If the current abuse of illegal immigrants is allowed to continue, the United States soon won't have to import a foreign peasantry. We will have created our own. "No business which depends for existence on paying less than living wages to its workers has any right to continue in this country," President Franklin Delano Roosevelt said in 1933, after the passage of the National Industrial Recovery Act. "By living wages I mean more than a subsistence level — I mean the wages of a decent living."

the visible hand

ADVOCATES OF THE FREE MARKET, who may be appalled by the idea of returning to such economic policies, must confront the fact that Adam Smith's invisible hand has always been celebrated far more in theory than in practice. Alexander Hamilton's *Report on Manufactures,* an early blueprint for America's commercial development, praised Smith's thoughts on specialization but ignored his faith in the free market. On the contrary, Hamilton urged the federal government to play an activist role in creating an urban, industrial society. The railroad construction that later provided the foundation for nineteenth-century economic growth was subsidized by massive federal land grants, as was the settlement of the American West. The tariff that protected American manufacturers for decades after the Civil War had more in common with mercantilism than with any of Smith's notions about free trade. The economic history of the twentieth century continued along the same lines: the New Deal rescue of capitalism, direct government investments in industry during the Second World War, the highway-building of the Eisenhower era, the military spending responsible for our current dominance of the aerospace, computer, and software industries. For some reason these facts are not mentioned in current debates over economic policy. The period of America's greatest economic supremacy — from the early 1950s until the late 1960s — was marked by high income taxes, vigorous antitrust enforcement, and unprecedented levels of union membership. No period of American history has remotely resembled the free market ideal described in *The Wealth of Nations.* Even Adam Smith was more concerned about the harmful influences of concentrated economic power than are many of his contemporary followers. Smith believed that the interests of consumers must always take precedence over those of producers, who often care little about the public good and always seek to avoid competition. "The sneaking arts of underling tradesmen," he warned, "are thus erected into political maxims for the conduct of a great empire."

Although Thomas Jefferson and Alexander Hamilton greatly admired *The Wealth of Nations,* Smith did not become an American icon until the early twentieth century, when his writings were used as a defense against government efforts to curtail monopoly power. Ever since, business groups hoping to avoid regulation have portrayed the workings of the invisible hand as an eternal and inviolable law. The idea of the marketplace as the fullest expression of democracy has a strong appeal. But it assumes that economic motives are the only human motives. If making money were all that mattered, there would be no nurses, teachers, poets, farmers, soldiers, police officers, or professors of medieval literature. The minimum wage, the abolition of child labor, and the creation of worker safety and environmental laws all express moral impulses that the market has neglected. The Founding Fathers saw the wisdom of a political system characterized by checks and balances. Despite the appeal of free market rhetoric, economic systems must be structured the same way, with diverse and competing centers of power.

minding your business

MY OWN VIEWS TEND TOWARD a suspicion of all absolute theories and a strong belief in thought that knows its limits. I like the idea of fewer laws, strictly enforced. The enormity of today's underground reveals the extent to which American society has become alienated and at odds with itself, like a personality beginning to decompose. The harshness of our marijuana laws and the frequency with which they are broken are a symptom of this larger problem. Almost everyone would agree murder is a crime that ought to be severely punished. But the morality of marijuana prohibition is so much more open to dispute, and the drug is so widely used without obvious harm, that its illegal status only breeds more alienation, more disrespect for the law, and more participation in the black market.

The arbitrary nature of America's marijuana laws seems all the more remarkable given the expensive marketing efforts now conducted for various legal drugs. Were Anthony Comstock alive today, he would no doubt consider Viagra — a drug widely promoted as a means of improving a man's sex life — to be the quintessence of Evil. But no social opprobrium is currently attached to this drug trade. American physicians write about 200,000 prescriptions for Viagra every week, and the drug's manufacturer, Pfizer, Inc., earned $1.75 billion from it in 2001. Bob Dole, the 1992 Republican candidate for president, was Viagra's first television spokesman. Elizabeth Dole, now a U.S. senator from North Carolina, apparently doesn't oppose this sort of recreational drug use. During her 2002 senatorial campaign, however, she drew the line. "We need an all-out revival of our crusade to rid America of illegal drugs," she declared. "I will be a champion for this cause."

In a nation where about one of every fourteen people takes antidepressants, the goal of a drug-free society seems a bit unrealistic. Arguments on behalf of legalizing marijuana have a strong inherent logic, but in the near term such a policy would be one more sign of America's wildly split personality. You cannot go overnight from being a society where someone may get a life sentence for possessing a single joint to being a society where someone may legally buy sensimilla, along with their Marlboros and Bud Lights. The immediate decriminalization of marijuana is a good first step toward a rational drug policy. States that have already decriminalized it do not have higher rates of pot use. Portugal and Spain have decriminalized the possession of all drugs, placing emphasis instead on prosecuting drug dealers and providing treatment for drug abusers. Both countries have lower rates of drug use than the United States, as do all the countries in Western Europe, where drug laws are less punitive.

Corporate greed and misbehavior have recently shaken faith in the free market, while the threat to America's security is no longer hypothetical. During wartime Americans have always been forced to think about the values that are worth fighting to defend. Things can no longer be taken for granted. Many abuses and injustices no longer seem tolerable. The certainties of the past twenty years have begun to crumble, and the world now seems a very different place. In the face of genuine terror, it becomes much more difficult to conjure fears of a weed.

The commodities we buy and sell may indeed reflect who we are—but they offer only a partial reflection. Our desires are now expressed in all sorts of other ways. And our government will become truly democratic when it acknowledges that complexity. Prison cells are an expensive commodity, and they should be reserved for people who commit violent acts, who exploit the weak and the poor. Economic crimes should be punished much more severely than behavior that is considered merely unconventional or distasteful. When it comes to interfering with what consenting adults do behind closed doors, the government should obey some useful advice: mind your own business. "Over himself, over his own body and mind," wrote John Stuart Mill, "the individual is sovereign." Black markets will always be with us. But they will recede in importance when our public morality is consistent with our private one. The underground is a good measure of the progress and the health of nations. When much is wrong, much needs to be hidden.

NOTES

BIBLIOGRAPHY

ACKNOWLEDGMENTS

INDEX

notes

the underground

Although I did a great deal of reporting and research for this book, I also benefited from the hard work of others. In these notes I've tried to give credit to the many people whose thinking, writing, and research helped mine. Adam Smith's economic and philosophic theories have been subject to numerous interpretations over the years. Robert L. Heilbroner's *The Essential Adam Smith* (New York: W. W. Norton, 1986) is a fine introduction to the world's most influential economist. In *Economic Sentiments: Adam Smith, Condorcet, and the Enlightenment* (Cambridge, Mass.: Harvard University Press, 2002), Emma Rothschild offers a provocative intellectual history of "the invisible hand," suggesting that Smith's use of the phrase was "a mildly ironic joke" and that it never played a major role in his worldview. Though I disagree with some of her arguments, Rothschild plausibly claims that Smith borrowed the phrase from Shakespeare's *Macbeth,* whose protagonist implores the darkness to hide his foul crimes "with thy bloody and invisible hand." As for the influence of Smith's theories on America's Founding Fathers, I learned much from Peter McNamara's *Political Economy and Statesmanship: Smith, Hamilton, and the Foundation of the Commercial Republic* (De Kalb: Northern Illinois University Press, 1998). My interpretation of Adam Smith's philosophy is based mainly on his own words, as expressed in two works that he continually revised: *The Theory of Moral Sentiments* and *An Inquiry into the Nature and Causes of the Wealth of Nations.*

The past twenty-five years have produced a growing literature about the underground economy. Most of it is fascinating but highly speculative. *The Underground Economy in the United States and Abroad* (Lexington, Mass.: Lexington Books, 1982), edited by Vito Tanzi, offers a good overview of the subject. Tanzi, director of the Department of Fiscal Affairs at the International Monetary Fund (IMF), is an influential scholar in the field. He believes that high taxes and excessive government regulation are responsible not only for shadow economies but for a variety of other social ills. I learned much from two of his papers on tax evasion and corruption: "A Primer on Tax Evasion," *International Monetary Fund Staff Papers,* December 1993, and "Corruption Around the World: Causes, Consequences, Scope, and Cures," *International Monetary Fund Staff Papers,* December 1, 1998. In *Off the Books: The Rise of the Underground* (New York: St. Martin's Press, 1986), Philip Mattera convincingly argues that low wages, deregulation, and high unemployment are also important factors in the growth of shadow economies. *The Underground Economy: Global Evidence of Its Size and Impact* (Vancouver: Fraser Institute, 1997), edited by Owen Lippert and Michael Walker, is a revealing collection of essays. Harry I. Greenfield has fine chapters on the monetary and criminal aspects of the underground in his book *Invisible, Outlawed, and Untaxed: America's Underground Economy* (Westport, Conn.: Praeger, 1993). I found these articles to be especially useful: Dominik Enste and Friedrich Schneider, "Increasing Shadow Economies All Over the World—Fiction or Reality?" Discussion Paper No. 26, Institute for the Study of Labor, Bonn, Germany, December 1998; Friedrich Schneider, "The Size and Development of the Shadow Economies of 22 Transition and 21 OECD Countries," Discussion Paper No. 514, Institute for the Study of Labor, Bonn, Germany, June 2002; Matthew H. Fleming, John Roman, and Graham Ferrell, "The Shadow Economy," *Journal of International Affairs,* Spring 2000; Yair Eilat and Clifford Zinnes, "The Shadow Economy in Transition Countries: Friend or Foe? A Policy Perspective," *World Development,* July 2002.

For more than three decades Peter Reuter has been using economic theory to understand the workings of illegal markets. He helped to create the RAND Corporation's Drug Policy Research Center and is now a professor at the University of Maryland's School of Public Affairs and its Department of Criminology and Criminal Justice. Reuter's *Disorganized Crime: The Economics of the Visible Hand* (Cambridge, Mass.: MIT Press, 1983) stresses the role of competition in shaping black markets and debunks some of the popular myths about Mafia cartels. I am extremely grateful to him for answering so many of my questions over the years and for reviewing portions of this manuscript. The remaining errors in these pages are entirely my own. Reuter's most recent book, *Drug War Heresies: Learning from Other Places, Times, and Vices* (New York: Cambridge University Press, 2001), written with Robert J. MacCoun, is a model of scholarship and common sense.

page

3 *"The happiness of mankind"*: Adam Smith, in Knud Haakonssen, ed., *The Theory of Moral Sentiments* (Cambridge: Cambridge University Press, 2002), p. 193.

"the invisible hand": See ibid, p. 215, and Adam Smith, in Edwin Canaan, ed., *The Wealth of Nations (An Inquiry into the Nature and Causes of The Wealth of Nations)* (New York: Modern Library, 2000), p. 285.

obeyed only his "passions": See Smith, *Theory of Moral Sentiments*, pp. 32–52.

"Life, liberty, and estate": See John Locke, *Political Writings of John Locke*, (New York: Mentor, 1993), p. 304.

5 *the Austrian economist Friedrich Schneider*: Throughout this chapter I have relied on Schneider's estimates, not because they are necessarily the most accurate, but because they are the most consistent. By using the same methodology to compare the shadow economies in dozens of countries, Schneider provides a sense of relative proportion. His research, funded in part by the IMF, seems rigorous and thorough. He shares Vito Tanzi's belief that high taxes are to blame for driving economic activity underground.

2.6 and 4.6 percent of America's gross domestic product: Cited in Dominik Enste and Friedrich Schneider, "Increasing Shadow Economies All Over the World — Fiction or Reality?" Discussion Paper No. 26, Institute for the Study of Labor, Bonn, Germany, December 1998.

By 1994 it had reached 9.4 percent: Ibid.

about $650 billion: In 1994 America's total GDP was $7,054.3 billion. See "Gross Domestic Product in Current and Real (1996) Dollars: 1960 to 1999," *Statistical Abstract of the United States* (Washington, D.C.: U.S. Government Printing Office, 2000), p. 451.

about $200 billion of federal taxes: Cited in Ralph Vartabedian, "Unpaid Tax Total Put at $195 Billion a Year by IRS," *Los Angeles Times,* May 2, 1998.

Americans spent about $5 billion a year on alcohol: Cited in Barry Molefsky, "America's Underground Economy," in Tanzi, *Underground Economy,* p. 47.

about 5 percent of the U.S. gross national product: Ibid.

Perhaps 5 percent of the nation's gasoline and 20 percent of its meat: Ibid., p. 48.

as much as 15 percent of their personal income: Ibid.

6 *According to Friedrich Schneider's estimates*: See Schneider, "Size and Development of the Shadow Economies."

In Estonia . . . in Russia . . . in Ukraine: Ibid.

7 *In Bolivia . . . In Nigeria*: Cited in Enste and Schneider, "Increasing Shadow Economies."

averaged about $2 billion a year: Cited in Douglas B. Weinberg, "International Flows of U.S. Currency," *Survey of Current Business,* U.S. Department of Commerce, October 1996.

about $20 billion in U.S. currency was being shipped: Ibid.

approximately three-quarters of all $100 bills: Cited in Michael J. Lambert and Kristin D. Stanton, "Opportunities and Challenges of the U.S. Dollar as an Increasingly Global Currency: A Federal Reserve Perspective," *Federal Reserve Bulletin,* September 1, 2001. See also John B. Carlson and Benjamin D. Keen, "Where Is All the U.S. Currency Hiding?" *Economic Commentary,* Federal Reserve Bank of Cleveland, April 15, 1996.

7　*an estimated $32.7 billion in interest:* Cited in Lambert and Stanton, "The U.S. Dollar."

The 1996 redesign of the $100 bill: See Edward J. Green and Warren E. Weber, "Will the New $100 bill Decrease Counterfeiting?" *Federal Reserve Bank of Minneapolis Quarterly Review,* Summer 1996.

reefer madness

The physiological and psychological effects of smoking marijuana have long been the subject of enormous debate. In order to describe them accurately, I did my best to interview some of the leading authorities on the subject. It was a pleasure speaking with the late Dr. Leo Hollister, a former president of the American College of Neuropsychopharmacology who taught at the University of Texas Medical School for many years. Hollister was highly regarded for his knowledge of marijuana toxicology and psychopharmacology. His summaries of the medical literature on the drug— "Health Aspects of Cannabis," *Pharmacological Reviews* 38: 1–20, 1986, and "Health Aspects of Cannabis: Revisited," *International Journal of Neuropsychopharmacology* 1: 71–80, 1998 — remain unsurpassed. Dr. John P. Morgan, a professor of pharmacology at the City University of New York Medical School, spent hours with me and patiently debunked many of the horror stories that have been spread about marijuana. Morgan wrote the section "Drug Use and Dependence" for the most recent edition of *The Merck Manual of Diagnosis and Therapy* (Rahway, N.J.: Merck, Sharp, & Dohme, 1999). He is also the author, with Lynn Zimmer, of *Marijuana Myths, Marijuana Facts* (New York: Lindesmith Center, 1997), an excellent guide to the real and imagined consequences of pot smoking. Two well-known and outspoken critics of marijuana use, Dr. Gabriel Nahas and Dr. Mitchell S. Rosenthal, offered a more alarming view of the drug. Nahas, a research professor of anesthesiology at New York University Medical Center, has been campaigning against marijuana for three decades. His books include *Marihuana—Deceptive Weed* (New York: Raven Press Publishers, 1973) and *Keep Off the Grass* (Middlebury, Vt.: Paul S. Erikkson, 1990). I found his opposition to be passionate and sincere, but his scientific claims about the drug were unconvincing. Nahas is also an editor of *Marihuana and Medicine* (Totowa, N.J.: Humana Press, 1999), along with Kenneth M. Sutin, David J. Harvey, and Stig Agurell. As president of the Phoenix House Foundation, Rosenthal has been providing treatment for substance abusers since 1970. I am grateful for his insights into marijuana's potential for abuse. Dr. Donald P. Tashkin, a professor in the Division of Pulmonary Diseases at the University of California at Los Angeles Medical Center, told me about his research on the respiratory harms of smoking marijuana. And Dr. Donald Abrams—assistant director of the AIDS Division at San Francisco General Hospital and assistant clinical professor at the Cancer Research Institute, University of California at San Francisco—described his work gauging marijuana's effects on the immune system.

The many government studies of marijuana have produced reports outlining its effects on health. Among those I consulted were Indian Hemp Drugs Commission, *Report of the Indian Hemp Drugs Commission* (Simla, India: Government Central Printing Office, 1894); Mayor's Committee on Marihuana, *The Marijuana Problem in the City of New York: Sociological, Medical, Psychological, and Pharmacological Studies* (Lancaster, Pa.: Jacques Cattel Press, 1944); Hallucinogens Subcommittee of the Advisory Committee on Drug Dependence, *Report on Cannabis,* British Home Office, November 1968; National Commission on Marihuana and Drug Abuse, *Marihuana: A Signal of Misunderstanding* (Washington, D.C.: Government Printing Office, 1972); Institute of Medicine, *Marijuana and Health: Report of the Committee to Study the Health-Related Effects of Cannabis and Its Derivatives* (Washington, D.C.: National Academy Press, 1982); House of Lords Science and Technology Committee, *Cannabis: The Scientific and Medical Evidence,* November 4, 1998; Institute of Medicine, *Marijuana and Medicine: Assessing the Science Base* (Washington, D.C.: National Academy Press, 1999); Swiss Federal Commission for Drug Issues, *Cannabis Report,* May 1999; Alex Sleator and Grahame Allen, *Cannabis,* Research Paper 00/74, House of Commons Library, August 3, 2000; Maurice Rickard, *Reforming the Old and Refining the New: A Critical Overview of Australian Approaches to Cannabis,* Research Paper No. 6, 2001–2, Department of the Parliamentary Library, Commonwealth of Australia, 2001. The scientific consensus about marijuana's harmful effects has changed remarkably little over the past century. Leslie L. Iverson offers an overview of the latest research in *The Science of Marijuana* (New York: Oxford University Press, 2000). I am grateful to Dr. Lester Grinspoon, an emeritus professor of psychiatry at Harvard Medical School, for his thoughts on why this herbal medicine has been so maligned for so long. His book *Marihuana: The Forbidden Medicine* (New Haven, Conn.: Yale University Press, 1993) suggests that cannabis will soon prove useful for a variety of ailments. Alice O'Leary, a founder of the Alliance for Cannabis Therapeutics, put me in contact with cancer patients and AIDS patients who have risked imprisonment to continue using marijuana as medicine.

Dr. David F. Musto's *The American Disease: Origins of Narcotic Control* (New York: Oxford University Press, 1999) is the definitive history of American drug control policy. I am grateful to Dr. Musto, a professor of child psychiatry and the history of medicine at the Yale School of Medicine, for the hours he spent discussing his work and his interviews with Harry J. Anslinger. Rufus King—who from 1956 to 1958 served as chairman of the Joint American Bar Association–American Medical Association Committee on Narcotic Drugs—also shared with me his reminiscences about Anslinger. King's book, *The Drug Hang-Up: America's Fifty-Year Folly* (Springfield, Ill.: Charles C Thomas, 1972), contains interesting material about Anslinger's heyday at the Federal Bureau of Narcotics. Lynn Zimmer, an associate professor of sociology at Queens College, City University of New York, spoke with me at length about the racial and cultural prejudices that have long been associated with marijuana use. Richard Bonnie helped me understand the origins of marijuana prohibition in the United States, the rise of the antidrug parents' groups in the 1970s, and the subsequent failure of marijuana law reform. Bonnie served from 1971 to 1973 as the associate director of the National Commission on Marihuana and Drug Abuse; he is now a professor of law at the University of Virginia Law School and director of its Institute of Law, Psychiatry, and Public Policy. I highly recommend his book *Marihuana Use and Criminal Sanctions* (Charlottesville, Va.: Michie Company, 1980) and the book that he wrote with Charles H. Whitebread II, *The Marihuana Conviction: A History of Marihuana Prohibition in the United States* (Charlottesville: University Press of Virginia, 1974). These two volumes should be the starting point for anyone curious about marijuana and the law in the United States.

Ernest L. Abel's *Marihuana: The First Twelve Thousand Years* (New York: Plenum Press, 1980) takes a broad, multicultural view and contains a great deal of fascinating material. John F. Hopkins's *A History of the Hemp Industry in Kentucky* (Lexington: University of Kentucky Press, 1951) looks at the days when cannabis was at the heart of a thriving, legal industry in the United States. *Reefer Madness: A History of Marijuana* (New York: St. Martin's Griffin, 1999), by Larry (Rats) Sloman, is a lively and entertaining look at our pot culture, with a fine section on Anslinger's hatred of jazz and an appropriate introduction by William Burroughs. I also enjoyed these two books, which strongly evoke their era: Harry J. Anslinger and William F. Thompkins, *The Traffic in Narcotics* (New York: Funk & Wagnall, 1953), and Harry J. Anslinger and Will Oursler, *The Murderers: The Story of the Narcotics Gangs* (New York: Farrar, Straus, and Cudahy, 1961). In a fine biography, *The Protectors: Harry J. Anslinger and the Federal Bureau of Narcotics, 1930–1962* (Newark: University of Delaware Press, 1990), John C. McWilliams offers a sober, nuanced, and well-researched account of the man. A recent documentary, *Grass* (Home Vision, 1999), features some memorable footage of Anslinger and antidrug propaganda films dating from the 1920s. Words can hardly do justice to old marijuana scare films such as *Marihuana: Weed with Roots in Hell* (1936), *Reefer Madness* (1937), *The Devil's Harvest* (1942), and *She Shoulda Said No!*

(*Wild Weed*) (1948), all currently distributed by Something Weird Video of Seattle. They say a great deal—and say it very badly.

The Marijuana Papers (New York: Signet Books, 1968), edited by David Solomon, is a useful collection of literary, historical, and scientific essays on the drug. Jerome Himmelstein's *The Strange Career of Marihuana: Politics and Ideology of Drug Control in America* (Westport, Conn.: Greenwood Press, 1983) is a thorough review of popular attitudes toward pot, as expressed in the mainstream media. John Kaplan's *Marijuana: The New Prohibition* (New York: World, 1970) was an early attempt to challenge conventional thinking about the drug and has interesting material on California's war on marijuana during the 1960s. As the full title amply reveals, Michael Massing's *The Fix: Under the Nixon Administration, America Had an Effective Drug Policy. We Should Restore It.* (*Nixon Was Right.*) has a surprising, unsettling, and ultimately persuasive central argument. Peggy Mann's *Marijuana Alert* (New York: McGraw-Hill, 1985), with a foreword by Nancy Reagan, played an important role in the 1980s backlash against pot. Mann's work was popular among antidrug parents' groups, supplying cultural, intellectual, and "scientific" arguments for making America's marijuana laws tougher. In *Smoke and Mirrors: The War on Drugs and the Politics of Failure* (New York: Little, Brown, 1996), Dan Baum gives an excellent account of how Ronald Reagan's war on marijuana began and where it eventually led.

As counsel to the House of Representatives Committee on the Judiciary, Eric E. Sterling helped draft the Anti–Drug Abuse Acts of 1986 and 1988. His thoughts on how those laws came to be passed were extremely useful to me. Mark A. R. Kleiman, a professor of policy studies and the director of the Drug Policy Analysis Program at the University of California at Los Angeles, shared his expertise on the causes and consequences of the war on marijuana that began in the 1980s. His books *Marijuana: Costs of Abuse, Costs of Control* (Greenwich, Conn.: Greenwood Press, 1989) and *Against Excess: Drug Policy for Results* (New York: Basic Books, 1992) offer well-reasoned critiques of our current drug control strategies. Steven B. Duke, a professor at Yale Law School, explained some of the intricacies of forfeiture law to me. His book *America's Longest War: Rethinking Our Tragic Crusade Against Drugs* (New York: G. P. Putnam's Sons, 1993) makes a compelling argument for why the war on drugs cannot succeed. A number of other drug war opponents took the time to speak with me: Kevin B. Zeese, president of Common Sense for Drug Policy; R. Keith Stroup, executive director of the National Organization for the Reform of Marijuana Laws (NORML); Richard Cowan, a former executive director of NORML; Dale Gieringer, the coordinator of NORML California; Ethan Nadelman, executive director of the Drug Policy Alliance; and Peter Gorman, former editor in chief at *High Times* magazine. Lee P. Brown, who at the time was head of the Office of National Drug Control Policy—serving as President Clinton's first "drug czar"—gave me a somewhat different point of view. I learned much from three special agents at the Drug Enforcement Administration, William Ruzzamenti, James McGiveny, and Steve White. I am grateful to the various law enforcement officers who, off the record, spoke bluntly to me about our tactics in the war on drugs.

As deputy staff director at the U.S. Sentencing Commission, Paul Martin not only took time to explain the details of federal sentencing guidelines but also used his authority to obtain information for me about federal prisoners serving lengthy terms for marijuana crimes. Judge William W. Wilkins, Jr., the first chairman of the U.S. Sentencing Commission, described how the guidelines were devised and implemented—and how their underlying goal conflicted with that of mandatory minimum sentences. A study conducted by the commission under Judge Wilkins—U.S. Sentencing Commission, *Special Report to Congress: Mandatory Minimum Penalties in the Federal Criminal Justice System* (St. Paul, Minn.: West Publishing Co., August 1991)—offers a strong critique of mandatory minimums from a conservative perspective. I also learned much from Henry Scott Wallace's "Mandatory Minimums and the Betrayal of Sentencing Reform," *Federal Bar News and Journal,* vol. 40, no. 3, 1993. Judge Jack B. Weinstein, of the U.S. District Court, Eastern District of New York, and Judge William Schwarzer, former head of the Federal Judicial Center, spoke to me on the record about congressional efforts to curtail judicial discretion. I am grateful to the other judges who spoke to me off the record. Jonathon Turley, a professor at George Washington University Law School, spoke to me about some of the pressures that mandatory minimum drug sentences have placed on the federal prison system. Marc Mauer, assistant director of the Sentencing Project, had a great influence on my thinking about prisons and their current role in American society. I recommend two books with which he has been involved: Marc Mauer, *Race to Incarcerate* (New York: New Press, 2001), and Marc Mauer and Meda Chesney-Lind, eds., *Invisible Punishment: The Collateral Consequences of Mass Imprisonment* (New York: New Press, 2002).

Julie Stewart, the founder and president of Families Against Mandatory Minimums (FAMM), has been fighting simplistic sentencing formulas with great intelligence and compassion since 1991. I hope that politicians will someday embrace her views on mandatory prison sentences. Monica Pratt, the director of communications at FAMM, helped me locate cases in which marijuana offenders received excessive punishments. I am grateful to the many criminal defense attorneys who described how the marijuana laws were being enforced in their communities and told me about some of their clients. Among those who deserve special thanks are Sam McKerral, in Alabama; William Logan, in California; Nancy Lord, in Georgia; George Taseff, in Illinois; Stephen W. Dillon, in Indiana; Dan Viets, in Missouri; and C. Rabon Martin, in Oklahoma. I must also thank the many marijuana offenders and family members who shared their stories with me, especially James Montgomery;

Orland Foster and his sister, Wendy Foster; William Bonner and his mother, Helen Bonner; Douglas Lamar Gray and his aunt Jo Ann Dean; and Edward M. Czuprynski.

I was fortunate to speak with former DEA agent Steve White and Ed Rosenthal—author of *The Big Book of Buds: Marijuana Varieties from the World's Great Seed Breeders* (Oakland: Quick American Archives, 2001), among other titles, and America's foremost guru of pot growing—about the marijuana industry. Few people know more about growing pot than these two men. Ralph A. Weisheit, a professor of criminal justice at Illinois State University, generously shared his knowledge of the subject. His book *Domestic Marijuana: A Neglected Industry* (Westport, Conn.: Greenwood Press, 1992) is a serious, academic study of the subject. Jon Gettman, a former policy analyst at NORML and for years the author of its annual "Crop Report," gave me his well-informed views on the size and location of America's pot harvest. I am grateful to "Dave" and a number of other marijuana growers for taking the risk and describing their work to me.

My account of Mark Young's case is largely based upon court transcripts (*United States of America v. Mark Young,* Case No. 91–37–CR, United States District Court, Southern District of Indiana, Indianapolis Division) and interviews with some of the leading participants. I am grateful to Young's defense attorney, Kevin McShane, for telling me about his efforts to save Young from a life sentence. Thomas M. Dawson, who argued Young's appeal, spent many hours outlining not only the details of this case, but also the workings of the federal system in a wide variety of drug cases. Had Dawson billed me for all the time we spent discussing these issues, he could have earned a small fortune. I am grateful to Donna Eide, the assistant U.S. attorney in the Southern District of Indiana who prosecuted the Young case, and to Deborah Daniels, who was the district's U.S. attorney at the time, for sharing their points of view. Daniels's successor as U.S. attorney, Judith Stewart, also helped me understand the government's policy in such cases. Dana York, NORML's Indiana coordinator at the time, spoke with me about the state's attitudes toward and market for marijuana. Mark Young's mother, Mary Fagel, and his ex-wife, Patricia Rowland, told me how his sentence had affected their lives. His sister Andrea Strong was invaluable to me, helping to track down sources and placing the story in the proper context. Her work on behalf of FAMM deserves great praise. I am extremely grateful to her and her husband, Don Strong, for their patience and support. And Mark Young was remarkably cordial, blunt, and helpful as I picked through the details of his life. I thank him sincerely. May he never spend another day behind bars.

For almost a decade Allen St. Pierre, executive director of the NORML Foundation, and I have been discussing, debating, and sharing information about marijuana. Though we disagree on a number of issues, he's consistently displayed real integrity, compassion, and a commitment to reform. When the reefer madness of the United States finally comes to an end, I hope St. Pierre gets much of the credit.

page

13 *a person convicted of armed robbery . . . someone convicted of rape . . . a convicted murderer can expect:* In 2001 the average prison sentence in Indiana for rape was 16.5 years, the average for robbery was 11.8 years, and the average for murder was 50.34 years. Interview with Pam Patterson, Indiana Department of Corrections.

eleven years and four months in prison: On average, a convicted murderer will spend 136 months in a state prison for the crime. See "Felony Sentences in State Courts, 1998," *Bureau of Justice Statistics Bulletin,* October 2001.

will serve no more than half the nominal sentence: Patterson interview.

14 *About 20,000 inmates in the federal prison system:* In 1999, the most recent year for which I obtained statistics, 7,128 marijuana offenders were convicted in federal court: 91.2 percent of them were sentenced to prison, and the average sentence length was 33.8 months. That means roughly 6,500 marijuana offenders go to federal prison every year and remain there for about three years. And that suggests there are at least 19,500 marijuana offenders in federal prison at the moment. The number may actually be higher, since marijuana offenders with sentences of ten years, twenty years, or life increase the total behind bars. It is interesting to note that the number of marijuana offenders sent to federal prison in 1999 was larger than the number of offenders sent to federal prison for methamphetamine, crack cocaine, or cocaine powder. More than twice as many people were sent to federal prison for marijuana crimes than for crimes involving heroin and other opiates. See "Federal Drug Offenders, 1999 with Trends 1984–99," Bureau of Justice Statistics, August 2001.

an additional 25,000 to 30,000: In 1998, the most recent year for which I obtained statistics, 927,717 people were convicted of felony offenses in state courts: 6.1 percent of those convictions were for marijuana crimes — 3.6 percent for possession and 2.5 percent for trafficking. That means in 1998 roughly 56,600 people were convicted of marijuana felonies in state court — 33,400 for possession and 23,200 for trafficking. The Bureau of Justice Statistics did not calculate how many of those marijuana felony offenders actually went to prison. It did conclude, however, that 36 percent of all drug offenders convicted of a felony in state court for possession and 45 percent of drug offenders convicted of a felony in state court for trafficking were sent to prison in 1998. Those convicted for possession spent an estimated 14 months in prison, and those convicted for trafficking spent an estimated 22 months in prison. That means in 1998 approximately 12,000 people convicted of felony possession of marijuana went sent to prison for a year, and 10,440 people convicted of marijuana trafficking felonies went to prison for two years. And that suggests there are about 32,880 marijuana offenders in state prison at the moment. I have used 25,000 to 30,000 as my estimate because the sentences given for marijuana felonies may be somewhat shorter than those given for other drug felonies. See "Felony Sentences in State Courts, 1998," *Bureau of Justice Statistics Bulletin*, October 2001.

Dozens of marijuana offenders: I was able to obtain information from the U.S. Sentencing Commission about the number of marijuana offenders given life sentences under federal law in 1992, 1993, and 1994. Sixteen people were sentenced to life in federal prison for marijuana during those three years. In a recent report the Bureau of Justice Statistics noted that 88 drug offenders were given life sentences under federal law in 1999, although the report did not specify the drugs involved. Since the number of offenders sent to federal prison for marijuana in 1999 was much larger than the number sent there for any other drug, it seems fair to assume that some of those 88 life sentences were pot-related. See "Federal Drug Offenders, 1999."

sentences of twenty or thirty or forty years: According to information from the U.S. Sentencing Commission, under federal law a total of 110 marijuana offenders were given prison sentences of 240 months or longer in 1992 and 1993. Since then the number of people sent to federal prison every year for marijuana crimes has risen by more than 50 percent.

life sentences in state correctional facilities: In at least a dozen states you can get a life sentence for marijuana (40 years or longer) by violating controlled substances acts. Those states are: Alabama (life), Florida (74 years), Louisiana (80 years), Mississippi (life), Missouri (life), Montana (life), Nevada (life), Oklahoma (life), Rhode Island (life), Tennessee (60 years), Texas (life), and Virginia (40 years). In states that have strict habitual offender laws, a marijuana crime may count as a third strike and lead to a life sentence. According to the Bureau of Justice Statistics, in 1998 life sentences represented 0.2 percent of all felony sentences for drug possession and 0.1 percent of all sentences for drug trafficking. There were about 121,000 felony sentences for drug possession that year and 214,600 for drug trafficking. That means about 1,000 people were given life sentences for state drug offenses in 1998. The Bureau of Justice Statistics did not record how many of those life sentences stemmed from marijuana crimes. See "Felony Sentences in State Courts, 1998" and National Criminal Justice Association, *A Guide to State Controlled Substances Acts,* January 1999.

used more frequently than all other drugs combined: In 2000 about 8 per-

cent of the American population over the age of twelve smoked marijuana and 6 percent used illicit drugs other than marijuana. See U.S. Department of Health and Human Services, Substance Abuse and Mental
Health Services Administration, *Summary of Findings from the 2000 National Survey on Drug Abuse* (Rockville, Md.: U.S. Department of Health
and Human Services, 2001), pp. 132–34, 141, 142.

14 *Approximately one-third of the American population:* In 2000 about 34 percent of the American population over the age of twelve had smoked
marijuana at least once. See ibid. All of the figures on marijuana use produced by federal surveys probably underestimate the real numbers by a
wide margin. In the current legal climate many people are understandably reluctant to tell anyone from the U.S. government how often they
smoke pot.
About twenty million Americans: Ibid.
More than two million: About 12 percent of the nineteen million Americans who smoked marijuana in 2000 smoked it on three hundred or
more days. See ibid.
anywhere from a quarter to half: Nobody really knows how much of
the marijuana smoked in the United States is grown there, too. Ralph
Weisheit, a professor of criminal justice at Illinois State University, includes this estimate in his book *Domestic Marijuana: A Neglected Industry* (Westport, Conn.: Greenwood Press, 1992), p. 31. Based on my conversations with pot growers, pot dealers, academics, and DEA agents, it
seems accurate.
plausible estimates start at $4 billion: The value of America's marijuana
crop can be measured either by consumption figures (how much pot
Americans smoke each year) or by production figures (how much pot is
grown in the United States). Unfortunately, nobody really knows how
much pot is grown or smoked. In 1997 the Office of National Drug
Control Policy (ONDCP) estimated the annual value of the marijuana
smoked by Americans based on the following assumptions: that the nation's 8.6 million monthly pot smokers smoked an average of 18.7 joints
a month in 1995; that each joint weighed 0.0136 of an ounce; and that
each ounce of pot cost $269. The ONDCP concluded that Americans
spent about $7 billion on marijuana in 1995 — but acknowledged that it
had most likely understated the real amount by 30 percent. Adjusted for
that error, the ONDCP's estimate comes to about $9 billion. My own at-
tempt to estimate the value of the pot being smoked in the United States
relied on the number of daily, not monthly, users. Daily users smoke
most of the marijuana that is grown or sold. One study of daily users
found that they smoke, on average, four to five joints a day. Two million daily users smoking four joints a day consume much more pot

than 8.6 million monthly users smoking 18.7 joints a month. The total value spent on pot also depends on how much each joint costs—$4? $8? Without belaboring the details, my estimates produced consumption values ranging from $11 billion to $30 billion a year. In 1989 Mark A. R. Kleiman, then at the Harvard School of Public Policy, used a consumption-based approach to estimate that the American market for marijuana was about $14 billion—of which $4 billion (18 percent) was produced in the United States. Production-based estimates also vary widely. Ralph Weisheit argues that the annual value of America's marijuana crop during the late 1980s ranged from $32 billion to $65 billion. John Gettman and Paul Armentano, in their NORML "1998 Crop Report," claim that during the previous year American growers earned $15.1 billion from marijuana with a retail value of $25.2 billion. It isn't easy to estimate the size of the annual marijuana crop; in 1982 the DEA seized 38 percent more domestic pot than was previously thought to exist. The DEA no longer speculates about how much marijuana is grown in the United States, indoors or outdoors. Perhaps that is a wise decision. See "What America's Users Spend on Drugs, 1988–1995," Office of National Drug Control Policy, September 29, 1997; Mark A. R. Kleiman, *Marijuana: Costs of Abuse, Costs of Control* (Westport, Conn.: Greenwood Press, 1989), pp. 33–46; Weisheit, *Domestic Marijuana*, pp. 31–35; John Gettman and Paul Armentano, "NORML Report on U.S. Domestic Marijuana Production, 1998 Marijuana Crop Report," October 1998.

In 2001 the value of the nation's largest legal cash crop: See USDA/ National Agricultural Statistics Service, "Crop Production Annual Summary," January 11, 2002.

16 *hailed as a "miracle drug":* Interview with Dr. Lester Grinspoon.

Other doctors think that Grinspoon: Dr. Gabriel Nahas, a research professor of anesthesiology at New York University Medical School, is foremost among those physicians who doubt the utility of marijuana as medicine. For a good sense of such views, see Gabriel Nahas, Kenneth M. Sutin, David J. Harvey, and Stig Agurell, eds., *Marihuana and Medicine* (Totowa, N.J.: Humana Press, 1999).

17 *inquiries by the National Academy of Science and Great Britain's House of Lords:* See the House of Lords Science and Technology Committee, *Cannabis: The Scientific and Medical Evidence,* November 4, 1998; Institute of Medicine, *Marijuana and Medicine: Assessing the Science Base* (Washington, D.C.: National Academy Press, 1999).

"You cannot patent this plant": Grinspoon interview.

It appears to be less addictive, however: In 1994 Dr. Jack Henningfield, chief of clinical pharmacology at the National Institute on Drug Abuse's Center for Addiction Research, ranked six popular drugs—heroin, cocaine, marijuana, alcohol, nicotine, and caffeine—according to their ability to produce dependence among users. He deemed marijuana the easiest to quit and nicotine the most habit-forming. See Philip J. Hilts, "Is Nicotine Addictive? It Depends on Whose Criteria You Use," *New York Times,* August 2, 1994.

17 *An occasional marijuana user . . . a heavy user:* Interview with Dr. John P. Morgan.

Studies of lifelong, heavy marijuana users: Dr. Morgan brought these studies to my attention. See V. Rubin and L. Comitas, *Ganja in Jamaica: A Medical and Anthropological Study of Chronic Marijuana Use* (The Hague: Mouton, 1975); A. Kokkevi and R. Dornbush, "Psychological Test Characteristics of Long-Term Hashish Users," in C. Stefanis et al., eds., *Hashish: Studies of Long-Term Users* (New York: Raven Press, 1977); P. Satz et al., "Neuropsychologic, Intellectual, and Personality Correlates of Chronic Marijuana Use in Native Costa Ricans," *Annals of the New York Academy of Medicine* 282: 266–306, 1976; J. B. Page et al., "Psychosociocultural Perspectives on Chronic Cannabis Use: The Costa Rican Follow-Up," *Journal of Psychoactive Drugs* 20: 57–65, 1988. In a twelve-year study of 65,000 men and women in California, researchers at the Kaiser Permanente Health Group found no statistically significant correlation between marijuana smoking and mortality. Excluding AIDS patients, pot smokers had no higher risk for early death than people who never smoked pot. See Stephen Sidney et al., "Marijuana Use and Mortality," *American Journal of Public Health,* April 1997.

short-term memory deficiencies: See L. Miller et al., "Marijuana: An Analysis of Storage and Retrieval Deficits in Memory with the Technique of Restricted Reminding," *Pharmacology, Biochemistry, and Behavior* 8: 327–32, 1978; R. I. Block et al., "Acute Effects of Marijuana on Cognition: Relationships to Chronic Effects and Smoking Techniques," *Pharmacology, Biochemistry, and Behavior* 43: 907–17, 1992; H. G. Pope and D. Yurgelun-Todd, "The Residual Cognitive Effects of Heavy Marijuana Use in College Students," *Journal of the American Medical Association* 275 (7), February 21, 1996.

18 *marijuana may have a mild immunosuppressive effect:* See H. Friedman et al., "Marijuana, Receptors, and Immunomodulation," *Advances in Experimental Medicine and Biology* 373: 103–13, 1995; S. Spector et al., Delta-9-Tetrahydrocannabinol Augments Murine Retroviral Induced Immunosuppression and Infection," *International Journal of Immunopharmacology* 13: 411–17, 1991; G. A. Cabral et al., "Effect of Delta-9-Tetrahydrocannibinol on Herpes Simplex Virus Tyrpe 2 Vaginal Infection in the Guinea Pig," *Proceedings of the Society for Experimental Biology and Medicine* 182: 181–86, 1986; Leo Hollister, "Marijuana and Immunity," *Journal of Psychoactive Drugs* 24: 159–64, 1992.

habitual marijuana smoking may cause chronic bronchitis: Interview with Dr. Donald P. Tashkin. See Tashkin, "Marihuana and the Lung," in *Marihuana and Medicine,* pp. 279–88.

occasional use of marijuana by a healthy adult: Interview with Dr. Leo Hollister. See "Health Aspects of Cannabis," *Pharmacological Reviews* 38: 1–20, 1986, and "Health Aspects of Cannabis: Revisited," *International Journal of Neuropsychopharmacology* 1: 71–80, 1998, both by Dr. Hollister.

kills thousands of people every year: See Leslie L. Iverson, *The Science of Marijuana* (New York: Oxford University Press, 2000), p. 179.

a hundred pounds of marijuana a minute: See Francis L. Young, "In the Matter of Marijuana Rescheduling Petition: Opinion and Recommended Ruling, Findings of Fact, Conclusions of Law, and Decisions of Administrative Law Judge," U.S. Department of Justice, Drug Enforcement Administration, September 6, 1988, p. 56.

19 *The first American law concerning marijuana:* "For hempe also both English and Indian," delegates at the first meeting of Virginia's House of Burgesses declared, "we do require and enjoine all householders of this Colony that have any of those seeds to make tryal thereof the next season." See Susan Myra Kingsbury, ed., *The Records of the Virginia Company of London,* vol. III (Washington, D.C.: Government Printing Office, 1933), p. 166. In 1639 the legislature of New Plymouth passed a law requiring that every household grow hemp, as did the legislature in Connecticut. See James F. Hopkins, *A History of the Hemp Industry in Kentucky* (Lexington: University of Kentucky Press, 1951), p. 7.

allowed hemp to be used as legal tender: Ibid., p. 8.

aroused a "lust for blood": Quoted in Richard J. Bonnie and Charles H. Whitebread, *The Marihuana Conviction: A History of Marihuana Prohibition in the United States* (Charlottesville: University Press of Virginia, 1974), p. 34.

"The dominant race and most enlightened countries": A. E. Fossier, "The Marihuana Menace," speech before the Louisiana State Medical Society, New Orleans, April 14–16, 1931.

20 *"Murder Weed Found Up and Down Coast":* Quoted in Larry (Ratso) Sloman, *Reefer Madness: A History of Marijuana* (New York: St. Martin's Griffin, 1999), p. 44.

"Marijuana: Assassin of Youth": Harry J. Anslinger and Courtney Riley Cooper, "Marijuana: Assassin of Youth," *American Magazine,* July 1937.

lectured Caldwell on the viciousness of marijuana: See John C. McWilliams, *The Protectors: Harry J. Anslinger and the Federal Bureau of Narcotics, 1930–1962* (Newark: University of Delaware Press, 1990), pp. 77–78.

"morphine feeding stations" and "barrooms for addicts": Quoted in David F. Musto, *The American Disease: Origins of Narcotic Control* (New York: Oxford University Press, 1999), p. 374, n. 42.

20 *"jail offenders, then throw away the key"*: Quoted in McWilliams, *Protectors*, p. 78.

21 *dismissed its authors as "dangerous" and "strange"*: Quoted in ibid., p. 104. Anslinger felt betrayed by the physicians who did the study; he'd supplied them with marijuana. Interview with Dr. David F. Musto.
"Marijuana and Musicians": For accounts of Anslinger's fierce hatred of jazz, see Sloman, *Reefer Madness*, pp. 133–51, and Bonnie and Whitehead, *Marijuana Conviction*, pp. 181–86.
collaborated with the Office of Strategic Services: For Anslinger's links to the OSS and the CIA, see McWilliams, *Protectors*, pp. 164–75.
MK-Ultra, a notorious mind control program: For a good account of MK-ULTRA, one of the strangest government programs ever conceived, see Martin A. Lee and Bruce Shlain, *Acid Dreams: The Complete Social History of LSD: The CIA, the Sixties, and Beyond* (New York: Grove Press, 1992), pp. 27–35.

22 *"I toiled wholeheartedly in the vineyards"*: Quoted in ibid., p. 35.
"one of the most influential members of Congress": Harry J. Anslinger and Will Oursler, *The Murderers: The Story of the Narcotic Gangs* (New York: Farrar, Straus, and Cudahy, 1961), pp. 181–82.
believes that well-connected addict was Senator Joseph R. McCarthy: See McWilliams, *The Protectors*, pp. 98–99.

23 *"Recognizing the extensive degree of misinformation"*: National Commission on Marihuana and Drug Abuse, *Marihuana: A Signal of Misunderstanding* (Washington, D.C.: Government Printing Office, 1972), p. 167.
"Considering the range of social concerns": Ibid., p. 167.
"the Jews": Quoted in Dan Baum, *Smoke and Mirrors: The War on Drugs and the Politics of Failure* (New York: Little, Brown, 1996), p. 54.
a backyard barbecue held in Atlanta: For the origins of the parents' antidrug movement, see Peggy Mann, *Marijuana Alert* (New York: McGraw-Hill, 1985), pp. 414–19, and Gabriel Nahas, *Keep Off the Grass* (Middlebury, Vt.: Paul S. Erikkson, 1990), pp. 230–36. The organized backlash against marijuana reform began two years before the Atlanta barbecue, at Senate hearings staged with assistance from Gabriel Nahas in 1974. The transcript of those hearings is a remarkable document. Among the claims that were made in testimony before the subcommittee: marijuana turned kids into "semi-zombies," caused irreversible brain damage, and led to chromosome damage among moderate pot smokers "roughly the same type and degree . . . as in persons surviving atom bombing with a heavy level of radiation exposure." See *Marihuana-Hashish Epidemic and Its Impact on National Security,* Hearings before the Subcommittee to Investigate the Administration of the Internal Security Act and Other Internal Security Laws of the Commit-

tee on the Judiciary, U.S. Senate, 93rd Congress, Second Session, May 9, 16, 17, 20, 21, and June 13, 1974 (Washington, D.C.: Government Printing Office, 1975), pp. ix, xi, 210.

24 *one out of twelve high school seniors:* Cited in Mann, *Marijuana Alert,* p. 414.
"The slogans of the revolution": The Yippie leader who made this prediction, Jerry Rubin, later embraced the values of the Reagan revolution. Quoted in William Powell, *The Anarchist Cookbook* (Secaucus, N.J.: Lyle Stewart, 1971), p. 31. See also Timothy Leary, "The Politics, Ethics, and Meaning of Marijuana," and Allen Ginsberg, "First Manifesto to End the Bringdown," in David Solomon, ed., *The Marijuana Papers* (New York: Signet Books, 1968).
"tumultuous change in values . . . the leading edge of this cultural change": Quoted in Mann, *Marihuana Alert,* pp. 23, 31.
"is probably the most dangerous drug": See "Text of GOP Debate," *Associated Press,* February 29, 1980.
"the present young-adult generation's involvement": Quoted in Baum, *Smoke and Mirrors,* p. 154.
smoking pot could turn young men into homosexuals: See "Reagan Aide: Pot Can Make You Gay," *Newsweek,* October 27, 1986, p. 95.

25 *Richard Bonnie . . . believes that advocates:* Interview with Richard Bonnie.

26 *Some states classify marijuana:* For an overview of state marijuana laws, see National Criminal Justice Association, *A Guide to State Controlled Substances Acts,* January 1999, and "NORML's State Guide to Marijuana Laws," www.norml.org.

27 *"smoke a joint, lose your license" statutes:* See Diana R. Gordon, "The Drug War Hits the Road," *The Nation,* May 31, 1993; Nate Hendley, "Smoke a joint, lose your license: Little-known U.S. penalty: Federal funding for highways tied to drug enforcement," *National Post,* May 10, 2002.
About 724,000 people were arrested: There were 723,627 marijuana arrests in 2001, and 641,108 were for possession (88.5 percent). For figures on all drug arrests, see *Crime in the United States, 2001,* FBI Uniform Crime Reporting Program, October 2002.
a few days in jail: It is extremely difficult to obtain information on how many people are sent to jail every year for marijuana crimes. The number nationwide may be 100,000 or more. A recent study in Maryland found that about one-quarter of those arrested for marijuana possession spent at least one day in jail and about one-sixth spent a week or more in jail before trial. See Peter Reuter, Paul Hirschfield, and Curt Davies, "Assessing the Crackdown on Marijuana in Maryland," Abell Foundation, May 2001.

35 *300,000 acres of marijuana:* Cited in Hopkins, *Hemp in Kentucky,* p. 212.
A bushel of corn . . . a bushel of manicured marijuana: In 2001 the average

price for a bushel of corn was between $1.85 and $2.15. A bushel of corn weighs 56 pounds. The marijuana growers in Mark Young's case received $1,200 a pound for their crop more than a decade ago. That means a bushel of their Indiana, farm-raised marijuana was worth $67,200. Marijuana grown indoors would have brought a much higher price. For the price of corn, see *Monthly Agricultural Newsletter,* National Agricultural Statistics Service, February 2002.

36 *a rare instance in which protectionism actually worked:* Interview with Mark A. R. Kleiman.
approximately $970 million: See Kleiman, *Marijuana,* pp. 74–77.
roughly $4 billion a year: In 2002 the federal government spent $18.8 billion fighting the war on drugs. It seems fair to assume that 20 to 25 percent of that money was used to fight marijuana (since about 30 percent of all federal drug arrests are for marijuana crimes). That means in 2002 between $3.76 billion and $4.7 billion was spent by the federal government in the war on marijuana. See "Federal Drug Offenders, 1999" and *National Drug Control Strategy, FY 2003 Budget Summary,* The White House, February 2002.
In 2000 the DEA eradicated: Cited in "Drugs and Crime Facts," Bureau of Justice Statistics, October 28, 2002.
finds only 10 to 20 percent of the marijuana: See Weisheit, *Domestic Marijuana,* pp. 31, 34.
prices ranging from $400 a pound: See "Drug Trafficking in the United States," DEA Domestic Strategic Intelligence Unit, September 2001.

37 *Weisheit first became interested:* Interview with Ralph Weisheit.

38 *Weisheit agrees that most of the marijuana:* Ibid.
Estimates of how many Americans grow marijuana: The number of people growing marijuana in the United Staes is as hard to determine as the size of their annual crop. For this estimate, see "Analysis of the Domestic Cannabis Problem and the Federal Response, Staff Report," National Drug Enforcement Policy Board, 1986.

43 *Members of Congress vied to appear tough:* For an account of the congressional debate over the Boggs Act, see Bonnie and Whitehead, *Marijuana Conviction,* pp. 206–21.
"would just about dry up the [drug] traffic": Quoted in ibid., p. 207.
attributed the passage of such laws to "hysteria": Quoted in ibid., p. 211.
"result in better justice": See *Congressional Record–House,* September 23, 1970, p. 33314.

45 *the most commonly cited justification:* See U.S. Sentencing Commission, *Special Report to Congress: Mandatory Minimum Penalties in the Federal Criminal Justice System* (St. Paul, Minn.: West Publishing Co., August 1991), pp. 14–15.

NOTES

Tora S. Brown — a nineteen-year-old: See Tom Jackman, "Woman's Silence Leads to Long Prison Term: She Won't Name Mother as Co-conspirator in PCP Case," *Kansas City Star,* January 26, 1994.

47 *"At the end, when we seen how bad it was":* Interview with Mary Fagel.

48 *"Mr. Young, it's a sad day":* Transcript, *U.S. v. Young,* February 8, 1992, p. 73.

"When I was in England I experimented: Quoted in Thomas B. Edsall, "Clinton Admits '60s Marijuana Use," *Washington Post,* March 30, 1992.

"Marijuana is illegal, dangerous, unhealthy": Quoted in Jacob Sullivan, "Weed Whackers," *Reason,* October 19, 1997. See also Donna E. Shalala, "Say 'No' to Legalization of Marijuana," *Wall Street Journal,* August 18, 1995.

annual marijuana arrests more than doubled: Some 342,000 people were arrested for marijuana in 1992, the year before Clinton took office; 734,498 (an all-time record) were arrested in 2000, the last year of his presidency. See "FBI Uniform Crime Reports," 1993, 2001.

Far more people were arrested . . . during the Clinton presidency: Some 4,909,438 people were arrested for marijuana during Clinton's presidency, from 1993 through 2000; during the Reagan years, from 1981 through 1988, 3,255,096 were arrested for pot. See "FBI Uniform Crime Reports," 1982–1989, 1994–2001.

49 *more than three times as many people:* During the Nixon presidency, from 1969 through 1974, there were 1,540,600 arrests for marijuana.

a twenty-six-fold increase in pot arrests: According to the New York State Department of Criminal Justice Statistics, in 1992, the year before Giuliani took office, there were fewer than 2,000 marijuana arrests in New York City. There were 52,000 marijuana arrests there in 2000.

"Are you now, or have you ever been, a pot smoker?": The sociologist David Wagner makes a similar argument in his fine book *The New Temperance: The American Obsession with Sin and Vice* (New York: Westview Press, 1997), but he phrases the crucial question somewhat differently: "Are you now or have you ever been a '60s'-style person?" There are some important differences, however, between the McCarthy-era witch-hunts and the War on Drugs. The McCarthy era was briefer and destroyed fewer lives.

50 *"so-called medicinal use of marijuana":* Quoted in "Barr Refutes Study on 'Medicinal' Marijuana," August 8, 1997.

"All civilized countries in the world": See "Medical Marijuana Referenda Movement in America," Hearing Before the Subcommittee on Crime of the House Judiciary Committee, One Hundred Fifth Congress, October 1, 1997.

a "subversive criminal movement": Quoted in Peter Schrag, "A Quagmire for Our Time," *American Prospect,* August 13, 2001.

50 *"legal, widely used, profitable, disfavored":* Bob Barr, "Is Janet Reno's RICO Lawsuit Against Big Tobacco Legally Justified?" *Insight Magazine,* October 15, 1999.

McConnell accepted more money from tobacco: See "Tobacco, Top 20 Recipients," www.opensecrets.org. This Web site, run by the Center for Responsive Politics, is an excellent source of information about the role of money in the American political system.

responsible for an estimated 440,000 deaths: Cited in J. L. Fellows et al., "Annual Smoking-Attributable Mortality, Years of Potential Life Lost, and Economic Costs—United States, 1995–1999," *Morbidity and Mortality Weekly Report,* Centers for Disease Control and Prevention, 51 (14), April 12, 2002.

about 3 percent of Fortune 200 companies . . . about 98 percent: In 1983, six of the Fortune 200 conducted drug tests; by 1991 that number had risen to 196. Cited in Kirstin Downey Grimsley, "Like It or Not, Here's the Cup," *Washington Post,* May 10, 1998.

A recent study of 14,000 employees: See "Study Highlights Casual Drinking's Effects on Productivity," *Alcoholism and Drug Abuse Weekly,* January 18, 1999.

51 *annual revenues of about $740 million:* Cited in Dana Hawkins, "Tests on Trial," *U.S. News & World Report,* August 12, 2002.

"marijuana has no direct, negative effect": Charles R. Schwenk and Susan L. Rhodes, *Marijuana and the Workplace: Interpreting Research on Complex Social Issues* (Westport, Conn.: Quorum Books, 1999), p. 177.

52 *"Kicking this guy out of his apartment":* Interview with Tom Condon.

"We must educate our children": Dan Burton, "Kill the Coca at Its Roots: Eradication of the Growing Fields Would Save American Lives and Aid the Environment," *Los Angeles Times,* April 26, 1990.

"We must get tough on drug dealers": Quoted in Marc Lacey, "Rep.'s Son Charged with Trafficking Drugs," *Los Angeles Times,* January 26, 1997.

53 *"My son has a good heart":* Quoted in "Rep. Cunningham Pleads for Leniency for Son," *National Journal's House Race Hotline,* November 20, 1998.

"de facto sentencing by police and prosecutors": Quoted in *Mandatory Minimum Penalties,* p. H-15.

54 *Clark was indicted under federal law:* Donald Clark was pardoned by President Clinton in January 2001 and released from prison.

55 *"They busted me completely":* Interview with Edward Czuprynski.

"naive, trusting, and childlike in comprehension": Quoted in "FAMM Case Study, Zodenta McCarter."

56 *"giant mausoleum adrift in a great sea":* Quoted in Pete Earley, *The Hot House: Life Inside Leavenworth Prison* (New York: Bantam, 1992), p. 30.

57 *a perfect microcosm of the federal prison system:* Interview with Jonathon Turley.

in the past year it has housed more than 1,700: According to the Federal Bureau of Prisons, there were 1,755 inmates at Leavenworth in November 2002.

about 30 percent above capacity: See Paige M. Harrison and Allen J. Beck, "Prisoners in 2001," *Bureau of Justice Statistics Bulletin,* July 2002.

more than 10,000 inmates a year: Between 2000 and 2001 the number of federal inmates increased by 11,465. See "Prisoners in 2001."

the Federal Bureau of Narcotics had only 300 agents: Cited in David F. Musto, *The American Disease* (New Haven: Yale University Press, 1973), p. 240.

the DEA, now has 4,600: Cited in "DEA Staffing and Appropriations, FY 1972–2003," U.S. Drug Enforcement Administration.

from $88 million to $1.3 billion: See *Drugs, Crime, and the Justice System: A National Report from the Bureau of Justice Statistics* (Washington, D.C.: U.S. Government Printing Office, 1992), p. 130.

In 1970 there were 3,384 drug offenders: See "Federal Prison Population, and number and percent sentenced for drug offenses, United States 1970–2001," Bureau of Justice Statistics, July 18, 2002.

Today there are more than 68,000: Ibid.

more than 330,000: See "Prisoners in 2001."

the number of people imprisoned for all crimes in 1970: There were 196,092 inmates in American prisons in 1970. See Bureau of Justice Statistics, *Sourcebook of Criminal Justice Statistics, 1996* (Washington, D.C.: U.S. Government Printing Office, 1997), p. 518.

61 *"The place is full of nuts":* Interview with Tom Dawson.

62 *spent about $25 million on its informers:* Cited in Mark Curriden, "Secret Threat to Justice," *National Law Journal,* February 20, 1995.

63 *"Criminals are likely to say and do almost anything":* Quoted in ibid.
Perhaps a hundred senior federal judges: I based this estimate on interviews with William Schwarzer and Jack B. Weinstein.
"I need a rest from the oppressive sense of futility": Quoted in Jack B. Weinstein, "No More Drug Cases," *New York Law Journal,* April 15, 1993.
"Every particle of real punishment": Jeremy Bentham, "Principles of Penal Law," in John Bowring, ed., *The Works of Jeremy Bentham* (New York: Russell and Russell, 1962), Vol. I, p. 398.

64 *"My position as a prosecutor":* Interview with Deborah Daniels. In the summer of 2001 President Bush appointed Daniels to be the assistant attorney general for the Office of Justice Programs.
sold more than a million copies: Interview with Ed Rosenthal.

66 *"The war on drugs is an absolute failure":* Quoted in "Leaders Debate Legalization of Drugs," *Associated Press,* November 16, 2001. See also Gary E. Johnson, "The Case for Drug Legalization," February 1, 2000.

66 *An opinion poll taken around the same time:* The poll was conducted by Zogby International between November 27 and 29, 2001.

67 *"You bet I did, and I enjoyed it.":* Quoted in Richard Brookhiser, "City Power: Bloomberg, End Pot Law Hypocrisy," April 19, 2002.

"escalate the war on drugs": Quoted in Schrag, "Quagmire."

"the latest manifestation of the liberals' commitment": John P. Walters and James F. X. O'Gara, "The Clinton Administration's Continuing Retreat in the War on Drugs," *Heritage Foundation Reports,* June 16, 1994. See also John P. Walters, "The Myth of 'Harmless' Marijuana," *Washington Post,* May 1, 2002.

"it would send the wrong message to children": Quoted in Schrag, "Quagmire."

"Many Americans do not know that hemp and marijuana": Quoted in Michael Ravnitsky, "DEA Moves to Ban Foods with Hemp," *National Law Journal,* December 11, 2001.

68 *"We have 960 patients out in the parks":* Quoted in David S. Broder, "DEA Marijuana Madness," *Washington Post,* November 11, 2001.

"The government antidrug policy is a big lie": Quoted in Jim Herron Zamora, "Profile: Ed Rosenthal; Pot-Growing Icon Takes Raid in Stride," *San Francisco Chronicle,* February 25, 2002.

69 *"We are after you":* Quoted in Martin Linton, " 'Relentless Drive' on Pushers," *The Guardian,* August 10, 1985.

"never legalize illicit drugs": Quoted in Michael George et al., "Pot Luck: Lax Prosecution of Drug-Related Cases," *New Statesman & Society,* March 17, 1995.

"the most chilling, evil industry": Quoted in Matthew Parris, "Deliver Us from Cowardice," *The Times,* January 1, 2000.

British arrests for marijuana nearly quadrupled: See Alex Sleator and Grahame Allen, *Cannabis,* Research Paper 00/74, House of Commons Library, August 3, 2000, Appendix 1, Table 7.

As many as 5,600 marijuana offenders: Ibid.

70 *the highest rate of marijuana use among young people:* See "Surveys: Lifetime Prevalence Among Students 15–16 Years," European Monitoring Centre for Drugs and Drug Addiction, 2002.

British teenagers were much more likely to smoke pot: See Tony Thompson, "The Drugs Debate: Two Countries Took the Test," *Observer,* February 24, 2002.

"draw up plans to legalise cannabis": Quoted in Mary Ann Sieghart, "Why Are Ministers So Scared of the Drug Debate?" *The Times,* March 31, 2000.

The Police Foundation recommended: See *Drugs and the Law, Report of the Independent Inquiry into the Misuse of Drugs Act, 1971,* Police Foundation, 2000.

a former deputy leader of the Tories: See Peter Lilley, "Common Sense on Cannabis: The Conservative Case for Change," Social Market Foundation, July 2001.

"the long-term consumption of cannabis": Report by the Advisory Committee on Drug Dependence (London: Her Majesty's Stationery Office, 1968), p. 7.

"very much less dangerous than the opiates": Ibid., p. 17.

"moderate indulgence in cannabis has little ill effect: "Dangerous Habits," *The Lancet* 352 (9140), November 14, 1998.

"moderate use practically produces no ill effects": Quoted in *Advisory Committee on Drug Dependence,* p. 7.

71 *when drug use is at its height:* Musto interview.

Marijuana use among the young peaked in 1979 . . . when use had already fallen by about 40 percent: Some 16.7 percent of teenagers aged 12 to 17 smoked pot at least once a month in 1979; by 1988 that proportion had fallen to about 10 percent. See "Estimated Prevalence of Drug and Alcohol Use During the Past Month," Bureau of Justice Statistics, *Sourcebook of Criminal Justice Statistics, 1994* (Washington, D.C.: U.S. Government Printing Office, 1995), p. 294.

the explanation most young people gave: See Lloyd D. Johnston, "Toward a Theory of Drug Epidemics," in Lewis Donohew, Howard E. Sypher, and William J. Bukoski, *Persuasive Communication and Drug Abuse Prevention* (Hillsdale, N.J.: Lawrence Erlbaum Associates, 1991), pp. 115–29.

more than doubling in the United States: See "Preliminary Estimates from the 1995 National Household Survey on Drug Abuse," Substance Abuse and Mental Health Services Administration, August 1996.

88.5 percent of America's high school seniors: See "High School Seniors' Perceptions of Availability of Drugs, By Type of Drugs, 1982–94," *Sourcebook, 1994,* p. 214.

In 2000 the proportion of seniors who said: See "High School Seniors' Perceptions of Availability of Drugs, 1988–2000," Bureau of Justice Statistics, *Sourcebook of Criminal Justice Statistics, 2000* (Washington, D.C.: U.S. Government Printing Office, 2001), p. 173.

72 *"but you've got to walk through the heroin":* Young interview.

74 *"Tobacco and alcohol are the most widely used":* Michael D. Newcomb, "Identifying High-Risk Youth: Prevalence and Petters of Adolescent Drug Abuse," *Adolescent Drug Abuse: Clinical Assessment and Therapeutic Interventions,* National Institute on Drug Abuse Research Monograph Series, 156 (Rockville, Md.: U.S. Department of Health and Human Services, 1995), p 37.

drink alcohol almost four times as often: See "Students Reporting Use of

Alcohol and Drugs, by Grade Level of Respondent, and Frequency of Use, 2000–2001," Bureau of Justice Statistics, 2002.

in the strawberry fields

The best book about California farmworkers was published more than sixty years ago. *Factories in the Field: The Story of Migratory Farm Labor in California,* by Carey McWilliams (Berkeley: University of California Press, 1999), describes a system of agricultural production that in many respects still operates the same way today. Published two months after *The Grapes of Wrath, Factories in the Field* never attracted as many readers as that epic novel. One reason, perhaps, is that the exploited migrants depicted by John Steinbeck were Caucasian, while those described by McWilliams were mainly Asian and Latino. In *North from Mexico: The Spanish Speaking People of the United States* (Philadelphia: J. B. Lippincott, 1948), McWilliams offers a history that mainstream historians had long ignored. *Mexican Americans/American Mexicans: From Conquistadors to Chicanos* (New York: Hill and Wang, 1993), by Matt S. Meier and Feliciano Ribera, is a more recent introduction to the subject. Cletus E. Daniel's *Bitter Harvest: A History of California Farmworkers, 1870–1941* (Ithaca, N.Y.: Cornell University Press, 1981) is a fine work of scholarship, adding new sources and much new information. *Migratory Labor in American Agriculture: Report of the President's Commission on Migratory Labor* (Washington, D.C.: U.S. Government Printing Office, 1951) gives a strong sense of how little has changed over the past fifty years.

The plight of Mexican farmworkers in the United States is inextricably linked to the racism they've encountered here for more than a century. John Higham's *Strangers in the Land: Patterns of American Nativism, 1860–1925* (New Brunswick, N.J.: Rutgers University Press, 1988) is a classic work on the roots of anti-immigrant sentiment in a nation of immigrants. *Unwanted Mexican Americans in the Great Depression: Repatriation Pressures, 1929–1939* (Tucson: University of Arizona Press, 1974), by Abraham Hoffman, tells an important story that has largely been forgotten: how the expulsion of Mexican farmworkers during the 1930s allowed Steinbeck's "Okies" to find work in rural California. Juan Ramon Garcia's *Operation Wetback: The Mass Deportation of Mexican Undocumented Workers in 1954* (Westport, Conn.: Greenwood Press, 1980) is another book that examines hidden American history: President Eisenhower's reliance on the U.S. Army to round up and deport poor Mexicans. The failure of America's first large-scale guest worker program is described in *Merchants of Labor: The Mexican Bracero Story; An Account of the Managed Migration of Mexican Farmworkers in California, 1942–1960* (Charlotte, N.C.: McNally & Loftin, 1964), by Ernesto Galarza. The lessons of the Bracero Program are the starting point for *"Temporary" Alien Workers in the*

United States: Designing Policy from Fact and Opinion (Boulder, Colo.: West-view Replica Edition, 1982), by Sidney Weintraub and Stanley R. Ross. Peter Matthiessen's *Sal Si Puedes: Cesar Chavez and the New American Revolution* (New York: Random House, 1969) is a poignant reminder of the years when meaningful change seemed not only possible but imminent.

I am grateful to the many experts on farm labor and immigration who took the time to speak with me. Don Villarejo, executive director of the California Institute for Rural Studies, gave me a good overview of the issues now surrounding migrant labor. The late Julian L. Simon, a professor at the University of Maryland's College of Business and Management, spent hours debating the virtues of unrestricted immigration with me. His book *The Economic Consequences of Immigration* (Cambridge, Mass.: Basil Blackwell, 1989) is essential reading on the subject. His arguments are brilliant, formidable, optimistic, and profoundly libertarian; nevertheless I don't agree with all of them. Marc Linder, a professor at the University of Iowa Law School, is equally brilliant—and even more contrarian. Linder's work on behalf of migrants in Texas, as well as a mastery of the academic literature, informs his book *Migrant Workers and Minimum Wages: Regulating the Exploitation of Agricultural Labor in the United States* (Boulder, Colo.: Westview Press, 1992). Philip L. Martin, a professor of agricultural economics at the University of California at Davis, shared his views on the size of America's migrant workforce and the best ways to improve their lives. His book *The Endless Quest: Helping America's Farmworkers* (Boulder, Colo.: Westview Press, 1994), written with David A. Martin, is calm, well reasoned, and convincing. I also recommend two other works of his: *Promises to Keep: Collective Bargaining in California Agriculture* (Ames: Iowa State University Press, 1996) and "Economic Integration and Migration: The Mexico-U.S. Case," United Nations World Institute for Development Economics Research, Conference on Poverty, International Migration and Asylum, September 18, 2002. Juan Vicente Palerm—director of the University of California's Institute for Mexico and the United States—served as my guide to the Santa Maria Valley in both literal and literary terms. He has a uniquely cross-cultural perspective on migrant labor. I benefited greatly from the following works of his: Palerm, "Farm Labor Needs and Farm-workers in California, 1970 to 1989," *California Agricultural Studies, 91–92*, Labor Market Information Division, State Employment Development Department, April 1991; "A Season in the Life of a Migrant Farmworker in California," *Western Journal of Medicine* 157: 362–66, September 1992; "A Binational System of Agricultural Production: The Case of the Mexican Bajio and California," with Jose Ignacio Urquiola, in Daniel G. Aldrich, Jr., and Lorenzo Meyer, *Mexico and the United States: Neighbors in Crisis* (San Bernardino, Calif.: Borgo Press, 1993); and "Immigrant and Migrant Farmworkers in the Santa Maria Valley, California," Center for Survey Methods Research, Bureau of the Census, 1994. Martin and Palerm helped to ensure that my writing about farm labor was factually correct. Any remaining errors or misjudgments are entirely my fault.

I learned a great deal from two books that examine the effects of technology on farm labor: David Runsten and Phillip LeVeen, *Mechanization and Mexican Labor in California Agriculture* (San Diego: University of California, 1981) and Barry L. Price, *The Political Economy of Mechanization in U.S. Agriculture* (Boulder, Colo.: Westview Press, 1983). Runsten—the associate director of the Center for North American Integration and Development at the University of California, Los Angeles—spoke to me about his research on farm labor, mechanization, the strawberry industry, and the advent of migrant workers from Oaxaca. His collaboration with Michael Kearney, a professor of anthropology at the University of California, Northridge, has produced a pair of fascinating reports on these new immigrants: "A Survey of Oaxacan Village Networks in California Agriculture," California Institute for Rural Studies, September 1994, and "Mixtec Migrants in California Agriculture," with Carol Zabin, Anna Garcia, and Carol Nagengast, California Institute of Rural Studies, May 1993. Kearney first traveled to Oaxaca in the 1960s, and I am grateful for the time he spent telling me about the ongoing exodus of Mixtecs. Two of his articles were particularly useful: "Border and Boundaries of State and Self at the End of Empire," *Journal of Historical Sociology* 4 (1): 52–74, March 1991, and "Mixtec Ethnicity: Social Identity, Political Consciousness, and Political Activism," with Carole Nagengast, *Latin American Research Review* 25 (2): 61–91. Manolo Gonzalez helped me understand the role of Mixtec labor in Santa Barbara County, and Fred Krissman told me about his anthropological research in the Mixtec. Krissman has served as a visiting fellow at the Center for U.S.-Mexican Studies, University of California, San Diego. Algimiro Morales, a founder of the Coalition of Indian Communities of Oaxaca, described some of the challenges that Mixtecs now face in California. Leo Chavez, a professor of anthropology at the University of California, Irvine, shared his experience with migrants in northern San Diego County. His book *Shadowed Lives: Undocumented Immigrants in American Society* (New York: Harcourt Brace Jovanovich, 1992) contains a fine account of the farmworker encampments there.

U.S.-Mexico Relations: Labor Market Interdependence (Stanford: Stanford University Press, 1992), edited by Jorge A. Bustamante, Clark W. Reynolds, and Raul A. Hinojosa Ojeda, is a provocative collection of essays. Maralyn Edid's *Farm Labor Organizing: Trends & Prospects* (Ithaca, N.Y.: ILR Press, 1994) outlines the huge difficulties that union organizers now confront in the fields. *Seasonal Agricultural Labor Markets in the United States,* ed. Robert D. Emerson (Ames: Iowa State University Press, 1984), provides an interesting economic analysis of the demand for farmworkers. Bonnie Lynn Bade's "Is

There a Doctor in the Field? Underlying Conditions Affecting Access to Health Care for California Farmworkers and Their Families," California Policy Research Center, University of California, September 1999, describes the poor living conditions and poor health of the state's migrants. Two recent books bring such conditions vividly to life: Daniel Rothenberg's *With These Hands: The Hidden World of Migrant Farmworkers Today* (New York: Harcourt Brace, 1998) and Ruben Martinez's *Crossing Over: A Mexican Family on the Migrant Trail* (New York: Henry Holt, 2001). *Coyotes: A Journey through the Secret World of America's Illegal Aliens* (New York: Vintage Books, 1987), by Ted Conover, is a brilliant investigation of a realm that most Americans never see.

The following government reports contain a great deal of useful information: Commission on Agricultural Workers, *Report of the Commission on Agricultural Workers* (Washington, D.C.: U.S. Government Printing Office, 1992); Robin Marsh, David Runsten, and David Zilberman, "Profile of the California Strawberry Industry: Production and Pest Management Characteristics," Report for the Environmental Protection Agency, Project 44-2, Modeling the Impacts of Pesticide Use in Specialty Crop Markets, Berkeley, California, July 1992; David C. Mountjoy, "Farming Practices Survey and Outreach Recommendations for the Elkhorn Slough Water Quality Management Plan," Association of Monterey Bay Governments, July 1, 1993; "California Findings from the National Agricultural Workers Survey: A Demographic and Employment Profile of Perishable Crop Farmworkers Survey," Research Report No. 3, U.S. Department of Labor, Office of Program Economics, 1993; "U.S. Farmworkers in the Post-IRCA Period," based on data from the National Agricultural Workers Survey (NAWS), Research Report No. 4, U.S. Department of Labor, Office of Program Economics, March 1993; "Migrant Farmworkers: Pursuing Security in an Unstable Labor Market," based on data from the National Agricultural Workers Survey (NAWS), Research Report No. 5, U.S. Department of Labor, Office of Program Economics, May 1994; "Findings from the National Agricultural Workers Survey (NAWS), 1997–1998: A Demographic and Employment Profile of United States Farmworkers," Research Report No. 8, U.S. Department of Labor, Office of Program Economics, March 2000; Alice C. Larson, "Migrant and Seasonal Farmworker Enumeration Profiles Study, California," Migrant Health Program, Health Resources and Services Administration, U.S. Department of Health and Human Services, September 2000.

A History of the Strawberry: From Ancient Gardens to Modern Markets (Berkeley: University of California Division of Agricultural Sciences, 1974), by Stephen Wilhelm and James E. Sagen, tells you just about everything you'd care to know about strawberries—and more. Stafford Whiteaker's *The Compleat Strawberry* (New York: Crown Publishers, 1985) takes a more idiosyncratic approach, featuring poems, etchings, history, folklore, gardening tips, and a recipe for strawberry toothpaste. Ernest Feder's *Strawberry Imperialism: An Enquiry into the Mechanisms of Dependency in Mexican Agriculture* (The Hague: Institute of Social Studies, 1977) has a much different tone, viewing the American investment in Mexico's strawberry industry as a manifestation of capitalist imperialism. Miriam J. Wells's *Strawberry Fields: Politics, Class, and Work in California Agriculture* (Ithaca: Cornell University Press, 1996), the culmination of two decades' research, has much fascinating material on sharecropping and the strawberry industry in the Pajaro and Salinas valleys, though I disagree with her class-based analysis. *Good Liberals & Great Blue Herons: Land, Labor, and Politics in the Pajaro Valley* (Santa Cruz, Calif.: Center for Political Ecology, 1994), by Frank Bardacke, evokes the unique culture and community of Watsonville.

I am grateful to Carrie Kahn—who at the time was an intrepid reporter at KPBS in San Diego—for taking me to the shantytowns of Tijuana. For seven years she reported from the border with great skill and compassion. Bill Hoerger, the executive director of California Rural Legal Assistance (CRLA), spent many hours telling me about the efforts of his organization on behalf of farmworkers. I'm grateful to the other CRLA attorneys who spoke to me at length about their work and helped me meet with farmworkers: Mike Meuter in Salinas, Jeannie Barrett in Santa Maria, Claudia Smith and Ricardo J. Soto in Oceanside. I'm also grateful to Jose Lopez and Sabino Lopez for introducing me to migrants in the central coast. Anne Hipshman—assistant chief counsel to the California labor commissioner—helped me understand the legal intricacies of the new sharecropping arrangements. At the United Farm Workers union, I learned much from Marc Grossman, Annabelle Cortez, and Lauro Navarro. Most of all, I'm grateful to the many farmworkers and sharecroppers who invited me to visit their encampments and homes. In trying to depict their lives in California, I was constantly struck by the inadequacy of words.

Victor Voth—an emeritus pomologist in the Department of Pomology at the University of California, Irvine—explained some of the challenges that strawberry growers now face. Voth is a legendary figure in the industry, having helped to develop many popular strawberry varieties. Amado Amarao, a plant breeder for Driscoll Associates, explained some of the details of strawberry cultivation and gave me a tour of one of the company's farms in Oxnard. Theresa Thorne, at the California Strawberry Commission, and David Owen, at the San Diego County Farm Bureau, were also quite helpful in providing the growers' perspective. Peter M. Gwosdof was friendly and helpful during all of our conversations about sharecropping, though I wish his legal skills were being put to a different use. I interviewed some of the leading strawberry growers in California—and disliked none of them. I was fortunate to hear their blunt opinions and have chosen not to publish their names. It was never my intention to demonize strawberry growers. The real blame lies not with a handful of individuals but with a system that encourages and rewards exploitation of the poor.

page

78 *about 600 acres of strawberries . . . about six times that amount:* In 1973 there were 690 planted acres, and in 2002 there were 4,450. Figures provided by the California Strawberry Commission.

produces more than half the fruits, nuts, and vegetables: Interview with Agnes Perez, Economic Research Service, U.S Department of Agriculture.

fallen 14 percent over the last two decades: Adjusted for inflation, California's gross income from farms fell from about $31 billion in 1980 to $27.2 billion in 2000. See "2000 California Agricultural Statistical Review," California Agriculture Statistics Service; "Consumer Price Index," U.S. Department of Labor.

roughly 300,000 acres of California farmland: California had 32,156,894 acres of farmland in 1982 and 27,698,779 in 1997. See "Farm Numbers, Land in Farms, and Average Size of Farms: California," U.S. Department of Agriculture, National Agricultural Statistics Service, 1982 and 1997.

anywhere from 30 to 60 percent . . . are illegal immigrants: Interview with Philip L. Martin. According to a recent federal report, about 52 percent of farmworkers nationwide are illegal immigrants. See "Findings from the National Agricultural Workers Survey (NAWS), 1997–1998: A Demographic and Employment Profile of United States Farmworkers," Research Report No. 8, U.S. Department of Labor, Office of Program Economics, March 2000, p. 22.

79 *despite the loss since 1964 of more than nine million acres:* In 1964 California had 37,012,000 acres of farmland; it had 27,698,779 in 1997. The 2002 Census of Agriculture will likely show that even more farmland has been lost. Figures supplied by the National Agricultural Statistics Service, U.S. Department of Agriculture.

it was commonly believed that within a decade there would be no more migrant farmworkers: See Philip L. Martin and David A. Martin, *The Endless Quest: Helping America's Farmworkers* (Boulder, Colo.: Westview Press, 1994), pp. 15, 169.

if a crop could not be harvested mechanically: Ibid., p. 169.

According to his estimates: Martin interview.

more than 50 percent since 1980: In 1978 farmworkers who picked table grapes earned $5.25 an hour—about $14.45 in today's dollars. Interview with Fred Krissman, Center for U.S/Mexican Studies, University of California, San Diego. Most table grape pickers now earn the California minimum wage of $6.75 an hour.

79 *a twenty-nine-year-old male . . . who earns less than $7,500 a year:* Twenty-nine is the median age of a migrant farmworker. See "NAWS, 1997–98," pp. 9, 39, 44, 49.

his life expectancy is forty-nine: Cited in Maralyn Edid, *Farm Labor Organizing: Trends & Prospects* (Ithaca, N.Y.: ILR Press, 1994), p. 5.

80 *a California industry whose annual sales are about $840 million:* Strawberry sales were $841,031,000 million in 2001. See "California's Top Twenty Commodities for 2001," California Agricultural Statistics Service.

American farmers now receive more money for fresh strawberries . . . except apples: Sales of fresh apples were $1.1 billion in 2001, followed by strawberry sales of $974 million. Interview with Agnes Perez, expert on noncitrus fruit, Agricultural Research Service, United States Department of Agriculture. See also "Non-citrus Fruits and Nuts 2001 Preliminary Survey," USDA, January 2002.

81 *In the early 1950s the state was responsible:* Cited in James E. Sagan and Stephen Willhelm, *A History of the Strawberry: From Ancient Gardens to Modern Markets* (Berkeley: University of California Division of Agricultural Sciences, 1974), p. 158.

California's strawberry output more than tripled: California strawberry output rose from 382,258 pounds in 1974 to 1,316,888 pounds in 1994. See "California Strawberry Production 1972 through 1994," California Strawberry Commission.

Americans doubled their consumption of fresh strawberries: Per capita consumption of fresh strawberries in the United States rose from 1.8 pounds in 1974 to 3.98 in 1994. See "United States Per Capita Consumption of Fresh and Frozen Strawberries, 1961 through 1994," California Strawberry Commission.

In 2001 California shipped 91 million boxes: See "Non-citrus Fruits and Nuts 2001 Preliminary Survey."

The state now accounts for more than 80 percent: California produces about 83 percent of the nation's strawberries. Ibid.

about one-quarter of the world's commercial strawberries: See "Strawberry Situation and Outlook, 2001," Foreign Agricultural Service, U.S. Department of Agriculture.

82 *profits of $12,000 to $30,000 an acre:* A sharecropper producing berries for processing would have lower costs; a grower producing fresh, premium berries would have much higher costs. For a recent breakdown of such costs, see Karen M. Klonsky and Richard L. De Moura, "Sample Costs to Produce Fresh Market Strawberries, Central Coast, Monterey-Santa Cruz," University of California Cooperative Extension, 2001.

labor costs constitute between 50 to 70 percent: The more productive the field, the higher the labor costs, since more berries need to be picked.

A typical fifty-acre farm in the central coast has annual labor costs of $18,500 and total operating costs of about $27,000. See "Sample Strawberry Costs, Central Coast."

83 *Sharecropping has a long history:* For a succinct account, see Miriam Wells, "The Resurgence of Sharecropping: Historical Anomaly or Political Strategy?" *American Journal of Sociology,* July 1984, pp. 1–29. For a good analysis of why sharecropping has reappeared in California agriculture, see Marc Linder, *Migrant Workers and Minimum Wages: Regulating Exploitation of Agricultural Labor in the United States* (Boulder, Colo.: Westview Press, 1992), pp. 215–74.

84 *The California supreme court ruled in 1989:* See *S. G. Borello & Sons, Inc. v. Department of Industrial Relations* (1989), 48 Cal. 3rd 341. The benefits of relying on "independent contractors" instead of employees are spelled out for growers in Trenna Grabowski, "Employee Versus Independent Contractor," *California Farmer,* October 19, 1991.

85 *as much as half of the strawberry acreage in his area:* Interview with Mike Meuter.
    A survey by CRLA staff members in Santa Maria: Interview with Jeannie Barrett, CRLA.
    "It's basically a form of debt peonage": Barrett interview.
    Kirk's contracts were such works of art: I obtained copies of "Kirk Produce, Inc., Agricultural Sublease," "Kirk Processing and Kirk Produce Inc., Fresh Strawberry Consignment Sales Agreement and Continuing Guaranty," "Kirk Produce, Processing Strawberry Agreement." For a skeptical view of how independent such "independent growers" really are, see the ruling of the California Court of Appeal, Second Appellate District, Division Six, in *Kirk Produce Inc., etc. v. Victoria L. Bradshaw, as Labor Commissioner,* 2nd Civil, No. B084308 (Super. Ct. No. 200797) (Santa Barbara County). The case addressed the employment status of a Kirk sharecropper, Rodolfo Contreras: "Kirk 'loaned' Contreras substantial sums of money on a regular, frequent basis as 'advances' on deliveries of the crop for items needed to raise the crop," the court found. "The 'loans' would be 'repaid' out of the proceeds of the 'sale' of the crop to Kirk. Contreras owed Kirk about $70,000 at all relevant times. The agreements afforded Contreras no real opportunity to make a profit. Because Contreras remained in debt to Kirk, the arrangement kept Contreras beholden . . . Contreras' only real investment in equipment and materials was a tractor and a pickup truck. These investments are *de minimis;* they do not constitute the means to independently run a business like this. [Contreras'] previous experience consisted of three years as a field laborer. He had never been an independent businessman and had no education in business."

86 *the equivalent of a fifth-grade education:* Cited in David C. Mountjoy, "Farming Practices Survey and Outreach Recommendations for the Elkhorn Slough Water Quality Management Plan," Association of Monterey Bay Governments, July 1, 1993, p. 9.

87 *such loans are designed to make the sharecropper appear:* Interview with Bill Hoerger.

88 *the search for a peasantry:* See Cletus E. Daniel, *Bitter Harvest: A History of California Farmworkers, 1870–1941* (Ithaca, N.Y.: Cornell University Press, 1981), p. 40.

89 *complete freedom of movement between California and Mexico:* See Matt S. Meier and Feliciano Ribera, *Mexican Americans–American Mexicans: From Conquistadors to Chicanos* (New York: Hill and Wang, 1993), pp. 118–19; Abraham Hoffman, *Unwanted Mexican Americans in the Great Depression: Repatriation Pressures, 1929–1939* (Tucson: University of Arizona Press, 1974), pp. 32–33.

70 to 80 percent of the migrant farmworkers: Martin interview.

the Mexican population of Los Angeles: See *Mexican Americans,* p. 120.

90 *In the early 1970s, the UFW had perhaps 80,000 members:* Cited in "Cesar Chavez Chronology," United Farm Workers.

Today it has about one-third that number: The UFW now has roughly 27,000 members. Interview with Marc Grossman, principal spokesman, UFW.

"Mexicanization": Interview with Juan Vicente Palerm.

93 *spends half the year working:* According to the latest NAWS survey, the average farmworker spent 47 percent of his or her time in the United States doing farmwork, 19 percent residing but not working, and 8 percent in nonfarm work. See "NAWS, 1997–98," p. 24.

Since 1980, the acreage around Watsonville and Salinas: In 1980 there were 4,270 acres of strawberries in the area that produced about 96,000 tons of strawberries. In 2000 there were 11,570 acres that produced about 365,000 tons of strawberries. See "California Strawberry Acreage and Yield by Major Areas, 1972 through 1994," California Strawberry Commission, and the Agricultural Commission crop reports for Monterey County and Santa Cruz County, 2000.

A survey of garages in Soledad: Meuter interview.

94 *hundreds of strawberry pickers have been found living in caves:* A decade ago, a large encampment was found near a strawberry farm in Prundedale. Smaller encampments are discovered from time to time in the area. See Roya Camp, "Shanty Camp Draws Aid; Field Workers Found Living in Makeshift Caves," *Salinas Californian,* August 28, 1991; Everett Messick and Susan Ferris, "Authorities to Move Laborers Out of Caves; Seeks Housing for 200 Migrants in Castroville, Salinas Areas," *Monterey Her-*

ald, August 29, 1991; "Back Wages Sought for Farmworkers," *Watsonville Register-Pajaronian,* September 3, 1991.

95 *Guadalupe's population was 18 percent Latino:* Cited in Juan Vicente Palerm, "Farm Labor Needs and Farmworkers in California, 1970 to 1989," *California Agricultural Studies, 91–92,* Labor Market Information Division, State Employment Development Department, April 1991, p. 21.
today it is about 85 percent Latino: According to the U.S. Census Bureau, Guadalupe's population was 84.5 percent Latino in 2000. The actual proportion was most likely higher, given the perennial undercount of Latinos by the census.
up to ten times as high as any wages Mexican peasants could earn: See Juan Vicente Palerm with Jose Ignacio Urquiola, "A Binational System of Agricultural Production: The Case of the Mexican Bajio and California," in Daniel G. Aldrich, Jr., and Lorenzo Meyer, eds., *Mexico and the United States: Neighbors in Crisis* (San Bernardino, Calif.: Borgo Press, 1993), p. 327.
preserved rural communities in Mexico that otherwise might have collapsed: According to Michael Kearney, a professor of anthropology at the University of California, Northridge, some villages in Oaxaca now derive 80 percent of their annual income from remittances sent home by migrant workers in California. Interview with Michael Kearney. See also "Binational System," pp. 311, 346; Michael Kearney, "Mixtec Ethnicity: Social Identity, Political Consciousness, and Political Activism," *Latin American Research Review* 25 (2): 74–77.

96 *Juan Vicente Palerm believes:* Palerm interview.
Perhaps 40 percent of the farm labor: Cited in Palerm, "Immigrant and Migrant Farmworkers in the Santa Maria Valley, California," Center for Survey Methods Research, Bureau of the Census, 1994, p. 11.
twenty-five times as labor-intensive as cultivating broccoli: Broccoli production requires 80 man-hours per acre; strawberry production requires about 2,000 man-hours per acre. See "Immigrant and Migrant," pp. 4, 6.

97 *The rural population of Mexico:* Palerm interview.
"Migrate or starve": Kearney interview.

98 *Perhaps one-fifth of the Mixtec farmworkers:* Interview with Agimiro Morales, Coalition of Indian Communities of Oaxaca.
Two or three migrants now die there from exposure: One hundred and three migrants were found dead in California's Imperial Desert during 2001. Cited in Kenny Klein, "Search Ended for Immigrants Missing in Imperial Desert," *Desert Sun* (Palm Springs), August 15, 2002. The official death toll no doubt understates the number of migrant deaths; many bodies lie undiscovered in remote areas of the desert. For a good account of why INS policies have made crossing the border so treacher-

ous, see Wayne A. Cornelius, "Death at the Border: Efficacy and Unintended Consequences of U.S. Immigration Control Policy," *Population and Development Review,* December 1, 2001.

98 *Wages in Oaxaca:* Morales interview.
 Wages in the strawberry fields of Baja California: Kearney interview.

99 *"virtually peonage": Migratory Labor in American Agriculture: Report of the President's Commission on Migratory Labor* (Washington, D.C.: U.S. Government Printing Office, 1951), p. 5.
 40 percent of the migrants in the United States: Ibid., p. 69.
 "unquestionable": Ibid., p. 80.
 "We depend on misfortune": Ibid., p. 3.

100 *almost 1.3 million illegal immigrants:* Cited in *Endless Quest,* p. 175.
 one of the greatest immigration frauds: Ibid., p. 176.
 an estimated 7 to 8 million illegal immigrants: See D'Vera Cohn, "New Census Information Reveals Larger Than Expected Number of Illegal Immigrants," *Washington Post,* October 25, 2001.
 About half of them are Mexican: See Frank del Olmo, "Migration Issue Needs Bush's Attention," *Los Angeles Times,* September 9, 2001.
 often more illegal immigrants than braceros: See *"Temporary" Workers,* p. 24.
 Palerm does not rule out lending his support: Palerm interview.

101 *a modern euphemism for an indentured laborer:* See *"Temporary" Workers,* pp. 2–3.
 "There's nothing more permanent": Martin interview. See also Philip L. Martin and Michael S. Teitelbaum, "The Mirage of Mexican Guest Workers," *Foreign Affairs,* November–December 2001.
 The majority of illegal immigrants in California: For an excellent description of the new migrant work force, see Wayne A. Cornelius, "From Sojourners to Settlers: The Changing Profile of Mexican Immigration to the United States," in Jorge A. Bustamante, Clark W. Reynolds, and Raul A. Hinojosa Ojeda, eds., *U.S.-Mexico Relations: Labor Market Interdependence* (Stanford, Calif.: Stanford University Press, 1992), pp. 155–95. For the proportions of illegals now employed outside agriculture, see pp. 178–79.

102 *"Cheap labor benefits agriculture in the short run":* Martin interview.
 the distinction between legal and illegal farmworkers: Interview with Joaquin Avila.

103 *The plight of immigrants has been deplored:* In 1908 President Theodore Roosevelt appointed a commission to investigate how the lives of American farmers and farmworkers could be improved. See United States Country Life Commission, *Report of the Commission on Country Life* (New York: Sturgis & Walton, 1911).
 Maintaining the current level of poverty among migrant farmworkers: The

typical American household spends roughly $5,031 a year on food—and about $500 of that is spent on fruits and vegetables. According to Philip L. Martin, the cost of farm labor represents less than 10 percent of the retail price for fruits and vegetables. If the wages of American farmworkers were doubled and the higher labor cost was directly passed to consumers, it would add about $50 to the average household's yearly food bill. Moreover, this estimate may be too high. Many processed fruits and vegetables are no longer picked by hand. The typical American household spends only $301 a year on fresh fruits and vegetables. Increasing that sum by about $30—less than the cost of two CDs—could eliminate most of the hardship and poverty among California's farmworkers. See *Endless Quest*, p. 4; "Average Annual Expenditures of All Consumer Units by Race, Hispanic Origin, and Age of Householder: 1999," *Statistical Abstract of the United States: 2001* (Washington, D.C.: U.S. Government Printing Office, 2002), p. 431.

"Five Cents for Fairness": See "Five Cents for Fairness: The Case for Change in the Strawberry Fields," Strawberry Workers Campaign, November 1996.

"Californians for Statewide Smoking Restrictions": For the Dolphin Group's concern about the health of smokers, see Dan Morain, "Pitch to Put Smoking Ban on Ballot Is Deceptive, Critics Say," *Los Angeles Times,* April 10, 1994; Bradley Johnson, "California Waiting for Smoke to Clear," *Advertising Age,* October 24, 1994; and John Stauber and Sheldon Rampton, "Smokin'!: How the American Tobacco Industry Employs PR Scum to Continue Its Murderous Assault on Human Lives," *Tucson Weekly,* November 22–29, 1995.

the "Grape Workers and Farmers Coalition": For the Dolphin Group's work on behalf of grape pickers, see Cesar Chavez, "PR Group Targets Grape Boycott," *Toronto Star,* November 15, 1989.

the Strawberry Workers & Farmers Alliance: For the Dolphin Group's concern for strawberry pickers, and the growers' efforts to impede the UFW, see "Seven Thousand Workers Demonstrate Against Union; Workers Denounce AFL-CIO Union Summer and United Farmworkers Attack on Strawberry Industry," *PR Newswire,* August 14, 1996; "Farmworkers Rights and Human Rights Embraced: Farmworkers and Farmers Champion the Strawberry Industry," *PR Newswire,* July 10, 1997; Susan Ferriss and George Raine, "Strawberry Fields Forever United?" *San Francisco Examiner,* November 24, 1996; David Bacon, "The U.F.W. Picks Strawberries," *The Nation,* April 14, 1997; Bob Egelko, "Growers Lose Court Ruling on Donations; Businesses Illegally Gave Money to Group Opposing Strawberry Workers' Union," *San Francisco Examiner,* September 29, 2000.

104   *perhaps 1,600 of California's roughly 20,000 strawberry workers:* Gross-man interview.
106   *Perhaps one-third of the farmworkers in northern San Diego County:* Cited in Dan Weisman, "Farmworkers Often Homeless: Estimated 7,000 in North Country Lack Housing," *North Country Times,* March 21, 2000.

an empire of the obscene

The sexual customs of two thousand years ago provide some insight into the deeply conflicted attitudes toward pornography in the United States today. I found Peter Brown's *The Body and Society: Men, Women, and Sexual Renunciation in Early Christianity* (New York: Columbia University Press, 1988) to be fascinating and thought-provoking. For a sense of the morality that early Christians defiantly rejected, I read a number of books that try to evoke distant, often mysterious realms: David M. Halperin, John J. Winkler, and Froma I. Zeitlin, eds., *Before Sexuality: The Construction of Erotic Experience in the Ancient Greek World* (Princeton: Princeton University Press, 1990); Amy Richlin, ed., *Pornography and Representation in Greece and Rome* (New York: Oxford University Press, 1991); Michael Grant, *Eros in Pompeii: The Secret Rooms of the National Museum of Naples* (New York: William Morrow, 1975). The discovery of erotica in the ruins of Pompeii had a strong impact on many conservative intellectuals who cherished classical ideals. Indeed, it completely blew their minds. The decision to hide those erotic relics from the public is a central metaphor in Walter Kendrick's fine book, *The Secret Museum: Pornography in Modern Culture* (New York: Viking, 1987). The slow and steady erosion of traditional values is also explored in Lynn Hunt, ed., *The Invention of Pornography: Obscenity and the Origins of Modernity, 1500–1800* (New York: Zone Books, 1993).

If you want to understand contemporary American sexuality, examining the life and times of Anthony Comstock is a good place to start. *Anthony Comstock: Roundsman of the Lord* (New York: Albert and Charles Boni, 1927), by Heywood Broun and Margaret Leech, is a harshly critical and amusing biography. Comstock's official biographer, Charles Gallaudet Trumbull, offers a laudatory but no less entertaining view of the man in *Anthony Comstock, Fighter: Some Impressions of a Lifetime Adventure in Conflict with the Powers of Evil* (New York: Fleming H. Revell, 1913). Neither of these biographies, however, is as revealing as Comstock's own words. His two books — *Frauds Exposed: How the People Are Deceived and Robbed, and Youth Corrupted* (New York: J. H. Brown, 1880) and *Traps for the Young* (New York: Funk & Wagnalls, 1883) — outline a moral philosophy that still permeates much of the nation's culture.

Edward de Grazia's *Girls Lean Back Everywhere: The Law of Obscenity and the Assault on Genius* (New York: Vintage, 1993) is an excellent survey of the Comstock Law's enduring legacy. The origins of federal obscenity law are also explored in Marjorie Heins's provocative book, *Not in Front of the Children: Indecency, Censorship and the Innocence of Youth* (New York: Hill and Wang, 2001). I learned much from *Censorship: The Search for the Obscene* (New York: Macmillan, 1964), by Morris L. Ernst and Alan U. Schwartz, a book published as Comstockery was coming under renewed attack. James R. Peterson's *The Century of Sex: Playboy's History of the Sexual Revolution, 1900–1999* (New York: Grove Press, 1999) offers an overview of the social changes that brought airbrushed nudes to American newsstands. The book rightly gives much credit to Hugh Hefner; yet Reuben Sturman's name never appears in its pages. Gay Talese covers some of the same ground in *Thy Neighbor's Wife: A Chronicle of American Permissiveness Before the Age of AIDS* (New York: Ivy Books, 1993). Talese's work contains fascinating historical material as well as some unusual firsthand reporting. Eric Schaefer's *Bold! Daring! Shocking! True!: A History of Exploitation Films, 1919–1959* (Durham, N.C.: Duke University Press, 1999) is a scholarly examination of the cinematic underground that preceded today's hard-core film industry. Charles Winick's essay — "From Deviant to Normative: Changes in the Acceptability of Sexually Explicit Material," in Edward Sagarin, ed., *Deviance and Social Change* (Beverly Hills, Calif.: Sage, 1977), pp. 219–46 — succinctly conveys the impact of the 1960s youth counterculture on sexual attitudes. Perhaps the best work on the history, effects, and legal implications of pornography in the United States is *The Report of the Commission on Obscenity and Pornography* (Washington, D.C.: U.S. Government Printing Office, 1970).

The Attorney General's Commission on Pornography (also known as the Meese Commission) produced a report that is less rigorous and reliable. While the 1970 commission sponsored extensive research by social scientists, the Meese Commission merely held hearings, then issued its report within a year. Nevertheless, the *Attorney General's Commission on Pornography, Final Report* (Washington, D.C.: U.S. Government Printing Office, 1986) is a useful historical document. "Beyond the Pornography Commission: The Federal Response," U.S. Department of Justice, July 1988, is also worth reading. Bill Thompson offers a scathing critique of the Meese Commission in *Soft Core: Moral Crusades Against Pornography in Britain and America* (London: Cassell, 1994). A much more favorable view can be found in *Sourcebook on Pornography,* edited by Franklin Mark Osanka and Sara Lee Johann (Lexington, Mass.: Lexington Books, 1989). The relative merits of the two commissions are examined in *Pornography in a Free Society* (New York: Cambridge University Press, 1988), a fine book by Gordon Hawkins and Franklin Zimring.

The controversy surrounding pornography that led to the Meese Commission also inspired many books. Although my aim was to investigate the economics of the sex trade, I tried to read widely in the literature debating the merits of porn. Catherine A. MacKinnon and Andrea Dworkin are two of the most articulate and important foes of pornography. Dworkin's *Pornography: Men Possessing Women* (New York: E. P. Dutton, 1989) is essential reading — an angry critique of porn as a tool of male domination and incitement to rape. "Defamation and Discrimination," the first chapter in MacKinnon's *Only Words* (Cambridge, Mass.: Harvard University Press, 1998), uses that premise to characterize pornography as a civil rights violation, not a form of protected speech. The unusual alliance between radical feminists and conservative Republicans on this issue finds expression in "The Legal Case Against Restricting Pornography," by Alan E. Sears, in Dolf Zillman and Jennings Bryant, eds., *Pornography: Research Considerations and Policy Considerations* (Hillsdale, N.J.: Lawrence Erlbaum, 1989), pp. 323–42. Sears, the executive director of the Meese Commission, believes that pornography violates both human and civil rights. In *The Case Against Pornography* (Wheaton, Ill.: Victor Books, 1986), Donald E. Wildmon argues that porn lies at the heart of a spiritual battle between Christianity and secular humanism. Wildmon is the founder of the National Federation for Decency and president of the American Family Association, based in Tupelo, Mississippi. *Sourcebook on Pornography* contains excerpts from various texts opposing porn on moral, religious, and feminist grounds.

A number of feminists have questioned whether the content of today's porn should determine the legality of all sexually explicit material. In *Hard Core: Power, Pleasure, and the "Frenzy of the Visible"* (Los Angeles: University of California Press, 1989), Linda Williams suggests that pornography has long reflected a male point of view — and might in the future embody a different set of values. *Dirty Looks: Women, Pornography, Power* (London: BFI Publishing, 1993), edited by Pamela Church Gibson and Roma Gibson, is a collection of essays by feminists who oppose the censorship of porn and any overly simplistic interpretation of its "meaning." A fine overview of the studies assessing porn's impact on its viewers can be found in *The Question of Pornography: Research Findings and Policy Implications* (New York: Free Press, 1987), edited by Edward Donnerstein, Daniel Linz, and Steven Penrod. The consensus among social scientists is that all sexually violent material encourages aggression, regardless of how explicit it may be — and that R-rated films contain much more violence against women than hard-core films. I found the work of the late Berl Kutchinsky — who studied the effects of pornography in Denmark after the revocation of its obscenity laws — to be particularly enlightening. His essay "Legalized Pornography in Denmark" appears in *Men Confront Pornography* (New York: Crown, 1990), edited by Michael S. Kimmel. Ernest D. Giglio attacks Kutchinsky's scholarship in "Pornography in Denmark: A Public Policy Model for the United States?"; Kutchinsky responds in "Pornography and Its Effects in Denmark and the United States: A Rejoinder and Beyond"; and both are published in *Comparative Social Research: Deviance* (Greenwich, Conn.: JAI Press, 1985), edited by Richard F. Tomasson. Pornography's impact on the people who watch it is one issue; the impact on those who make it is another. In *Porn: Myths for the Twentieth Century* (New Haven, Conn.: Yale University Press, 1991) the psychoanalyst Robert J. Stoller offers edited transcripts of his interviews with porn actors, actresses, and filmmakers. *Sex Work: Writings by Women in the Sex Industry* (Pittsburgh: Cleis Press, 1987), edited by Frederique Delacoste and Priscilla Alexander, presents voices that are rarely heard.

In addition, I spoke to a number of people whose views of pornography influenced mine. Vagn Greve, chairman of the Danish Society for International Criminal Law and EU-Law, described his country's experience after legalization. "Dana"—who prefers to remain anonymous, a therapist whose patients are sex workers—gave me a much better understanding of their complex, often self-destructive lives. The photographer Ian Gittler shared his knowledge of the sex industry, gained during the preparation of his poignant and unsettling book *Porn Star* (New York: Simon & Schuster, 1999). Nadine Strossen made strong arguments against using the legal system to restrict sexually explicit material or women's choices. Strossen is a professor at New York Law School, the president of the American Civil Liberties Union, and the author of *Defending Pornography: Free Speech, Sex, and the Fight for Women's Rights* (New York: Scribner, 1995). Bruce A. Taylor, president and chief counsel of the National Law Center for Children and Families, expressed sincere concern about the anger, brutality, and misogyny in much of today's porn. The conclusion I've reached, however, is that some problems cannot be solved with laws.

The economics of porn has received less serious attention than its legal and cultural ramifications. Both federal commissions on pornography investigated the subject. Volume III of the 1970 report, "The Marketplace: The Industry," contains much historical information. The Meese Commission's inquiry, though worth reading, must be viewed with greater skepticism. Gary W. Potter's *The Porn Merchants* (Dubuque, Iowa: Kendall/Hunt, 1986) is the most thorough work on the subject, featuring some impressive organizational charts of Reuben Sturman's holdings. *Porn Gold: Inside the Pornography Business* (London: Faber and Faber, 1988) contains interesting material on the European trade. A number of journalists have produced first-rate work—indeed, the IRS investigation of Reuben Sturman was inspired by a magazine article, Edward P. Whelan's "Reuben Sturman and His Amazing Porno Empire!" *Cleveland* magazine, May 1976. Other notable articles are James Cook's "The X-Rated Economy," *Forbes*, September 18, 1978; Michael

Satchell's "The Big Business of Selling Smut," *Parade*, August 19, 1979; and "Family Business," by Ellen Farley and William K. Knoedelseder, Jr., *Los Angeles Times*, June 13, 20, 27, 1982. Stephen Kurkjian, Peter Mancusi, and Thomas Palmer wrote an excellent series of articles for the *Boston Globe* in February 1983, including "Pornography Industry Finds Big Profits in New Markets," "Home Viewing of X-Rated Tapes Popularizes 'Adult' Fare," "A Quick Route to Profits for Region's Top Porn Dealer," "A Rift Within Organized Crime," and "How Two FBI Agents Stalked the Top U.S. Porn Dealers." James Neff wrote an informative profile, "Reuben Sturman: Cleveland's Own King of Porn," that appeared in Cleveland's *Plain Dealer* on June 30, 1985, and Mark Rollenhagen did a fine job covering Sturman's downfall for the paper.

My own investigative piece, "The Business of Pornography," was published in *U.S. News & World Report* on February 10, 1997. Since then a number of articles have addressed the subject and its wider implications: "The Sex Industry: Giving the Customer What He Wants," *The Economist*, February 14, 1998; Richard C. Morais, "Porn Goes Public," *Forbes*, June 14, 1999; Timothy Egan, "Erotica, Inc.," *New York Times*, October 23, 2000; Holman W. Jenkins, Jr., "Pornography, Main Street to Wall Street," *Policy Review*, February 1, 2001; Frank Rich, "Naked Capitalists," *New York Times*, May 20, 2001; Janet M. LaRue, "Porn Nation," *World and I*, August 1, 2001; and William F. Buckley, "Porn, Pervasive Presence: The Creepy Wallpaper of Our Daily Lives," *National Review*, November 19, 2001.

Bob Peters, who at the time was supervising detective in the Pornography Section of the LAPD Vice Squad, briefed me on the local trade and its key players. The Pornography Section is like a municipal regulatory agency, keeping a close eye on who's doing what to whom and where. I'm grateful to the many people in the sex industry who not only answered my questions but also invited me to visit their offices, warehouses, sound stages, editing facilities, and, on one memorable occasion, a factory that made rubber articles for immoral use. At *Adult Video News*, publisher Paul Fishbein and senior editor Mark Kernes shared their extensive knowledge of the business. Dave Manach, the editor of *Exotic Dancer* magazine, and Rob Abner, the former publisher of *Stripper* magazine, provided some statistics about an increasingly popular form of live entertainment. Bill Margold talked to me at length about his experiences as a porn actor, screenwriter, and industry spokesman. Fred Hirsch and his children, Steve and Marci Hirsch at Vivid Video, described their family's involvement in the business over the past thirty years. John Stagliano, a popular hard-core director and the founder of Evil Angel Video (the "Evil Empire"), spoke bluntly about his production costs, company finances, and work on behalf of the Cato Institute. Candida Royalle—an outspoken feminist and porn director—discussed some of her career's contradictions. Another articulate and well-read feminist, the porn actress Nina Hartley, was an invaluable source on the industry's labor issues. Tim Lake told me the story of his company, Homegrown, and the rise of amateur porn. Philip D. Harvey gave me a tour of PHE's headquarters, explained why he sells porn through the mail, and introduced me to the fundamentals of nonprofit, social marketing. Harvey's book, *The Government vs. Erotica: The Siege of Adam & Eve* (Amherst, N.Y.: Prometheus Books, 2001), offers an impassioned defense of his trade. First Amendment attorney John Weston spoke about the legal challenges his porn clients routinely face. Larry Flynt outlined, among other things, porn's future in cyberspace. And I'm grateful to the many performers, directors, and executives throughout the industry who spoke to me but preferred not to be named.

The role of organized crime in the distribution of pornography has long been the focus of rumors and speculation. It was difficult to separate fact from fiction, and I did my best not to make categorical statements unsupported by hard evidence. The Meese Commission concluded that organized crime played a major role in the industry; its reasoning is skillfully dissected by Hawkins and Zimring in *Pornography in a Free Society.* Potter's lengthy consideration of the subject in *The Porn Merchants* is well worth reading. Few would dispute that various criminal organizations have been engaged in the production and distribution of pornography. Whether those groups fit traditional definitions of "organized crime" and the extent of their control by the Cosa Nostra have been the source of much disagreement. *The Handbook of Organized Crime in the United States* (Westport, Conn.: Greenwood Press, 1994), edited by Robert J. Kelly, Ko-Lin Chin, and Rufus Schatzberg, was extremely useful as I wrestled with these questions—as was Charles Winick's essay in the book, "Organized Crime and Commercial Sex." I learned much from a report prepared at the request of President Ronald Reagan: President's Commission on Organized Crime, *Report to the President and Attorney General, The Impact: Organized Crime Today* (Washington, D.C.: U.S. Government Printing Office, 1986). The fact that it devoted so few pages to pornography is significant. The nature of Reuben Sturman's relationship with Robert DiBernardo and the Gambino family is an important element in my narrative. For background on DiBernardo and the Gambinos I read John H. Davis, *Mafia Dynasty: The Rise and Fall of the Gambino Crime Family* (New York: HarperCollins, 1993), and Howard Blum, *Gangland: How the FBI Broke the Mob* (New York: Simon & Schuster, 1993). Neither book mentions Reuben Sturman. He does appear briefly in *The Last Mafioso: The Treacherous World of Jimmy Fratianno* (New York: Times Books, 1980), by Ovid Demaris. Luke Ford has a chapter on the Cosa Nostra in *A History of X: 100 Years of Sex in Film* (Amherst, N.Y.: Prometheus Books, 1999). Ford's reporting is vivid and entertaining and not always accurate. One of the first people I interviewed was George Burgasser, who at the time headed the Justice Department's Child Exploitation and Obscenity Unit. Burgasser suggested many places to look for evidence of Cosa Nostra involvement in the distribution of pornography. I'm grateful to two experts on the Gambino family who spoke to me at length about its role in the porn industry: James Kossler, who headed the FBI's Organized Crime Squad in New York City during its successful pursuit of John Gotti, and Ronald Goldstock, a professor at Cornell University Law School who headed the New York State Organized Crime Task Force in the 1980s. And I'm grateful to William P. Kelly, a legendary FBI agent, for telling me about his many run-ins with DiBernardo and other mobsters in the porn trade and for sending me clippings about the Cosa Nostra.

I met Reuben Sturman at a time when he felt abandoned by his longtime associates. Sturman was engaging and friendly during our prison interview and subsequent telephone conversations. He never refused to answer a question. He spoke proudly about his businesses, sharing the details of their legal and illegal activities. I had the feeling that, after a long and secretive career, Sturman wanted to be remembered. None of his assertions about the industry later turned out to be false — although I could never prove, nor disprove, his claims of independence from the Gambino family. Nor could I ascertain whether he lied about being broke. In addition to interviewing Sturman, I learned a great deal from some of the attorneys who worked long and hard to keep him out of jail: Herald Price Fahringer and the late Stanley Fleishman, whom Sturman regarded as the "kings" of First Amendment law; J. Michael Murray, who defended Sturman in the Cleveland tax case and the Las Vegas obscenity case; and Adam Bourgeois, an old friend of Sturman's who defended him in the Chicago extortion case. I also interviewed a number of prosecutors who sought to put Sturman behind bars: Bruce A. Taylor, who tried without success to convict him in an Ohio obscenity case; Stephen Jigger, who headed Cleveland's Organized Crime Strike Force and helped to convict Sturman in the tax case; and Mark Prosperi, now the U.S. attorney for the Northern District of Illinois, who helped to convict him for extortion. All of these attorneys helped me understand the legal complexities of such cases. And Tony Olivo, who as a U.S. marshal pursued Sturman after the prison escape, told me a great deal about the effort to capture him.

Most of all, I am indebted to Richard N. Rosfelder, Jr., now the president of International Research Group Inc., and Craig S. Morford, who is still an assistant U.S. attorney with Cleveland's Organized Crime Strike Force. My account of Sturman's downfall is largely based on thousands of pages of court transcripts and government documents obtained with their assistance. They not only spent countless hours patiently answering my questions but displayed even greater patience while helping to ensure that my work was factually correct. I have enormous respect for the personal honor and integrity of these two men. Without their help, this story might never have been told.

page

111 *sent a letter to the nation's leading drugstore:* See Robert Pear, "Playboy and Justice Department Trying to Settle Lawsuit," *New York Times,* November 8, 1986.

homosexuality should be denounced: See Charles M. Sennott, *Broken Covenant: The Story of Father Bruce Ritter's Fall from Grace* (New York: Simon & Schuster, 1992), pp. 199–201.

112 *The Meese Commission had found that one man:* See *Attorney General's Commission on Pornography, Final Report* (Washington, D.C.: U.S. Government Printing Office, 1986), p. 1066.

"Every legal subterfuge": Matthew Josephson, *The Robber Barons: The Great American Capitalists, 1861–1901* (New York: Harcourt Brace, 1934), p. 275.

might be the wealthiest man in the state of Ohio: See James Neff, "Reuben Sturman: Cleveland's Own King of Porn," *Plain Dealer,* June 30, 1985.

the only photograph of Sturman: See Edward P. Whelan, "Reuben Sturman and His Amazing Porno Empire!" *Cleveland Magazine,* May 1976.

113 *According to* Adult Video News: The sales, rental, and release data regarding American hard-core videos were provided to me by Paul Fishbein, the publisher of *Adult Video News,* and Mark Kernes, the magazine's senior editor.

Americans now spend as much as $8 billion: Nobody really knows how much money is being spent on sexually explicit materials. In 1997 I spent a great deal of time trying to come up with a reasonable estimate. I conducted off-the-record interviews with prominent figures in the magazine, video, cable, satellite television, audiotext, and sex industries. I arrived at an estimate of about $8 billion, comprised of the following: hard-core video rentals and sales, $3.9 billion; strip clubs, $2 billion; telephone sex, $1 billion; sex magazines, $400 million; pay-per-view in homes and hotels, $325 million; peep booths, $300 million; sex toys, $100 million. Since then, the revenues from pay-per-view have doubled, the revenues from sex magazines have fallen, and the Internet has been transformed from a negligible part of the business to one with annual sales of as much as $1 billion. The continued growth of the Internet may actually cause the sex industry's revenues to plateau or decline, because so much porn is now available online for free. In 2001 Frank Rich estimated in the *New York Times Magazine* that the annual revenues from porn were about $10 billion, which seems plausible to me. Rich's estimates were attacked by Dan Ackman, a contributor to *Forbes.com,* who suggested that *Adult Video News* has long exaggerated the number of

NOTES

adult films being rented and sold. That number is a crucial determinant of the total revenues from porn. Ackman suggested that $2.6 billion to $3.9 billion was a much more accurate estimate of the total revenue from all sources. A couple of days before Ackman's article appeared, an equity analyst in another *Forbes* article was quoted as saying that the porn industry has annual revenues of $11 billion. A 1999 article in *Forbes* estimated that the worldwide revenue from porn was $56 billion, with the United States by far the largest market. Americans currently spend about $25 billion a year on the rental and purchase of videos and DVDs. It seems reasonable to conclude that anywhere from one-tenth to one-fifth of that money is spent on porn. The actual size of the sex industry will be impossible to determine until its products are fully legal and taxable. Annual revenues of even $3 billion or $4 billion from porn would be impressive. Americans now spend about $2 billion a year on rock, hip-pop, and pop music concerts. See Eric Schlosser, "The Business of Pornography," *U.S. News & World Report*, February 10, 1997; Richard C. Morais, "Porn Goes Public," *Forbes*, June 14, 1999; Timothy Egan, "Erotica, Inc.," *New York Times*, October 23, 2000; Frank Rich, "Naked Capitalists," *New York Times*, May 20, 2001; Davide Dukcevich, "Stock Focus: Adult Entertainment Companies," *Forbes.com*, May 23, 2001; Dan Ackman, "How Big Is Porn?" *Forbes.com*, May 25, 2001; transcript, "Growing Pornography Business," *Talk of the Nation*, June 14, 2001.

113 *roughly the same as Hollywood's domestic box office receipts:* In 2002 Hollywood's domestic box office revenues exceeded $9 billion, an all-time record. Cited in Rick Lyman, "A Big Fat Box Office Increase," *New York Times*, December 30, 2002. The largest sector of the American sex industry is the oldest and the least reliant on technology. In 1986 the economist Helen Reynolds estimated that the United States had about half a million prostitutes, whose annual revenues were about $20 billion ($33 billion in today's dollars). See Helen Reynolds, *The Economics of Prostitution* (Springfield, Ill.: Charles C. Thomas, 1986), p. 5.

revenue generated by rock or country-and-western: Rock music recordings generated about $3.4 billion in sales during 2001; country-western, about $1.4 billion. Cited in "2001 Consumer Profile," the Recording Industry Association of America.

more money at strip clubs: There are roughly 2,300 strip clubs in the United States, and each one generates between $250,000 and $5 million a year. Assuming that the average club has annual revenues of about $1 million, Americans now spend about $2 billion a year at such establishments. In 2002 Broadway theaters had total revenues of $705.2 million, regional and nonprofit theaters had revenues of about $555 million, and American orchestras sold $504 million worth of tickets. American tastes in live entertainment are no longer highbrow; in 2000 the opera generated just $284 million in ticket sales. For the revenues of the strip clubs, I relied on information provided by Dave Manach, the editor of *Exotic Dancer* magazine, and Rob Abner, the former publisher of *Stripper* magazine. For Broadway revenues, see League of American Theaters and Producers, "Theatre League Releases Calendar-Year Stats," press release, December 26, 2002. For regional and nonprofit theaters, see "Theater Facts 2001," Theater Communications Group. For American orchestras, see "Quick Orchestra Facts from the 2000–2001 Season," American Symphony Orchestra League.

114   *the sexual content of American culture:* Charles Winick, "From Deviant to Normative: Changes in the Acceptability of Sexually Explicit Material," in Edward Sagarin, ed., *Deviance and Social Change* (Beverly Hills, Calif.: Sage, 1977), p. 220.

no more than $10 million: Cited in U.S. Commission on Obscenity and Pornography, *The Report of the Commission on Obscenity and Pornography* (Washington, D.C.: U.S. Government Printing Office, 1970), p. 19.

115   *two hundred and eleven new titles every week:* According to *Adult Video News*, 10,800 new hard-core titles were released in 2001.

116   *press run of 70,000 copies:* For the early days of *Playboy*, see James R. Peterson, *The Century of Sex* (New York: Grove Press, 1999), pp. 229–31.

118   Sex Life of a Cop: Aside from its minor role in the history of American obscenity law, the only memorable thing about *Sex Life of a Cop* is its title. Sanford E. Aday published the novel under a pseudonym. For those who are interested in what the fuss was about, see Oscar Peck, *Sex Life of a Cop* (Fresno, Calif.: Mid-Tower Publishing, 1959).

"terrible stuff": Quoted in Edward de Grazia, *Girls Lean Back Everywhere* (New York: Vintage, 1993), p. 519.

119   *"Evil one":* Anthony Comstock, *Frauds Exposed* (New York: J. H. Brown, 1880), p. 416.

with an overpowering compulsion to masturbate: According to Gay Talese, Comstock "masturbated so obsessively during his teens that he felt it might drive him to suicide." See Talese, *Thy Neighbor's Wife* (New York: Ivy Books, 1993), p. 43. See also Marjorie Heins, *Not in Front of the Children* (New York: Hill & Wang, 2001), p. 30; and Morris L. Ernst and Alan U. Schwartz, *Censorship* (New York: Macmillan, 1964), p. 21.

"Like a cancer it fastens itself": Anthony Comstock, *Traps for the Young* (New York: Funk & Wagnalls, 1883), p. 132.

"deadens the will . . . and damns the soul": Comstock, *Frauds Exposed*, p. 416.

119 *"obscene literature" and "beastly transparencies":* Ibid., p. 388.
120 *"obscene, lewd, or lascivious" materials:* Quoted in Ernst and Schwartz, *Censorship,* p. 31.
     "long-haired men" and "short-haired women": Comstock, *Frauds Exposed,* p. 408.
     "No sect nor class": Ibid., p. 392.
     "Irish smut dealer": Quoted in Heywood Broun and Margaret Leech, *Anthony Comstock* (New York: Albert and Charles Boni, 1927), p. 18.
121 *202,679 obscene pictures and photographs:* Cited in Comstock, *Frauds Exposed,* p. 435.
     "The United States is one great society": Quoted in Broun and Leech, *Comstock,* p. 89.
     "to deprave and corrupt": Quoted in Heins, *Not in Front of the Children,* p. 28.
     keeping mistresses and collecting rare erotica: According to Ron Chernow, one of J. P. Morgan's biographers, "While protecting public morals, Pierpont conducted amorous escapades aboard his yachts, in private railroad cars, and at European spas." Chernow says that Morgan liked to collect "old masters and old mistresses." See Chernow, *The House of Morgan* (New York: Touchstone, 1991), pp. 114–16.
     the obscenity conviction of Samuel Roth: See *Roth v. United States,* 354 U.S. 476 (1957).
     "I know it when I see it": See *Jacobellis v. Ohio,* 378 U.S. 184, 197 (1964).
122 *As Gay Talese observed:* Talese, *Thy Neighbor's Wife,* pp. 37–39.
     a three-part test for obscenity: See *Memoirs v. Massachusetts,* 383 U.S. 413 (1966).
     If a book had consecutive page numbers: Interview with Herald Price Fahringer.
     the Supreme Court overturned a Georgia law: See *Stanley v. Georgia,* 394 U.S. 447 (1969).
     the Supreme Court ruled that Sex Life of a Cop: See *Aday et al. v. United States,* 388 U.S. 447 (1967).
123 *"the Kings":* Interview with Reuben Sturman.
124 *"I'm tired of pussyfooting around with smut":* Quoted in Robert J. Holmes, "U.S. Indicts 5 in Smut Racket," *Plain Dealer,* September 7, 1968.
125 *"What's your name?":* Sturman interview.
     second largest in the state of California: Cited in James Cook, "The X-Rated Economy," *Forbes,* September 18, 1978.
126 *first public exhibitions of hard-core films:* My account of the stag film's origins is based on Arthur Knight and Hollis Alpert, "The History of Sex in Cinema: The Stag Film," *Playboy,* November 1967, and *Report on Obscenity,* pp. 184–92.
127 *roughly $50:* Cited in *Report on Obscenity,* p. 190.

270

the legislatures of two states: See Knight and Alpert, "History of Sex," p. 170.

perhaps 2,000 hard-core films were made: Cited in *Report on Obscenity,* p. 189.

"muck merchants": Quoted in Holman Harvey, "Help Stamp Out This Vile Traffic!" *Reader's Digest,* March 1959.

"Obscene File": For details, see Athan Theoharis and John Cox, *The Boss* (Philadelphia: Temple University Press, 1988), pp. 94–96; Athan Theoharis, *J. Edgar Hoover, Sex and Crime* (Chicago: Ivan Doe, 1995), pp. 61–65.

129 *hoped his machines would show children's cartoons:* See Gary W. Potter, *The Porn Merchants* (Dubuque, Iowa: Kendall/Hunt, 1986), p. 105.

roughly fifty to seventy-five new peep loops: Sturman interview.

130 *An average-sized store earned at least $2,000 a week:* Interview with Richard N. Rosfelder.

Sturman formed a joint venture with the Holloway family: My account of the Holloway family's travails and its links to Sturman's empire is partly based on these articles from the British press: "Sturman Drang," *Private Eye,* December 19, 1980; "SoHo News," *Private Eye,* January 2, 1981; "SoHo News," *Private Eye,* September 11, 1981; David May and Mark Hosenball, "Worldwide Tentacles of Mister Porn," *Sunday Times,* September 6, 1981; Tony Dawe, "The Porn Family Holloway: Father, Sons, and Daughter Jailed," *Daily Express,* January 12, 1984.

131 *Linda Lovelace . . . later wrote that her performance had been coerced:* When Lovelace became an antipornography activist during the 1980s, many journalists regarded her account of sexual abuse with skepticism. She later changed her mind about the harms of porn, casting further doubt on the accuracy of her memoir. It now appears that Lovelace was indeed brutalized and coerced by her manager. See Linda Lovelace with Mike McGrady, *Ordeal* (Secaucus, N.J.: Citadel Press, 1980), and Mark Kermode, "Desperately Seeking Linda," *The Independent,* September 20, 2002.

Anthony Peraino and his two sons: For an excellent account of the Peraino family and its porn business, see Ellen Farley and William Knoedelseder, "Family Business: Episode 1, The Pornbrokers," *Los Angeles Times,* June 13, 1982. See also Nicholas Gage, "Organized Crime Reaps Huge Profits from Dealing in Pornographic Films," *New York Times,* October 12, 1975; *Commission on Pornography,* p. 1219; Potter, *Porn Merchants,* pp. 26–34; and Warren Bates, "Arguments Heard in Porn Film Trial," *Las Vegas Review-Journal,* July 11, 1996.

Produced for about $22,000: Cited in Knoedelseder, "Pornbrokers."

annual revenues of America's peep booths were much larger: See Cook, "X-Rated Economy," and Potter, *Porn Merchants,* p. 20.

132 *"the filth flooding our newsstands":* Quoted in Michael Binstein and Charles Bowden, *Trust Me* (New York: Random House, 1993), p. 87.

"capable of poisoning any mind": See "Mailing of Obscene Matter," House Subcommittee No. 1, House Committee on Judiciary, January 27, 30, 1958, p. 74.

133 *"part of the Communist conspiracy":* See ibid., p. 74. In his testimony, Keating was quoting from the "United States Senate Committee on the Judiciary re. Internal Security Report," May 9–10, 1956, which says: "Part of the Communist conspiracy was to print and deposit for mailing and delivery obscene, lewd, lascivious, and filthy books, etc." Keating concluded that "surely the danger evidenced by these reports warrants the strongest type of legislation."

"noxious and obscene matter and materials": See U.S. Congress, House of Representatives, Education and Labor Committee, *To Create a Commission on Noxious and Obscene Matters and Materials: Hearings Before the Select Subcommittee on Education on H.R. 7465* (Washington, D.C.: U.S. Government Printing Office, 1965).

"I positively urge; beg you, if necessary": Ibid., p. 19.

"most notorious": Ibid., p. 31.

"spare the committee": Ibid., p. 15.

"sex drugged revelers": Ibid., p. 28.

134 *"so foul and revolting":* Quoted in *Girls Lean Back Everywhere,* p. 298n.

"Target Smut": For a thorough account of the campaign against the Fortas nomination, see ibid., pp. 525–50.

offers a description of the scene: Ibid., p. 538.

"There is no warrant": Report on Obscenity, p. 52.

"crime, deliquency, deviancy": Ibid.

sex offenders were less likely: Ibid.

raised in a conservative household: Ibid., p. 242.

135 *tough restrictions on the sale of sexually explicit material:* Ibid., p. 56.

demanded that its chairman, William Lockhart: For Keating's letters to Nixon on the subject, see Jules Witcover, "Civil War Over Smut," *Nation,* May 11, 1970.

filed a lawsuit to prevent the publication of its report: See "Complaint for Declaratory Judgment, Injunction, Temporary Restraining Order, and Other Relief," *Charles H. Keating, Jr., Commissioner, Plaintiff, v. William B. Lockhart, Commissioner, et al., defendants,* U.S. District Court for the District of Columbia, September 9, 1970.

"moral anarchy" and "a libertine philosophy!": Report on Obscenity, p. 515.

"not a valid part of the American political system": Ibid.

more sex-obsessed than Sodom and Gomorrah: Ibid., p. 541.

"french ticklers, vibrators . . . penis-shaped candy": Ibid.

"intrinsically evil": Ibid., p. 542.

"a blank check for pornographers": Ibid., p. 549.

"the ultimate answer lies not with the Government": See "Text of Nixon Message on Rise in Obscene Mail," *New York Times,* May 3, 1969.

"condoning anarchy in every other field": See "Text of Nixon's Statement Rejecting the Report of the Obscenity Panel," *New York Times,* October 25, 1970. See also Warren Weaver, Jr., "Nixon Repudiates Obscenity Report as Morally Void," *New York Times,* October 25, 1970.

"diabolical": Quoted in "Graham Assails Report," *New York Times,* October 14, 1970.

136 *denied that consenting adults had a right:* See *Paris Adult Theatre I v. Slaton,* 413 U.S. 49 (1973). See also *Miller v. California,* 413 U.S. 15 (1973).

or any right to privacy which might allow the sale: See *United States v. Reidel,* 402 U.S. 351, 354–56 (1971); *United States v. Thirty-seven Photographs,* 402 U.S. 363, 375–76 (1971).

"utterly" without social value: See *Memoirs v. Massachusetts,* 383 U.S. 413 (1965).

"serious literary, artistic, political": See *Miller v. California,* 413 U.S. 15 (1973).

"to protect the weak, the uninformed": See *Paris Adult Theatre I v. Slaton,* 413 U.S. 49 (1973).

the first year that Deep Throat *was in general release:* For details of how the film was distributed, see Knoedelseder, "Pornbrokers."

137 *A particularly bitter feud developed in Pennsylvania:* For an account of the "porn war" between Morrow and Krasner, see Potter, *Porn Merchants,* pp. 95–96.

"a piece of the porno": Quoted in Ovid Demaris, *The Last Mafioso* (New York: Times Books, 1980), p. 311.

138 *helpful in referring interested customers:* See Potter, *Porn Merchants,* p. 70.

obscenity conviction of an Albany, Georgia, theater owner: See *Jenkins v. Georgia,* 418 U.S. 153 (1974).

139 *"one of the most disgusting, nauseating, films"*: Quoted in Neff, "King of Porn."

"nervous nellies": Fahringer interview.

sent a two-and-a-half-page note to the judge: For the text of the note, see Katherine L. Hatton, "Sturman Is Acquitted in Obscenity Case", *Plain Dealer,* July 25, 1978.

140 *massage parlors, strip clubs, and a topless billiard hall:* See "Organized Crime Involvement in Pornography, a 1977 Justice Department report included in *Commission on Pornography,* p. 1229–30.

sold porn to outlets in all fifty states: Cited in Neff, "King of Porn."

143 *an exposé of Sturman's empire in* Cleveland *magazine:* See Whelan, "Amazing Porno Empire!"

143 *"You're out of your mind"*: Rosfelder interview.

145 *"I don't like to pay the tax"*: See transcript of *United States of America, Plaintiff, v. Reuben Sturman, et al.,* U.S. District Court, Northern District of Ohio, Eastern Division, CR 85–133, Direct Examination of Alfred Graf, p. 1000.

   "It's the same for me": See ibid.

146 *"a couple of dogs waiting for a scrap of meat"*: Rosfelder interview.

   the nation's tax laws seemed to offer more promise: For Wassenaar's views on how the IRS could help fight obscenity, see Robert L. Jackson, "IRS Probing Alleged Money Laundering Abroad by Far-Flung Pornographer," *Los Angeles Times,* March 16, 1985.

148 *"the future lies in audio-visual tape"*: Quoted in Whelan, "Amazing Porno Empire!"

   75 percent of all the videotapes sold: Cited in John Tierney, "Porn, The Low-Flung Engine of Progress," *New York Times,* January 9, 1994.

149 *FBI undercover investigation code-named "Miporn"*: For a good account of the Miporn investigation, see Stephen Kirk, Peter Mancust, Thomas Palmer, and M. E. Malone, "How Two FBI Agents Stalked the Top U.S. Porn Dealers," *Boston Globe,* February 18, 1983.

150 *a total taxable income, after expenses, of $1,237:* See transcript, *U.S. v. Sturman,* p. 41.

151 *"Bingo"*: Rosfelder interview.

152 *"upper echelon of an organized criminal group"*: Quoted in "Report & Recommendation," *U.S. v. Sturman,* Magistrate David S. Perelman, August 21, 1986, p. 4.

153 *"We have been instructed"*: Rosfelder interview.

154 *"You idiot, you don't own anything"*: Interview with Craig S. Morford.

155 *Holloway and four of his children were sent to prison:* See Dawe, "Porn Family Holloway."

   "I'll probably regret this": Quoted in transcript, *U.S. v. Sturman,* p. 101.

156 *"Scotland Yard, the Swiss Federal Police, Interpol"*: "Press Release," Indictment of Reuben Sturman, U.S. Department of Justice, June 28, 1985.

157 *"never have been a member of organized crime"*: "Brief in Support of Defendant Reuben Sturman's Motion to Dismiss, or in the Alternative, to Suppress and For an Evidentiary Hearing," Affidavit of Reuben Sturman, (Exhibit A), *U.S. v. Sturman,* May 1, 1987.

158 *"Combining old-fashioned muscle with sizable payoffs"*: James K. Barrett, "Inside the Mob's Smut Rackets," *Reader's Digest,* November 1973, p. 129.

   national pornography consortium: For the claim that the Cosa Nostra did control the pornography industry, see David Alexander Scott, *Pornography: Its Effects on the Family, Community and Culture* (Washington, D.C.: Free Congress Foundation, 1985), pp. 25–26, 51–52, excerpted in

Franklin Mark Osanka and Sara Lee Johann, eds., *Sourcebook on Pornography* (Lexington, Mass.: Lexington Books), pp. 73–76.

an obvious national control [of the porn business]": Quoted in "Beyond the Pornography Commission: The Federal Response, July 1988," U.S. Department of Justice, July 1988, p. 8.

as much as 90 percent of the porn industry: Cited in "Beyond the Pornography Commission," p. 8.

159 *eighteen principal sources of income for the Cosa Nostra:* The commission found only "anecdotal evidence about specific incidents" of organized crime involvement in porn. President's Commission on Organized Crime, *Report to the President and Attorney General, The Impact: Organized Crime Today* (Washington, D.C.: U.S. Government Printing Office, 1986), pp. 455–63.

three-quarters of them could find no verifiable evidence: Cited in *Commission on Pornography,* p. 292.

never among the top dozen sources of income: Interview with Ronald Goldstock.

agreed with Goldstock's assessment: Interview with James Kossler.

"When a Cosa Nostra member goes and gets a haircut": Goldstock interview.

New York City's largest wholesale distributor of porn: In his book on the Gambino family, John H. Davis claims that DiBernardo was "the biggest pornographer in the United States" — without offering substantiation. Although the nature of DiBernardo's relationship with Sturman may never be fully known, there's little doubt that Sturman's share of the market was much larger. During an off-the-record interview, a prominent industry figure who knew both men well scoffed at the idea that DiBernardo ever had a bigger porn empire. "DiBernardo's operation," he told me, "was the size of a dime compared to Sturman's, which was more like the size of this desktop." See John H. Davis, *Mafia Dynasty* (New York: HarperCollins, 1993), p. 254.

160 *"almost a total takeover [of the porn business]":* Quoted in Neff, "King of Porn."

Homer Young: See Whelan, "Amazing Porno Empire!"

"serious trouble": Quoted in Neff, "King of Porn."

claimed that Reuben Sturman could safely ignore: According to Fratianno's account, Sturman thwarted the L.A. mob's extortion efforts by paying $200,000 in protection money to Terry Zappi of the Gambino family. See Demaris, *Last Mafioso,* pp. 290–91, 295, 312, 404.

161 *"I wouldn't be surprised if he did":* Interview with William P. Kelly.

Robert DiBernardo was shot twice in the back of the head: See Federal Bureau of Investigation memo, "Investigation on 11/15/91 at Undisclosed,

File #BQ 183A-3507 by SAS George D. Gabriel and Carmine F. Russo."
Sonny Gravano arranged the hit. See also Davis, *Mafia Dynasty,* pp. 327,
348, 362, 380; and Howard Blum, *Gangland* (New York: Simon & Schuster, 1993), pp. 104–5, 150–53.

161 *"to an upper echelon of an organized criminal group":* Quoted in "Report and Recommendation," p. 4.
"significantly . . . in any important activity": Ibid.
"significant adverse effect": Ibid.
"Denying a defendant": Ibid., pp. 6–7.

163 *"I wanted to bring [money] to Switzerland":* Quoted in transcript of *U.S. v. Sturman,* Direct Examination of Walter Butti, p. 1093.

164 *"My approach . . . was to take the white pages":* Quoted in Greg Stricharchuk, "Sex, Money, and the IRS: How Greed Dethroned the King of Smut," *Corporate Cleveland,* May 1993.

165 *"you just forget everything you ever said":* Quoted in "Sex, Lies, Videotape . . . and Perhaps Tax Evasion," *National Law Journal,* October 9, 1989.
"no case against me from day one": Quoted in "Jury Deadlock Leads to Mistrial in Obscenity Case," *Reuters,* October 25, 1991.

167 *Los Angeles once had thirty to forty adult theaters:* Interview with Bob Peters, former supervising detective, Pornography Section, LAPD Vice Squad.
Perhaps three-quarters of the hard-core videos: Ibid.
may cost the retailer $60 per tape: This estimate does not apply to Blockbuster, the nation's largest video chain, which enjoys revenue-sharing agreements with Hollywood studios and pays an average of just $23 per tape. See Gerard P. Cachon and Martin A. Lariviere, "Turning the Supply Chain into a Revenue Chain," *Harvard Business Review,* March 2001.

168 *approximately 25,000 video stores:* Kernes interview.
"cash cow": Quoted in John Dempsey, "Cablers Comforted by Softcore Services," *Variety,* June 19, 1994.
splits the revenue fifty-fifty: Cited in Timothy Egan, "Erotica, Inc.," *New York Times,* October 23, 2000.
Americans spent about $465 million: According to Kagan World Media, Americans spent $465 million on pay-per-view adult movies in 2000. Cited in Sallie Hofmeister and Ralph Frammolino, "Playboy Sheds 'Gentleman' Cloak, Buys 'XX' TV Channels," *Los Angeles Times,* July 3, 2001.
Americans spend an additional $200 million: Cited in Jerry Hirsch, "Hotel Movie Firms Expect Upgrades to Turn Profits," *Los Angeles Times,* April 24, 2001.
about half of all the films: Ibid.
get a cut of up to 15 percent: Ibid.

new hard-core titles . . . increased about sevenfold: Some 1,500 new hard-core films were released in 1991, and 10,800 were released in 2001. Kernes interview.

perhaps a hundred hard-core feature films . . . at a typical cost in today's dollars of about $320,000: See Cook, "X-Rated Economy." See also Winich, "Organized Crime and Commercial Sex," in Kelly, Chin, and Schatzberg, *Handbook of Organized Crime*, p. 305.

about 11,000 hard-core videos: Kernes interview.

169 *Today about one-fifth of the hard-core videos . . . are classified as "amateur":* Interview with Tim Lake.

170 *"The imagination's the only limit":* Ibid.

"I thought I could outwit": Quoted in Mark Rollenhagen, "Sturman May Have Left the U.S.," *Plain Dealer,* December 10, 1992.

171 *"This guy is amazing":* Rosfelder interview.

172 *Nine months before Reuben Sturman escaped:* My account of Sturman's extortion attempts and escape from prison is based largely on interviews with Richard Rosfelder, Craig Morford, and Mark Prosperi, now the U.S. attorney in the Northern District of Illinois. Prosperi kindly sent me court documents from the case. See also "Statement of Facts," *United States of America v. Reuben Sturman and Herbert Michael Feinberg,* U.S. District Court, Northern District of Illinois, Case No. 93CR0167 (1993).

174 *"Whatever you owed Sturman":* Rosfelder interview.

"I got your message": Ibid.

176 *"I have no idea what you're talking about":* Ibid.

177 *"So do your best":* Quoted in transcript, *United States of America, Plaintiff, v. Sanford I. Atkin, Defendant,* U.S. District Court, Northern District of Ohio, Eastern Division, Case #94CR 378 (1994), Direct Examination of Reuben Sturman, p. 822.

178 *For more than five centuries, radical social movements:* See Lynn Hunt, ed., *The Invention of Pornography: Obscenity and the Origins of Modernity, 1500–1800* (New York: Zone Books, 1993).

San Francisco led the way in forging a new morality: See William Murray, "The Porn Capital of America," *New York Times Magazine,* January 3, 1971. For a fine account of how that idealistic revolution frequently ended in drug addiction and self-destruction, see John Hubner, *Bottom Feeders: From Free Love to Hard Core — The Rise and Fall of Counterculture Heroes Jim and Artie Mitchell* (New York: Dell, 1992).

"premature anti-Fascist": Interview with Nina Hartley.

179 *between $80,000 and $100,000 a year:* The estimated salaries of porn actresses were derived from interviews with a variety of people in the industry.

181 *roughly doubled between 1987 and 1992:* Interview with Rob Abner, founder and former publisher, *Stripper* magazine.

181 *$15,000 to $20,000 a week:* Interview with Dave Manach, editor, *Exotic Dancer* magazine.

182 *like his "kids":* Interview with William Margold.

A young woman who called herself "Rose": Although our interview was on the record, I chose not to include her real name.

187 *"Sex Is Your Business (Birth Control Is Ours)":* Quoted in Philip D. Harvey, *The Government vs. Erotica* (Amherst, N.Y.: Prometheus Books, 2001), p. 44.

The case reached the U.S. Supreme Court: See *Carey v. Population Services International,* 431 U.S. 678 (1977).

How to Start and Operate a Mail-Order Business: One of the nation's leading immigration scholars was also an expert on mail-order catalogues. See Julian L. Simon, *How to Start and Operate a Mail-Order Business* (New York: McGraw-Hill, 1965).

188 *"the most powerful agent":* Comstock, *Frauds Exposed,* p. 391.

"rot in prison": See *Noxious and Obscene Matters,* p. 19.

189 *"Yours Truly in Christ":* Quoted in Jim McGee, "U.S. Crusade Against Pornography Tests the Limits of Fairness," *Washington Post,* January 11, 1993.

"We always used to worry about being extorted": Interview with a leading porn company executive who preferred to remain anonymous.

outlined by a CDL attorney in 1983: See "U.S. Crusade Against Pornography." See also two other articles by Jim McGee: "U.S. Settles Obscenity Case with Mail Order Distributor," *Washington Post,* December 7, 1993, and "U.S. Reviews Reagan-Bush Obscenity Tactic," *Washington Post,* November 24, 1993. An excellent account of Project Postporn can be found in "Above the Law: The Justice Department's War Against the First Amendment", ACLU Arts Censorship Project, 1991.

190 *"multiple prosecutions (either simultaneous or successive)":* See "Brent D. Ward, United States Attorney, District of Utah, to Edwin Meese III, Attorney General, Re.: Nationwide Strategy for Pornography Prosecution," September 6, 1985, p. 2.

"unfairness": Quoted in "Above the Law," p. 6.

"encouraged": Quoted in McGee, "Crusade Against Pornography."

"There comes a point in life": Interview with Philip D. Harvey.

191 *"It just seems like the government is trying too hard":* Quoted in McGee, "Crusade Against Pornography."

"We must regain momentum": Ibid.

H. Robert Showers selected the mail-order companies: For an account of the centrally planned and controlled assault on mail-order companies, see Paul C. McCommon III, Special Attorney, National Obscenity Enforcement Unit, to H. Robert Showers, Executive Director, National Obscenity Enforcement Unit, "'Project Postporn' and the Danger of

Multiple District Prosecutions Coordinated from Washington, D.C.," September 14, 1988.

192 *"constitutionally protected activities"*: Quoted in James Rowley, "Justice Might Drop Multi-State Pornography Prosecutions," *Associated Press,* November 23, 1993.

"repeated criminal prosecutions": Quoted in "10th Circuit Finds Prosecution of NC Company Improper," *Entertainment Litigation Reporter,* July 13, 1992.

About 30 million copies of the Adam & Eve catalogue: Harvey interview.

194 *Sturman thought he'd been betrayed:* Sturman interview.

197 *"I've know Reuben for fourteen years"*: Quoted in Randall Samborn, "Dethroned 'King of Porn' Makes Last Stand in Court," *National Law Journal,* September 13, 1993.

198 *"They want me and everyone around me"*: Quoted in Mark Rollenhagen, "Sturman Pleads Guilty to Jury Tampering," *Plain Dealer,* April 27, 1994.

"All I've got is my prison commissary account": Quoted in Matt O'Connor, "Porn King Sentenced in Extortion," *Chicago Tribune,* June 20, 1994.

199 *Larry Flynt had known Sturman for decades:* Interview with Larry Flynt.

Reverend Jerry Falwell sued Flynt: For an account of the trial, see Rodney A. Smolla, *Jerry Falwell v. Larry Flynt: The First Amendment on Trial* (New York: St. Martin's Press, 1988).

200 *When Keating's Lincoln Savings & Loan crashed:* For an account of Keating's downfall, see Michale Binstein and Charles Bowden, *Trust Me* (New York: Random House, 1993), and Stephen Pizzo, Mary Fricker, and Paul Muolo, *Inside Job* (New York: McGraw-Hill, 1989).

shifted $840,000 from Lincoln Savings & Loan: Cited in Claudia Dreifus, "The Keating Papers: Charles Keating's Crusade Against Pornography," *Playboy,* June 1993.

allegedly used Covenant House funds to have sex: See Sennott, *Broken Covenant,* pp. 199–201. See also Michael Powell and Paul Moses, "A Rapid Fall from Grace," *Newsday,* February 25, 1990, and M. A. Farber, "Covenant Report Is Said to Find Sex Misconduct," *New York Times,* August 3, 1990.

at the forefront of technological innovation: See Doug Bedell, "Unlikely Innovators; Many Online Technologies Were First Perfected by the Adult Industry," *Dallas Morning News,* April 26, 2001.

201 *Americans now spend about $1 billion a year for online pornography:* The estimate was made in 2001 by Forrester Resarch. Cited in Robert P. Libbon, "Who's Getting the Most out of Erotic Content on the Net?" *American Demographics,* April 2001. See also Seth Lubove, "See No Evil: The Outfits Behind the Internet Porn Biz," *Forbes,* September 17, 2001.

31.9 percent of the nation's men: Cited in Libbon, "Who's Getting the Most?"

a poll conducted by Christianity Today: Cited in Joe Woodard, "Into Temptation: Pornography on the Web: The 'Silent Mistress That Is Always There' Is a Problem for Some Pastors," *Calgary Herald,* July 14, 2001.

201 *In 1997 perhaps 22,000 Web sites . . . today the number:* Cited in "Questioning Porn," *Los Angeles Times,* May 19, 2001.

difficult to earn money from pornography on the Internet: See Edward Cone, "The Naked Truth: Stiff Competition. Deadbeat Customers. Backend Hell. Welcome to the Real World of Internet Porn," *Wired,* February 2002.

"Some of the stuff on there": Flynt interview.

202 *"vigorously enforcing federal antipornography laws":* Quoted in "Presidential Candidates' Stand on Pornography," press release, Concerned Women for America, November 2, 2000.

"Do not include any of the following": Personal communication with Paul Cambria.

203 *"pimp for the porn industry":* Interview with Bruce A. Taylor.

"the market for pornography has been shrinking": Interview with Vagn Greve.

204 *"uninteresting" and "repulsive":* Berl Kutchinsky, "Pornography and Its Effects in Denmark and the United States: A Rejoinder and Beyond," *Comparative Social Research* (Greenwich, Conn.: JAI Press, 1985), p. 310. See also Kutchinsky, "Legalized Pornography in Denmark," in *Men Confront Pornography,* Michael S. Kimmel, ed. (New York: Crown, 1990).

"The most common immediate reaction": Kutchinsky, "Pornography and Its Effects in Denmark," p. 310.

"The smut lord is dead": "The Evil That Men Do," *Chattanooga Free Press,* November 16, 1997.

"Why do we target organized crime?": Morford interview.

205 *"Sturman created an illusion":* Rosfelder interview.

206 *treated his wife "abominably":* Sturman interview.

207 *Even the Meese Commission had acknowledged:* The Meese Commission argued that Sturman's business was "highly organized" and sold material that was probably obscene—and therefore could be considered an "organized crime" group. "We also have strong reason to believe," the Meese *Report* concluded, "that neither Sturman's organization nor some substantially smaller ones are themselves part of La Cosa Nostra . . . We do not say that there are no connections with La Cosa Nostra. On the contrary, there seems to be evidence, frequently quite strong evidence, of working arrangements, accommodations, assistance, some sharing of funds, and the like, as well as evidence of control by La Cosa Nostra, but nothing that would justify saying that these organizations are La Cosa Nostra or are part of La Cosa Nostra." See *Commission on Pornography,* pp. 292–97.

209 The Body and Society: See Peter Brown, *The Body and Society: Men, Women, and Sexual Renunciation in Early Christianity* (New York: Columbia University Press, 1988).
"I see another law in my members": Romans 7:23, *The Holy Bible*, King James Version.

210 *"temple of the Holy Ghost"*: 1 Corinthians 6:19.
"Be not deceived": 1 Corinthians 6:9–10.

out of the underground

Gambling is another American industry that rose from the underground to the mainstream over the past twenty-five years. In 1978 Nevada was the only state with legalized betting at casinos; today there are more than 800 casinos in twenty-eight states. The annual revenues from gambling have risen from about $1 billion in 1980 to more than $60 billion in 2001. Only three states — Tennessee, Hawaii, and Utah — now lack some form of legalized betting. The sort of lotteries that until recently could land their operators in prison are now widely promoted by state agencies. As Peter Reuter notes in *Drug War Heresies* (p. 142), "Moneys that previously went to criminals and corruption have been diverted to public coffers." The legalization of gambling has reduced a major source of illegal income for organized crime. But legalization has been accompanied by huge social costs. Public lotteries are essentially regressive taxes imposed on the poor.

Money laundering no longer occurs at the distant fringes of society. At least two publications — *Money Laundering Alert* and *World Money Laundering Report* — now chronicle the latest developments in the field. I find the whole subject not only fascinating but also a revealing sign of the times. "Turning Black Money into Green: Money Laundering," an essay by Robert J. Kelly, Rufus Schatzberg, and Ko-Lin Chin in *Handbook of Organized Crime*, is a good introduction to the art. I also learned a great deal from the following articles: Lawrence Malkin and Yuval Elizur, "The Dilemma of Dirty Money," *World Policy Journal*, March 22, 2001; William R. Schroeder, "Money Laundering," *FBI Law Enforcement Bulletin*, May 1, 2001; Nigel Morris-Cotterill, "Money Laundering," *Foreign Policy*, May 1, 2001; and William F. Wechsler, "Follow the Money," *Foreign Affairs*, July/August 2001. Having toured a fair number of prisons, I do not recommend trying any of these techniques.
page
213 *"The chief business of the American people"*: Calvin Coolidge, "The Press Under a Free Government," speech before the American Society of Newspaper Editors, January 17, 1925.
"How can they tell?": Quoted in Marion Meade, *Dorothy Parker: What Fresh Hell Is This?* (New York: Villard, 1988), p. 231.

214 *"There is nothing written in the sky":* Quoted in Michael Pertschuk, "Confessions of a Chronic Dissenter," *New York Times,* May 6, 1984.

Only Yesterday: I strongly recommend Frederick Lewis Allen's *Only Yesterday and Since Yesterday: A Popular History of the 20's and 30's, Two Volumes in One* (New York: Bonanza Books, 1986).

"The era of big government is over": Clinton made the comment during his 1996 State of the Union address. See "Text of the State of the Union Address," *Washington Post,* January 24, 1996.

215 *More prisons were built during Clinton's two terms:* See U.S. Department of Justice, Bureau of Justice Statistics, *Sourcebook of Criminal Justice Statistics 1996* (Washington, D.C.: U.S. Government Printing Office, 1997), p. 502, and "Prisoners in 2001," *Bureau of Justice Statistics Bulletin,* July 2002.

900 subsidiaries overseas: Cited in David Cay Johnston, "Enron's Collapse: The Havens," *New York Times,* January 17, 2002.

paid no income tax ... collected nearly $400 million: Ibid.

"inversion transactions": See David M. Hryck, "Taxation: Saving Money by Moving Offshore," *Start-Up & Emerging Companies Strategist,* June 2002.

"an estimated $4 billion a year in lost tax revenue": Cited in "Corporate Offshore Tax Avoidance," statement of Representative Richard E. Neal, testimony before the Subcommittee on Select Revenue Measures House Ways and Means Committee, Hearing on Corporate Inversions, June 25, 2002.

216 *population of 35,000—and 45,000 offshore:* Cited in William F. Wechsler, "Follow the Money," *Foreign Affairs,* July/August 2001.

about 2 to 5 percent of the world's GDP: Cited in Lawrence Malkin and Yuval Elizur, "The Dilemma of Dirty Money," *World Policy Journal,* March 22, 2001.

an estimated $70 billion: Cited in Jack Hitt, "The Billion-Dollar Shack," *New York Times,* December 10, 2000.

about $7 million per person: The island has about 10,000 inhabitants. Ibid.

meatpacking was one of the highest-paid industrial jobs: See Martin E. Personick and Katherine Taylor-Shirley, "Profiles in Safety and Health: Occupational Hazards of Meatpacking," *Monthly Labor Review,* U.S. Department of Labor, January 1989; and Eric Schlosser, *Fast Food Nation* (New York: Houghton Mifflin, 2001), pp. 149–90.

an estimated 28 percent of the workers are now paid in cash: Cited in "A Downward Spiral: L.A. Suffers as Its Massive Shadow Economy Booms," *Daily News of Los Angeles,* May 9, 2002.

between 9 and 29 percent of the city's economic activity: Cited in Nancy

Cleeland, "Off-the-Books Jobs Growing in Region," *Los Angeles Times,* May 6, 2002. For more on Los Angeles' underground economy, see Enrico A. Marcelli and Manuel Pastor, Jr., "Estimating the Effects of Informal Economic Activity: Evidence from Los Angeles County," *Journal of Economic Issues,* September 1999.

217 *less education than workers in any other American metropolitan area:* Cited in Beth Barrett, "Shadow Work Force Expanding: Trend Puts Real Economy in L.A. at Risk," *Los Angeles Times,* May 6, 2002.
roughly 11 percent of the working-age population: Ibid.
declined by about 37 percent since 1968: The federal minimum wage is currently $5.15. It was $1.60 in 1968 — about $8.20 in today's dollars.

218 *"No business which depends for existence":* Franklin D. Roosevelt, "Statement on N.I.R.A.," June 16, 1933.

219 *"The sneaking arts of underling tradesmen":* In the same passage Smith argued that England's duties on imported wines raised the price of alcohol — and encouraged drunkenness. Smith believed that in countries where wine was freely available, people drank less. See Smith, *Wealth of Nations,* p. 526.

220 *physicians write about 200,000 prescriptions:* Cited in Geoffrey Cowley, "Looking Beyond Viagra," *Newsweek,* April 24, 2000.
Pfizer, Inc., earned $1.75 billion: Cited in John Simons, "The $10 Billion Pill," *Fortune,* January 20, 2003.
"We need an all-out revival": Quoted in Jim Morrill, "Dole Calls for Revival of Anti-Drug Sentiment," *Charlotte Observer,* July 24, 2002. For an insightful examination of the arbitrary distinctions between many legal and illegal drugs, see Joshua Wolf Shenk, "America's Altered States," *Harper's,* May 1, 1999.
about one of every fourteen people: In 2000 Randolph M. Nesse, a professor of psychiatry at the University of Michigan, estimated that 20 million Americans are now taking antidepressants. Cited in Robert Wright, "Is Prozac Driving Wall Street?" *Slate,* March 4, 2000.

221 *"Over himself, over his own body and mind":* John Stuart Mill, *On Liberty, Representative Government, the Subjection of Women* (London: Oxford University Press, 1971), p. 15.

bibliography

Abel, Ernest L. *Marihuana: The First Twelve Thousand Years* (New York: Plenum Press, 1980).

Advisory Committee on Drug Dependence. *Cannabis: Report by the Advisory Committee on Drug Dependence* (London: Her Majesty's Stationery Office, 1968).

Aldrich, Daniel G., Jr., and Lorenzo Meyer. *Mexico and the United States: Neighbors in Crisis* (San Bernardino: Borgo Press, 1993).

Allen, Frederick Lewis. *Only Yesterday and Since Yesterday: A Popular History of the 20's and 30's, Two Volumes in One* (New York: Bonanza Books, 1986).

Anslinger, Harry J., and Will Oursler. *The Murderers: The Story of the Narcotics Gangs* (New York: Farrar, Straus, and Cudahy, 1961).

Anslinger, Harry J., and William F. Tompkins. *The Traffic in Narcotics* (New York: Funk & Wagnall, 1953).

Bade, Bonnie Lynn. "Is There a Doctor in the Field? Underlying Conditions Affecting Access to Health Care for California Farmworkers and Their Families" (California Policy Research Center, University of California, September 1999).

Bardacke, Frank. *Good Liberals & Great Blue Herons: Land, Labor, and Politics in the Pajaro Valley* (Santa Cruz: Center for Political Ecology, 1994).

Baum, Dan. *Smoke and Mirrors: The War on Drugs and the Politics of Failure* (New York: Little, Brown, 1996).

Binstein, Michael, and Charles Bowden. *Trust Me: Charles Keating and the Missing Billions* (New York: Random House, 1993).

Blum, Howard. *Gangland: How the FBI Broke the Mob* (New York: Simon & Schuster, 1993).

Bonnie, Richard. *Marihuana Use and Criminal Sanctions* (Charlottesville: Michie Company, 1980).

Bonnie, Richard, and Charles H. Whitebread II. *The Marihuana Conviction: A History of Marihuana Prohibition in the United States* (Charlottesville: University Press of Virginia, 1974).

Broun, Heywood, and Margaret Leech. *Anthony Comstock: Roundsman of the Lord* (New York: Albert and Charles Boni, 1927).

Brown, Peter. *The Body and Society: Men, Women, and Sexual Renunciation in Early Christianity* (New York: Columbia University Press, 1988).

Bureau of Justice Statistics, *Sourcebook of Criminal Justice Statistics, 1996* (Washington, D.C.: U.S. Government Printing Office, 1997).

——. *Sourcebook of Criminal Justice Statistics, 2000* (Washington, D.C.: U.S. Government Printing Office, 2001).

Bustamante, Jorge A., Clark W. Reynolds, and Raul A. Hinojosa Ojeda. *U.S.-Mexico Relations: Labor Market Interdependence* (Stanford: Stanford University Press, 1992).

California Findings from the National Agricultural Workers Survey. A Demographic and Employment Profile of Perishable Crop Farm Workers. Research Report No. 3 (U.S. Department of Labor, Office of the Assistant Secretary for Policy, Office of Program Economics, 1993).

Chavez, Leo R. *Shadowed Lives: Undocumented Immigrants in American Society* (New York: Harcourt Brace Jovanovich, 1997).

Chernow, Ron. *The House of Morgan: An American Banking Dynasty and the Rise of Modern Finance* (New York: Touchstone, 1991).

Commission on Agricultural Workers. *Report of the Commission on Agricultural Workers* (Washington, D.C.: U.S. Government Printing Office, 1992).

Comstock, Anthony. *Frauds Exposed: How the People Are Deceived and Robbed, and Youth Corrupted* (New York: J. H. Brown, 1880).

——. *Traps for the Young* (New York: Funk & Wagnalls, 1883).

Conover, Ted. *Coyotes: A Journey through the Secret World of America's Illegal Aliens* (New York: Vintage Books, 1987).

Conrad, Chris. *Hemp: Lifeline to the Future* (Los Angeles: Creative Xpressions, 1994).

Daniel, Cletus E. *Bitter Harvest: A History of California Farmworkers, 1870–1941* (Ithaca, N.Y.: Cornell University Press, 1981).

Davis, John H. *Mafia Dynasty: The Rise and Fall of the Gambino Crime Family* (New York: HarperCollins, 1993).

de Grazia, Edward. *Girls Lean Back Everywhere: The Law of Obscenity and the Assault on Genius* (New York: Vintage, 1993).

Delacoste, Frederique, and Priscilla Alexander, eds. *Sex Work: Writings by Women in the Sex Industry* (Pittsburgh: Cleis Press, 1987).

Demaris, Ovid. *The Last Mafioso: The Treacherous World of Jimmy Fratianno* (New York: Times Books, 1980).

Donnerstein, Edward, Daniel Linz, and Steven Penrod. *The Question of Pornography: Research Findings and Policy Implications* (New York: Free Press, 1987).

Drugs, Crime, and the Justice System: A National Report from the Bureau of Justice Statistics (Washington, D.C.: U.S. Government Printing Office, 1992).

Duke, Steven B. *America's Longest War: Rethinking Our Tragic Crusade Against Drugs* (New York: Putnam, 1993).

Dworkin, Andrea. *Pornography: Men Possessing Women* (New York: Dutton, 1989).

Earley, Pete. *The Hot House: Life Inside Leavenworth Prison* (New York: Bantam, 1992).

Edid, Maralyn. *Farm Labor Organizing: Trends & Prospects* (Ithaca, N.Y.: ILR Press, 1994).

Emerson, Robert D. *Seasonal Agricultural Labor Markets in the United States* (Ames: Iowa State University Press, 1984).

Ernst, Morris L., and Alan U. Schwartz. *Censorship: The Search for the Obscene* (New York: MacMillan, 1964).

Feder, Ernest. *Strawberry Imperialism: An Enquiry into the Mechanisms of Dependency in Mexican Agriculture* (The Hague: Institute of Social Studies, 1977).

Ford, Luke. *A History of X: 100 Years of Sex in Film* (Amherst, N.Y.: Prometheus Books, 1999).

Galarza, Ernesto. *Merchants of Labor: The Mexican Bracero Story. An Account of the Managed Migration of Mexican Farm Workers in California, 1942–1960* (Charlotte, N.C.: McNally & Loftin, 1964).

Garcia, Juan Ramon. *Operation Wetback: The Mass Deportation of Mexican Undocumented Workers in 1954* (Westport, Conn.: Greenwood Press, 1980).

Gentry, Curt. *J. Edgar Hoover: The Man and His Secrets* (New York: Norton, 1991).

Gibson, Pamela Church, and Roma Gibson. *Dirty Looks: Women, Pornography, Power* (London: BFI Publishing, 1993).

Gittler, Ian. *Porn Star* (New York: Simon & Schuster, 1999).

Grant, Michael. *Eros in Pompeii: The Secret Rooms of the National Museum of Naples* (New York: William Morrow, 1975).

Greenfield, Harry I. *Invisible, Outlawed, and Untaxed: America's Underground Economy* (Westport, Conn.: Praeger, 1993).

Grinspoon, Lester, and James B. Bakalar. *Marihuana, the Forbidden Medicine* (New Haven: Yale University Press, 1993).

Halperin, David M., John J. Winkler, and Froma I. Zeitlin, eds. *Before Sexu-*

ality: The Construction of the Erotic Experience in the Ancient Greek World (Princeton: Princeton University Press, 1990).

Harvey, Philip D. *The Government vs. Erotica: The Siege of Adam & Eve* (Amherst, N.Y.: Prometheus Books, 2001).

Hawkins, Gordon, and Franklin E. Zimring. *Pornography in a Free Society* (Cambridge: Cambridge University Press, 1989).

Hebditch, David, and Nick Anning. *Porn Gold: Inside the Pornography Business* (London: Faber and Faber, 1988).

Heilbroner, Robert L. *The Essential Adam Smith* (New York: W. W. Norton, 1986).

Heins, Marjorie. *Not in Front of the Children: "Indecency," Censorship, and the Innocence of Youth* (New York: Hill & Wang, 2001).

Herrer, Jack. *The Emperor Wears No Clothes: The Authoritative Historical Record of Cannabis and the Conspiracy Against Marijuana* (Austin, Tex.: Ah Ha, 2000).

Higham, John. *Strangers in the Land: Patterns of American Nativism, 1860–1925* (New Brunswick, N.J.: Rutgers University Press, 1988).

Himmelstein, Jerome. *The Strange Career of Marihuana: Politics and Ideology of Drug Control in America* (Westport, Conn.: Greenwood Press, 1983).

Hoffer, Eric. *The True Believer: Thoughts on the Nature of Mass Movements* (New York: Harper and Row, 1951).

Hoffman, Abraham. *Unwanted Mexican Americans in the Great Depression: Repatriation Pressures, 1929–1939* (Tucson: University of Arizona Press, 1974).

Hopkins, John F. *A History of the Hemp Industry in Kentucky* (Lexington: University of Kentucky Press, 1951).

The House of Lords Science and Technology Committee. "Cannabis: The Scientific and Medical Evidence" (London: November 4, 1998).

Hunt, Lynn, ed. *The Invention of Pornography: Obscenity and the Origins of Modernity, 1500–1800* (New York: Zone Books, 1993).

Indian Hemp Drugs Commission. *Report of the Indian Hemp Drugs Commission* (Simla, India: Government Central Printing Office, 1894).

Institute of Medicine. *Marijuana and Health: Report of the Committee to Study the Health-Related Effects of Cannabis and Its Derivatives* (Washington, D.C.: National Academy Press, 1982).

——— . *Marijuana and Medicine: Assessing the Science Base* (Washington, D.C.: National Academy Press, 1999).

Iverson, Leslie L. *The Science of Marijuana* (New York: Oxford University Press, 2000).

Jones, Richard C. *Patterns of Undocumented Migration: Mexico and the United States* (Totowa, N.J.: Rowman & Allanheld, 1984).

Kaplan, John. *Marihuana: The New Prohibition* (New York: World, 1970).

Kelly, Robert J., Ko-Lin Chin, and Rufus Schatzberg, eds. *The Handbook of Organized Crime in the United States* (Westport, Conn.: Greenwood Press, 1994).

Kendrick, Walter. *The Secret Museum: Pornography in Modern Culture* (New York: Viking, 1987).

Kimmel, Michael S., ed. *Men Confront Pornography* (New York: Crown, 1990).

King, Rufus. *The Drug Hang-Up: America's Fifty-Year Folly* (Springfield, Ill.: Charles C. Thomas, 1972).

Kleiman, Mark A. R. *Against Excess: Drug Policy for Results* (New York: Basic Books, 1992).

——— . *Marijuana: Costs of Abuse, Costs of Control* (Greenwich, Conn.: Greenwood Press, 1989).

Linder, Marc. *Migrant Workers & Minimum Wages: Regulating the Exploitation of Agricultural Labor in the United States* (Boulder, Colo.: Westview Press, 1992).

Lippert, Owen, and Michael Walker. *The Underground Economy: Global Evidence of Its Size and Impact* (Vancouver: Fraser Institute, 1997).

MacKinnon, Catherine A. *Only Words* (Cambridge, Mass.: Harvard University Press, 1998).

Mann, Peggy. *Marijuana Alert* (New York: McGraw-Hill, 1985).

Martin, Philip L., and David A. Martin. *The Endless Quest: Helping America's Farm Workers* (Boulder, Colo.: Westview Press, 1994).

Martinez, Ruben. *Crossing Over: A Mexican Family on the Migrant Trail* (New York: Henry Holt, 2001).

Massing, Michael. *The Fix: Under the Nixon Administration, America Had an Effective Drug Policy. We Should Restore It. (Nixon Was Right.)* (New York: Simon & Schuster, 1998).

Mattera, Philip. *Off the Books: The Rise of the Underground* (New York: St. Martin's Press, 1986).

Matthiessen, Peter. *Sal Si Puedes: Cesar Chavez and the New American Revolution* (New York: Random House, 1969).

Mauer, Marc. *Race to Incarcerate* (New York: New Press, 2001).

Mauer, Marc, and Meda Chesney-Lind, eds. *Invisible Punishment: The Collateral Consequences of Mass Imprisonment* (New York: New Press, 2002).

Mayor's Committee on Marihuana. *The Marijuana Problem in the City of New York: Sociological, Medical, Psychological, and Pharmacological Studies* (Lancaster, Pa.: Jacques Cattel, 1944).

McNamara, Peter. *Political Economy and Statesmanship: Smith, Hamilton, and the Foundation of the Commercial Republic* (Dekalb: Northern Illinois University Press, 1998).

McWilliams, Carey. *Factories in the Field: The Story of Migratory Farm Labor in California* (Berkeley: University of California Press, 1999).

———. *North from Mexico: The Spanish Speaking People of the United States* (Philadelphia: Lippincott, 1948).

McWilliams, John C. *The Protectors: Harry J. Anslinger and the Federal Bureau of Narcotics, 1930–1962* (Newark: University of Delaware Press, 1990).

Meier, Matt S., and Feliciano Ribera. *Mexican Americans/American Mexicans: From Conquistadors to Chicanos* (New York: Hill and Wang, 1993).

Morgan, John P., and Lynn Zimmer. *Marijuana Myths, Marijuana Facts* (New York: New York, Lindesmith Center, 1997).

Muolo, Paul. *Inside Job: The Looting of America's Savings and Loans* (New York: McGraw-Hill, 1989).

Musto, David F. *The American Disease: Origins of Narcotic Control* (New York: Oxford University Press, 1999).

Nahas, Gabriel. *Keep Off the Grass* (Middlebury, Vt.: Paul S. Erikkson, 1990).

———. *Marihuana—Deceptive Weed* (New York: Raven Press, 1973).

Nahas, Gabriel, Kenneth M. Sutin, David J. Harvey, and Stig Agurell, eds. *Marihuana and Medicine* (Totowa, N.J.: Humana Press, 1999).

National Commission on Marihuana and Drug Abuse. *Marihuana: A Signal of Misunderstanding* (Washington, D.C.: U.S. Government Printing Office, 1972).

Osanka, Franklin Mark, and Sara Lee Johann. *Sourcebook on Pornography* (Lexington, Mass.: Lexington Books, 1989).

Peck, Oscar. *Sex Life of a Cop* (Fresno, Calif.: Mid-Tower, 1959).

Peterson, James R. *The Century of Sex: Playboy's History of the Sexual Revolution, 1900–1999* (New York: Grove Press, 1999).

Pollan, Michael. *The Botany of Desire: A Plant's-Eye View of the World* (New York: Random House, 2001).

Potter, Gary W. *The Porn Merchants* (Dubuque, Iowa: Kendall/Hunt, 1986).

President's Commission on Migratory Labor. *Migratory Labor in American Agriculture: Report of the President's Commission on Migratory Labor, 1951.* Maurice T. Van Heeke, chairman (Washington, D.C.: U.S. Government Printing Office, 1951).

President's Commission on Organized Crime, *Report to the President and Attorney General, The Impact: Organized Crime Today* (Washington, D.C.: U.S. Government Printing Office, 1986).

Preston, Brian. *Pot Planet: Adventures in Global Marijuana Culture* (New York: Grove Press, 2002).

Price, Barry L. *The Political Economy of Mechanization in U.S. Agriculture* (Boulder, Colo.: Westview Press, 1983).

Reuter, Peter. *Disorganized Crime: The Economics of the Visible Hand* (Cambridge, Mass.: M.I.T. Press, 1983).

Reuter, Peter, and Robert J. MacCoun. *Drug War Heresies: Learning from Other Places, Times, and Vices* (New York: Cambridge University Press, 2001).

Reynolds, Helen. *The Economics of Prostitution* (Springfield, Ill.: Charles C. Thomas, 1986).

Richlin, Amy, ed. *Pornography and Representation in Greece and Rome* (New York: Oxford University Press, 1991).

Rosenthal, Ed. *The Big Book of Buds: Marijuana Varieties from the World's Great Seed Breeders* (Oakland, Calif.: Quick American Archives, 2001).

Rosenthal, Ed, and William Logan. *Ask Ed: Marijuana Law, Don't Get Busted* (Oakland: Quick American Archives, 2000).

Rothenberg, Daniel. *With These Hands: The Hidden World of Migrant Farmworkers Today* (New York: Harcourt Brace, 1998).

Rothschild, Emma. *Economic Sentiments: Adam Smith, Condorcet, and the Enlightenment* (Cambridge: Harvard University Press, 2002).

Runsten, David, and Phillip Leveen. *Mechanization and Mexican Labor in California Agriculture* (San Diego: University of California, 1981).

Sagarin, Edward, ed. *Deviance and Social Change* (Beverly Hills, Calif.: Sage, 1977), pp. 219–46.

Schaefer, Eric. *Bold! Daring! Shocking! True!: A History of Exploitation Films, 1919–1959* (Durham, N.C.: Duke University Press, 1999).

Schlosser, Eric. *Fast Food Nation* (Boston: Houghton Mifflin, 2001).

Schwenk, Charles R., and Susan L. Rhodes. *Marijuana and the Workplace: Interpreting Research on Complex Social Issues* (Westport, Conn.: Quorum Books, 1999).

Scott, David Alexander. *Pornography: Its Effects on the Family, Community and Culture* (Washington, D.C.: Free Congress Foundation, 1985).

Sennott, Charles M. *Broken Covenant: The Story of Father Bruce Ritter's Fall from Grace* (New York: Simon & Schuster, 1992).

Shorris, Earl. *Latinos: A Biography of the People* (New York: Avon Books, 1992).

Simon, Julian L. *The Economic Consequences of Immigration,* 2nd ed. (Ann Arbor: University of Michigan Press, 1999).

——. *How to Start and Operate a Mail-Order Business* (New York: McGraw-Hill, 1965).

Sloman, Larry. *Reefer Madness: A History of Marijuana* (New York: St. Martin's/Griffin, 1999).

Smith, Adam. *The Theory of Moral Sentiments,* Knud Haakonssen, ed. (Cambridge: Cambridge University Press, 2002).

——. *The Wealth of Nations (An Inquiry into the Nature and Causes of The Wealth of Nations),* Edwin Canaan, ed. (New York: Random House, 2000).

Smolla, Rodney A. *Jerry Falwell v. Larry Flynt: The First Amendment on Trial* (New York: St. Martin's Press, 1988).

Solomon, David, ed. *The Marijuana Papers* (New York: Signet Books, 1968).

Stoller, Robert J. *Porn: Myths for the Twentieth Century* (New Haven, Conn.: Yale University Press, 1991).

Storm, Daniel. *Marijuana Hydroponics: High-Tech Water Culture* (Berkeley: And/Or Books, 1987).

Strossen, Nadine. *Defending Pornography: Free Speech, Sex, and the Fight for Women's Rights* (New York: Scribner, 1995).

Talese, Gay. *Thy Neighbor's Wife: A Chronicle of American Permissiveness Before the Age of AIDS* (New York: Ivy Books, 1993).

Tanzi, Vito, ed. *The Underground Economy in the United States and Abroad* (Lexington, Mass.: Lexington Books, 1982).

Theoharis, Athan, ed. *From the Secret Files of J. Edgar Hoover* (Chicago: I.R.D., 1991).

———. *J. Edgar Hoover, Sex and Crime: An Historical Antidote* (Chicago: Ivan Doe, 1995).

Thompson, Bill. *Soft Core: Moral Crusades Against Pornography in Britain and America* (London: Cassell, 1994).

Tomasson, Richard F., ed. *Comparative Social Research: Deviance* (Greenwich, Conn.: JAI Press, 1985).

Trumbull, Charles. *Anthony Comstock, Fighter: Some Impressions of a Lifetime Adventure in Conflict with the Powers of Evil* (New York: Fleming H. Revell, 1913).

U.S. Attorney General's Commission on Pornography. *Attorney General's Commission on Pornography: Final Report* (Washington, D.C.: U.S. Government Printing Office, 1986).

U.S. Commission on Obscenity and Pornography. *The Report of the Commission on Obscenity and Pornography* (Washington, D.C.: U.S. Government Printing Office, 1970).

———. *Technical Report* (Washington, D.C.: U.S. Government Printing Office, 1971).

U.S. Country Life Commission. *Report of the Commission on Country Life* (New York: Sturgis & Walton, 1911).

U.S. Sentencing Commission. *Special Report to Congress: Mandatory Minimum Penalties in the Federal Criminal Justice System* (St. Paul: West, August 1991).

Wagner, David. *The New Temperance: The American Obsession with Sin and Vice* (New York: Westview Press, 1997).

Weintraub, Sidney, and Stanley R. Ross. *"Temporary" Alien Workers in the United States: Designing Policy from Fact and Opinion* (Boulder, Colo.: Westview Replica Edition, 1982).

Weisheit, Ralph. *Domestic Marijuana: A Neglected Industry* (Westport, Conn.: Greenwood Press, 1992).

Whiteaker, Stafford. *The Compleat Strawberry* (New York: Crown, 1985).

Wildmon, Donald E. *The Case Against Pornography* (Wheaton, Ill.: Victor Books, 1986).

Wilhelm, Stephen, and James E. Sagen. *A History of the Strawberry: From Ancient Gardens to Modern Markets* (Berkeley: University of California Division of Agricultural Sciences, 1974).

Williams, Linda. *Hard Core: Power, Pleasure, and the 'Frenzy of the Visible.'* (Los Angeles: University of California Press, 1989).

Zillman, Dolf, and Jennings Bryant, eds. *Pornography: Research Considerations and Policy Considerations* (Hillsdale, N.J.: Lawrence Erlbaum, 1989).

acknowledgments

The three essays in this book all began, one way or another, at the *Atlantic Monthly* while William Whitworth was the editor and Cullen Murphy the managing editor. I benefited immensely from their criticism, skepticism, encouragement, and willingness to publish long articles challenging the conventional wisdom. In many ways the *Atlantic* served as my journalism school, and I was fortunate to have been taught by these two wonderful, tough-minded editors. I'm grateful to James Fallows, one of the magazine's national editors, for saving my pornography investigation from oblivion and for insisting that the story of Reuben Sturman must appear in a book someday. Other editors at the *Atlantic* deserve many thanks: Jack Beatty, Avril Cornel, Corby Kummer, Amy Meeker, Lucie Prinz, Martha Spaulding, and Barbara Wallraff. Lowell Weiss fact-checked "Reefer Madness" for the *Atlantic,* and Yvonne Rolzhausen fact-checked "In the Strawberry Fields." They contradicted me with extraordinary skill and in the process became my dear friends.

Cullen Gerst began the unenviable task of fact-checking the new material in this book and helping me track down old sources for the footnotes. He did a fine job until impending marriage provided a convenient escape. Charles William Wilson somehow wound up doing most of the fact-checking work, as he did for *Fast Food Nation.* His ability to offer substantive criticism, as well as to find obscure information, is remarkable. We've spent countless late-night hours debating the minutiae of my work. We are constantly amazed that these things are true. Any remaining errors in the text are entirely my responsibility.

At Penguin Daniel Hind deserves many thanks for his faith that British readers might find these stories interesting. I'm grateful to Stefan McGrath for encouraging me to revisit the material and bring it up to date and make the underlying connections clear. Without his great enthusiasm and support, this book might not have appeared. Rosie Glaisher and Jennifer Todd have done a brilliant job of gaining attention for my work. Although I've thus far refused to dress up like a french fry or a joint for bookstore appearances, most of their ideas have been marvelous, creative, and effective.

A special thanks to Mark Mann for taking the cover photograph at such short notice and to Miranda for inhaling so much smoke on my behalf.

Ellis Levine, a former chief counsel at Random House, once again provided me with an independent legal reading. And once again his literary, as well as legal, advice was invaluable.

Andrew Lichtenstein, one of the nation's finest documentary photographers, kindly allowed me to include his photo of a strawberry worker.

At *Rolling Stone* Jann Wenner, Bob Love, and Will Dana asked me to look at the war on marijuana during the Clinton years, and some of the work I did for them appears in this book. For years the editors at *Rolling Stone* have been brave critics of America's misguided drug policies.

I am grateful to the friends who read a rough draft of this book and offered their blunt opinion of it: Michael Clurman, Jordan Katz, and John Seabrook.

I am profoundly grateful to my agent, Tina Bennett, whose intelligence, integrity, and determination never cease to amaze me. It can be said, without any exaggeration, that she is simply the best. Svetlana Katz, also at Janklow & Nesbit Associates, has helped me in innumerable ways. And Cecile Barendsma has done a marvelous job of bringing my work to readers outside the United States.

Most of all, I am grateful to my family for their love and support. For years they never expressed the slightest disapproval of my spending time with drug dealers, labor contractors, and pornographers. Billie and Bob, George and Lola, Lynn and Craig, James and Kyle, Amy, Mark, and my parents have given me more than I could ever ask for. My children, Mica and Conor, have been quite kind and understanding about my frequent absences from the house. I hope someday to write a book that they're allowed to read. As for my dear Red, without her love none of this would have been written, nor worth writing.

index